SOFTWARE ENGINEERING
AND MODULA-2

Prentice-Hall International
Series in Computer Science

C. A. R. Hoare, Series Editor

BACKHOUSE, R. C., *Program Construction and Verification*
BACKHOUSE, R. C., *Syntax of Programming Languages, Theory and Practice*
de BAKKER, J. W., *Mathematical Theory of Program Correctness*
BJORNER, D., and JONES, C. B., *Formal Specification and Software Development*
CLARK, K. L. and McCABE, F. G., *micro-PROLOG: Programming in Logic*
DROMEY, R. G., *How to Solve it by Computer*
DUNCAN, F., *Microprocessor Programming and Software Development*
ELDER, J., *Construction of Data Processing Software*
GOLDSCHLAGER, L., and LISTER, A., Computer Science: A Modern Introduction
HEHNER, E. C. R., *The Logic of Programming*
HENDERSON, P., *Functional Programming: Application and Implementation*
HOARE, C. A. R., *Communicating Sequential Processes*
HOARE, C. A. R., and SHEPHERDSON, J. C., (Eds.) *Mathematical Logic and Programming Languages*
INMOS LTD., *Occam Programming Manual*
JACKSON, M. A., *System Development*
JOHNSTON, H., *Learning to Program*
JONES, C. B., *Systematic Software Development Using VDM*
JOSEPH, M., PRASAD, V. R., and NATARAJAN, N., *A Multiprocessor Operating System*
LEW, A., *Computer Science: A Mathematical Introduction*
MacCALLUM, I., *Pascal for the Apple*
MacCALLUM, I., *USCD Pascal for the IBM PC*
MARTIN, J. J., *Data Types and Data Structures*
POMBERGER, G., *Software Engineering and Modula-2*
REYNOLDS, J. C., *The Craft of Programming*
TENNENT, R. D., *Principles of Programming Languages*
WELSH, J., and ELDER, J., *Introduction to Pascal, 2nd Edition*
WELSH, J., ELDER, J., and BUSTARD, D., *Sequential Program Structures*
WELSH, J., and HAY, A., *A Model Implementation of Standard Pascal*
WELSH, J., and McKEAG, M., *Structured System Programming*

SOFTWARE ENGINEERING AND MODULA-2

GUSTAV POMBERGER

University of Zürich

Prentice/Hall International

Englewood Cliffs, NJ   London   Mexico   New Delhi   Rio de Janeiro
Singapore   Sydney   Tokyo   Toronto   Wellington

Library of Congress Cataloging in Publication Data

Pomberger, Gustav, 1949 –
    Software engineering and modula-2.

    Bibliography: p.
    Includes index.
    1. Modula-2 (Computer program language) 2. Computer software – Development.
I. Title. II. Title: Software engineering and Modula two.
QA76.73.M63P6613   1986   005.13'3   85-28168
ISBN 0-13-821794-7
ISBN 0-13-821737-8 (Pbk)

British Library Cataloguing in Publication Data

Pomberger, Gustav
    Software engineering and Modula-2.
    1. Programming (Electronic computers)
    2. Computer engineering
    I. Title   II. Softwaretechnik und Modula-2,
    English
    005.1'2   QA76.6
    ISBN 0-13-821794-7
    ISBN 0-13-821737-8 (Pbk)

© 1984 Carl Hanser Verlag München Wien
The original edition of this work was published in German by Carl Hanser Verlag under
the title *Softwaretechnik und Modula-2*.

Prentice-Hall Inc., Englewood Cliffs, New Jersey
Prentice-Hall International (UK) Ltd, London
Prentice-Hall of Australia Pty Ltd, Sydney
Prentice-Hall Canada Inc., Toronto
Prentice-Hall Hispanoamericana S.A., Mexico
Prentice-Hall of India Private Ltd, New Delhi
Prentice-Hall of Japan Inc., Tokyo
Prentice-Hall of Southeast Asia Pte Ltd, Singapore
Editora Prentice-Hall do Brasil Ltda, Rio de Janeiro
Whitehall Books Ltd, Wellington, New Zealand

Printed and bound in Great Britain for
Prentice-Hall International (UK) Ltd,
66 Wood Lane End, Hemel Hempstead, Hertfordshire, HP2 4RG
by A. Wheaton & Co. Ltd, Exeter.

1   2   3   4   5   90   89   88   87   86

ISBN 0-13-821794-7
ISBN 0-13-821737-8 PBK

Table of Contents

Foreword

"Software engineering" is a concept that was coined towards the end of the 60's. The intention is to imply that the technique of creating complex, programmed systems is subject to laws similar to those for the manufacture of machines (engines). In both cases a critical requirements analysis and a careful choice of solution methodology is necessary. On the other hand fundamental differences must not be ignored. The most obvious is certainly that the products of the software engineer, as opposed to those of the mechanical engineer, are immaterial, as we say, "soft." They are represented as programs, as formal texts which are first brought to life by the computer.

The fact that texts--especially with the aid of a computer--are easily changeable, has the advantage that any shortcomings which may arise can be eliminated (or hidden) quickly, and at the same time the disadvantage of seducing the engineer to abuse this advantage. Experience demonstrates that it is precisely here that a sound initial concept is essential for success, because numerous after-the-fact adaptations rapidly lead to a system complexity which--and here is another difference to mechanical engineering--is cheap to introduce, but which later, in use, turns out to be expensive.

The merit of this book is that it handles the field of software engineering comprehensively. First a modern foundation is laid for the technical tools, and then they are applied. All phases of a project are carefully discussed, and not just programming; requirements analysis, specification of the requirements, design of a solution, documentation, and finally testing and maintenance receive their deserved attention. In conclusion, a chapter is dedicated to project management, whereby its scope in comparison with that of the technical aspect is, happily, kept within bounds. Thus clear priorities are set, and the trend of placing the blame on management for failures due to a lack of technical competence has been checked.

The book thus distinguishes itself fundamentally from the usual introductions to programming. In spite of this, an important chapter is dedicated to the technique of programming, the pillar of all software engineering. I am pleased that the author based it on the language Modula-2, which was developed especially for projects of the nature treated herein, and which represents a natural evolution of the language Pascal, which, in the meantime, has itself become globally accepted. This book is a welcome guide to its competent application.

N. Wirth

Preface

This book is intended for everyone who plans, designs and implements software. The writer has occupied himself for years with the production of software, at first in industry, and in the past years, in teaching and research at the university level. This book is a result of the experience collected in the process.

The term "software crisis," applicable even today, indicates that software is often incorrect, that immense difficulties appear in mastering complexity in the production of software, and that programs are often only understood by their own authors. One question also often discussed in this connection is that of the generality and acceptability of a programming language. Most of the programming languages in practical use today are conceptually outdated by the present standards of software engineering, and lend themselves little or not at all to the support of the new concepts in software engineering (such as data capsuling).

This book is intended to guide the reader to a new area, which is in no way supported by a secure basis of facts, but which, rather, is still in the beginning stages. It represents an attempt to depict personal and outside experiences in the field of software engineering systematically. It describes the phases of a software project (software life cycle), the problems which occur and how they are solved by formal, workable methods of software engineering. Because the choice of programming language is of great importance to the implementation, efficiency, quality and portability of software, a major part of the book is dedicated to the description of a modern programming language which corresponds to today's technological level. For this the writer, after serious consideration, has chosen the programming language Modula-2, developed by N. Wirth. Modula-2 is a simple, widely machine independent language and, because of its descendency from Pascal, easily learned by many programmers. The volume of the language is modest in comparison to other new programming languages (as, for example, Ada). The language lends itself, therefore, also to implementation on microcomputers and supports many of the software engineering concepts known today. In addition, Modula-2 lends itself, in the view of the writer, equally well to systems and applications programming.

The author is primarily interested in handling the fundamental principles and methods of software engineering in detail and in depth. From this the reader should be left in a position to apply these techniques on his own. To this end each section contains carefully commented examples. Detailed descriptions of methods which were developed for extremely specialized tasks of software engineering are intentionally omitted. These methods are discussed briefly, and the reader is referred to the appropriate literature. The author has also taken pains to ease access to advanced literature for the more intensively interested reader, by referencing it in many places, especially where it was important to keep the book within bounds.

It is expected of the reader that he have an elementary knowledge of algorithms, data structures and programming languages. He should be acquainted with the fundamentals of mathematics and logic, and above all have an interest in the subject.

March 1984, Linz   G. Pomberger

Acknowledgments

For me it is an honor and a pleasure, at this time, to express my thanks for the help rendered and the many suggestions received.

I am most especially indebted to *Prof. Peter Rechenberg*, my teacher and mentor. During the past years he has exerted a great influence on my thinking. Much of what I have recorded in this book is particularly influenced by his work. Whenever a question arose during the writing of this book, it was my habit to note in the margin of the manuscript, "Ask Rechenberg." *Prof. Rechenberg* was always supportive in word and deed. His priceless suggestions place me in his debt.

I wish to express my special gratitude also to *Prof. Niklaus Wirth* from Zürich. His work on algorithms and data structures, systematic programming, compiler construction and, above all, the definition of the programming languages Pascal and Modula-2 are of great importance for software engineering and have strongly influenced much of my work. I also owe to *Prof. Wirth* the possibility of a three month research stay at the ETH in Zürich. In this time it was possible for me to complete my understanding of the language Modula-2 and to discourse with him, the inventor of the language.

Still further I wish to express my thanks to the many other people who helpfully stood by my side during the long task. It is impossible for me to list each by name. However, I am most especially obligated to thank:
Günther Blascheck for the continuous exchange of thoughts, which, for me, were a great source of inspiration, and for his inspection of the manuscript,
Peter Mössenböck for helpful discussions, and because he read the entire manuscript and accorded me invaluable advice,
Prof. Jörg Mühlbacher, to whom I owe the contact to the publisher,
Mrs. Ingrid Kirchmaier for her excellent typing and because she was always at my side in good spirits,
the *students* who attended my software work sessions, and who provided the stimulating environment for my work through many discussions,
the original publisher, *Carl-Hanser-Verlag* , for their understanding and patience concerning the late delivery of the manuscript.

SOFTWARE ENGINEERING
AND MODULA-2

1. Introduction to the Problem

1.1 The Development of Software Engineering

The first computing machines were primarily used in the field of pure and applied science. The task of the programmer was not so much to discover complex algorithms as to formulate already known algorithms in a programming language in order to execute them on a computer. To this end no special knowledge was required except the command of a programming language. The programmer was ordinarily also the user. The programs were only occasionally used, and the tasks were seldom respecified. The only difficulties were to guarantee correctness and efficiency. The problems to be solved were comparatively simple, relative to those of today, and the programs were therefore relatively small. As a result the number of programming errors was small, and first became a major problem only when program systems came to be used in the solution of complex scientific and commercial applications. After this, whole teams of programmers worked on the production of program systems which were to be employed by various users. The specification of the problem and the demands placed on the system changed often during the design phase, and also long after the program system had been in use. Besides correctness and efficiency, the mastering of complexity through the decomposition of a problem into problem pieces, the specification of interfaces, security and reliability, flexibility, documentation, maintenance and project organization became major problems in the production of large program systems. This led to difficulties in the design and production of software to such an extent that in 1965 the term "*software crisis*" was coined. There is no comparison to this in the development of hardware. This is not to say that hardware is error-free, but in practice the reasons for difficulties which occur in large computer systems can usually be found in software errors.

Dijkstra (1972a) described this situation as follows:

"To put it quite bluntly: as long as there were no machines, programming was no problem at all; when we had a few weak computers, programming became a mild problem, and now we have gigantic computers, programming has become an equally gigantic problem. In this sense the electronic industry has not solved a single problem, it has only created them--it has created the problem of using its products."

The possibilities which were created by new computer generations vastly exceeded the programming techniques which had been developed up to that time. But the growing economical importance of software production (see *Boehm* 1973), and the enormous expansion of the data processing industry, which forced the development of numerous large program systems, pressed the demand for an improved *programming technology* more and more into the focus of research in the field of computer science.

The attempts at researching acceptable programming technology resulted in two software engineering conferences organized by NATO, in Garmisch in 1968 (*Naur* and *Randell*, 1969) and in Rome in 1969 (*Buxton* and *Randell*,1969). It was indicated at these two conferences that programs are industrial products, and that there was therefore the requirement for: Renunciation of the "art" of tricky, egotistical programming by the individual and adoption of planned, co-operative team programming (see also *Kimm* et al., 1979).

Since then an attempt has been made to analyse *software production* scientifically, considering it as a coherent process, and above all to place the questions of specification, methodical program design, requirements on a programming language, project organization, quality control, documentation and the automation of software production at the center of research interests.

1.2 The Concept of Software Engineering

What lies behind the term "*software engineering*"? Is this just an alternative phrase for programming, or is it a new technology? The term *software engineering* is obviously intended as provocation and indicates that the economical production of programs is an *engineering discipline*. There is to date, however, no generally acceptable, fixed definition of the concept.

Boehm (1979) defines software engineering as follows:

"The practical application of scientific knowledge in the design and construction of computer programs and the associated documentation required to develop, operate, and maintain them."

In *Dennis* (1975) we find the definition:

"Software Engineering is the application of principles, skills and art to the design and construction of programs and systems of programs."

D.L. Parnas (1974) writes:

" . . . software engineering is programming under at least one of the following two conditions:

(1) More than one person is involved in the construction and/or use of the program and

(2) more than one version of the program will be produced."

Finally, *F.L. Bauer* (1975) writes:

[The aim of software engineering is:] "To obtain economically software that is reliable and works efficiently on real machines."

The definitions given above show that the production of *large programs* involves new problems of a different nature to those of the production of *small programs*, and exhibits many similarities with the production of other technical products. The main problems here are:

* the mastering of complexity,
* the decomposition of a problem into pieces, which are then solved by various groups,
* project organization,
* the specification of interfaces between pieces,

* efficiency,
* the documentation and maintenance of the systems,
* portability and adaptability.

Common sense alone is not sufficient for solving all of these problems. It is necessary to examine the entire complex scientifically in order to create the prerequisites for the development of methods and tools which support software development and production. Therefore, it is expected of *good software engineering* that it provide methods, tools, norms and aids which make it possible to handle technical problems (such as *specification, design, construction, testing, efficiency, documentation and maintenance*) and organizational problems (such as *project organization* and *interface specification*) which occur in the production of software, and, in the process, to produce and apply software economically.

Based on this, *software engineering* can be defined as follows:

"*Software engineering* is the practical application of scientific understanding to the economical production and use of reliable and efficient software."

1.3   The Programming Language Modula-2

The development of computing machines was accompanied by the development and implementation of programming languages, in conjunction with compilers for these languages. *Rechenberg* (1983) writes in relation to this: "There already exist many hundreds of programming languages, and new ones are constantly being invented. The (computer) public takes absolutely no notice of most of these and they lead an insignificant life in the surroundings of their inventors." This is not surprising, if one considers which conditions must be satisfied for the general acceptance of a programming language (see *Goos*, 1982):

* The language must satisfy a factual need, because otherwise the effort spent on re-schooling programmers cannot be justified.
* The existence of the language and its compiler must be secured for long time spans (20 years and more, but at least for the life of the program system).
* Reliable compilers must exist for all important target machines, and maintenance and development of these compilers must be secured. In particular, the use of a language cannot be dependent on any given computer manufacturer.
* The implementation should be compatible with programming languages already in use, so that frictionless transition and rational co-existence of the languages is possible.
* The language should be easy to learn.

Until now, only Fortran, Cobol, PL/I, Basic and, increasingly, Pascal have been able to meet these primarily economic demands. Fortran and PL/I owe their success to the fact that they were offered and supported by the leading hardware producer, IBM. Cobol succeeded because the US Department of Defense, one of the larger computer and software customers, stipulated its use. Pascal and Basic are purely university products. Basic, although widespread, does not even begin to satisfy present day requirements on a programming language. Pascal is the only language which has become universally known on the basis only of its own qualities.

However, in the meantime software technology has continued to develop, and ever more stringent requirements have been placed on programming languages. Because none of the conventional programming languages could meet these requirements, new languages have been developed, the most important of which are *Ada* (*Ichbiah* et al., 1979) and *Modula-2* (*Wirth*, 1982).

Because this book handles the entire complex of software engineering, and thus the problem of the implementation and choice of a programming language, the author must consider which language he should recommend to the reader in order to emphasize correct software engineering techniques. Since only Ada and Modula-2 in some way meet the requirements of modern day software engineering the choice lies between them.

Striking similarities are apparent in a comparison of these languages, although they differ completely in volume, intended application and historical development. In Modula-2, as in Ada, the specification and implementation sections of programs are separated, both languages allow separate compilation and the program structure "module" in Modula-2 corresponds almost exactly to the "package" of Ada. Modula-2 allows the formulation of parallel processes, as does Ada, although at a lower level, but then again with more flexibility. The handling of exceptions and generic programs is missing from Modula-2, but these were purposely omitted in order to limit the size of the language.

In this connection *Rechenberg* (1983) writes: "The result of these similarities is that one may use Modula-2 instead of Ada in the vast majority of applications. The clarity of programming in Modula-2, the documentational value of Modula-2 programs and the extent to which the principles of modern software engineering may be applied by Modula-2 programs is just as great as for the corresponding Ada programs, if not in some respects even greater." The small size of Modula-2 is just as appealing; the language definition is only 25 pages long, that of Ada a few hundred. Modula-2 was also developed with an eye to its implementation on microcomputers, and there already exist effective compilers (for example for the workstation Lilith (*Wirth*, 1981) from *N. Wirth*, for Apple computers, Motorola 68000 processors and Intel 8080/8086 processors), which permit practical examination. Not only were the high expectations placed on Modula-2 completely satisfied in an intensive practical test by the author, they were surpassed. Modula-2 is easier to learn than was originally assumed.

Modula-2 was originally developed as a systems programming language for tasks for which Pascal was not sufficient. The language is largely machine independent and supports many software engineering concepts known today. This new language is thus suited to systems as well as to applications programming. The most important *advantages* which become apparent with the use of Modula-2, and which fundamentally add to increased programmer productivity are:

* The capability of separate compilation. This saves much unnecessary compilation time during the test phase.

* Complete type and interface checking, even if modules are compiled separately. This exposes a number of programming errors at compilation time and thus shortens the test phase.

* Modules, which constitute a program structure encompassing procedures, and which admit the implementation of data capsules. They not only increase the documentational value of programs, but also guarantee that large program systems be implemented faster than usual, through the minimization of error sources and the adaptability of modules independently from each other.

* The capability of formulating parallel processes, which extends the range of application markedly.

All these advantages, especially the simplicity of Modula-2 and the ability in Modula-2 to utilize all known software engineering concepts have led the author to present this language to those interested in software design.

2. Quality Standards for Software Products

In the last chapter it was shown that the production of software has the characteristics of an engineering discipline and exhibits similarities to the manufacture of many other technical products. Software is now produced by teams and applied by numerous users. Also, the software being produced is increasingly becoming used as components in more complex technical and commercial systems. This means that the reliable functioning of software products is a decisive factor in the functioning of the systems which they compose. And so the question arises: How can the *quality control requirements*, common in industry today, be applied to software products, and how can their observance be tested?

Software quality is not precisely defined. There is, however, unity among professionals that the *quality* of a software product entails much more than just its correctness. What then are the *quality features* which are derived from quality control stipulations and which determine the excellence of a software system? How can these features be measured? What are the consequences for software engineering?

To a certain extent the professional world is in agreement as to what features determine software quality. These matters are frequently discussed in the literature and at conferences (see *Boehm* et al., 1976; *Bowen*, 1978; *McCabe*, 1976; *McCall* et al., 1977a, 1977b; *Ramamoorthy* et al., 1982; *Yin* and *Winchester*, 1978). But methods and quantitative results, which are necessary for precision quality control, similar to those for other industrial products, for example the machine industry, do not, in general, exist.

In this chapter the discussion will first concentrate on the most important element of *quality planning*, the determination of *quality features*. Second the *implications of quality in software production* are discussed, followed by a few remarks about the *interactions between quality features*. Quantitative results which measure the fulfillment of a quality feature have been left out because, in the view of the writer, research developments in this field are not, as yet, sufficiently mature to warrant a discussion.

2.1 Software Quality Features

The quality requirements for software products resulted in the definition of quality features. But in practice one often meets unsolved problems. *Cavano* (1978) observes two problem areas in this connection: on the one hand there exists no generally accepted definition of the concepts *quality* and *quality feature*, on the other hand an unequivocal, objective evaluation of quality, for example in the completion of a software product, is not possible. But quality must necessarily be an aim of software development, and it affects not only the *planning* but also the *realization* and *supervision* of software production. The arthor wishes therefore, to define the most important, and in practice most recognized, *quality features-- correctness, reliability, user convenience* (adequacy, learnability, robustness), *maintainability* (readability, expandability, testability), *efficiency* and *portability*--(see illustration 2.1).

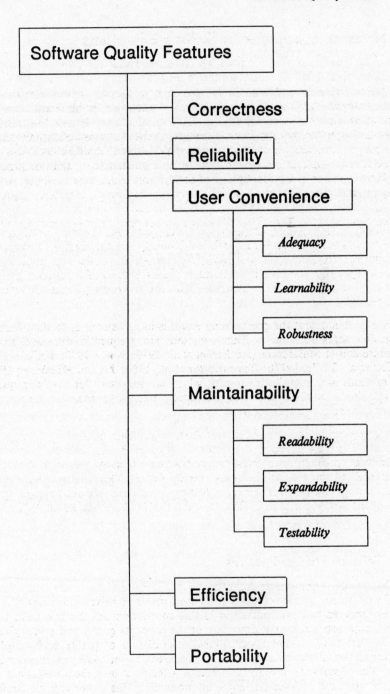

Illustration 2.1 Software Quality Features

Correctness

By the *correctness* of a program we understand that the program satisfy the functional specifications, which are the foundation of program development. The correctness of a program, then, relates only to the conformity of *functional specifications* and *program text*, and is therefore unrelated to the actual use of the program (compare *Kopetz*, 1979). The problem of the correctness of a program which is later to be embedded in a larger program system is especially critical. If p is the probability that an individual program is correct, then the probability P, that a program system which is made up of n programs is correct, is given by $P = p^n$. If n is large, p must be very nearly 1 if P is to be appreciably different from 0 (compare *Dijkstra*, 1972b):

n \ P	0.99	0.95	0.90
1	0.99	0.95	0.90
10	0.90	0.60	0.35
50	0.61	0.08	0.01
100	0.37	0.01	0.00

P

Reliability

The *reliability* of a program is determined on the one hand by its *correctness* and on the other by its *availability*. The correctness of a program is defined above without any mention of the time interval during which a program must satisfy a given specification. The time dependent fulfillment of a given specification determines the reliability of a program.

The reliability of a program can be defined in accordance with *Kopetz*, (1976) as the probability that the program can provide a function (determined by the specification) for a given number of input cases under fixed input conditions during a given time interval (under the assumption that hardware and input are free of errors). Thus the reliability of a program is its survival probability. It may be described by the reliability function R_t (see *Kopetz*, 1976). R has the following properties:

$R_0 = 1$ It is assumed that the program is working at the start of the time interval.

$R_\infty = 0$ It is assumed that the program is certainly not working at time $t = \infty$.

If Q_t is the unreliability of a program, then we have for all t: $Q_t + R_t = 1$.

User convenience

We consider *user convenience* to be a collective term for the *adequacy*, *learnability* and *robustness* of a system.

The requirement of *adequacy* relates to

(1) the required input
(2) the service provided by the system
(3) the output produced

Concerning (1)

The required input should be limited to a minimum, that is it should be as concise as possible but as detailed as necessary. The program should demand information of the user only when it is required for a task chosen by the user. The program should offer the user unformatted data input and conduct plausibility checks of the input. Uniformity and clarity in directing the user are of special importance in dialog oriented systems.

Concerning (2)

With due consideration to expandability, the services a program provides should be tailored to the desires of the user; this means that the functions offered should be limited to those given in the specification.

Concerning (3)

The output of a program should be readable, well structured and easy to interpret. The program should offer the user flexibility with respect to the volume, amount of detail and the format of printed results. Any error messages must be in understandable form for the user.

The *learnability* of a program depends directly on the form of the user interfaces and the clarity and simplicity of the user manual. The user manual should have a clear and simple structure, free of unnecessary ballast. It should explain to the user what the program can do on the whole, how individual functions are activated, which connections exist between functions, which exceptional conditions can occur and how they must be handled. In addition it should serve as a *reference manual* which permits the user to find answers to concrete questions quickly and easily.

By the *robustness* of a program we mean the property which weakens the effects of operating errors, erroneous input and hardware failures for a given application, and define according to *Kopetz* (1976):

"A software system is said to be robust when the consequences of an input or hardware error related to a given application are inversely proportional to the probability of the occurrence of that error in that application."

This means that frequent errors (for example command errors, typing errors, etc.) must be handled with special care, whereas less frequent errors may be dealt with more generously, as long as they can do no irreparable damage.

Maintainability

By the *maintainability* of a program we mean the ease with which errors can be localized and corrected and the ease with which the program functions can be altered or expanded. This definition indicates that the maintainability of a program depends on its readability, expandability and testability.

The *readability* of a program is dependent on the way in which it is represented, on the programming style and its consistency, on the readability of the implementation language, on how structured the system is and, most decisively, on the quality of the documentation.

The *expandability* of a program is dependent on whether or not it is possible to insert the desired changes at the logically appropriate point in the program, with no undesired side effects. This is especially dependent on the modularity and the amount of structure of the program, but is also, of course, dependent on the readability (in order to find "appropriate points") and the availability of an understandable program documentation.

By the *testability* of a program we mean how well the program facilitates testing of the program run (run time behavior, susceptibility to error, output behavior under predetermined conditions) and localization of program errors. Testability depends primarily on the modularity and the amount of structure of the program. Modular, well structured programs lend themselves better to systematic, stepwise testing than do monolithic, unstructured programs. Test aids, such as switchable output mechanisms contained in source code, assertions and comments in the documentation of algorithms, reduce the difficulty of testing and create the prerequisites for a general, systematic test of all program components.

Efficiency

By the *efficiency* of a program we mean the ability of the program to fulfill its task with the optimal use of all resources. Here "resources" must be interpreted very broadly and refers to memory space, CPU-time, I/O channels and peripheral devices, but it also refers to the volume and preparation of the input and output data.

Portability

By the *portability* of a program we mean the convenience with which the program can be implemented on various hardware systems. The portability of a program is therefore a function of its hardware independence. Hardware independence is determined, for example, by the choice of the implementation language and by the degree to which special operating system functions and hardware properties are used. Thus the portability depends in large measure on whether or not the program is so organized that the system dependent parts are grouped into easily exchangeable units. A program can be considered portable if the effort required to adapt the program is much less than the effort required to reprogram (compare *Tanenbaum* et al., 1978).

2.2 The Importance of Quality Features in Software Production

The quality requirements for a software product are not only limited to the final (ready to use) product. Rather, the quality of the final product is dependent on the quality of the intermediate products, which means that the quality requirements relate to all levels of the production process. Poor quality of the intermediate products (for example in the general design) always implies poor quality in the final product. Concerning the quality features and their implications for the production process we can distinguish between:

* quality features which concern the final product
* quality features which concern the intermediate products

The quality features for *final products* can be grouped according to *Bons* and *van Megen* (1982), *Cavano* (1978) and *Schmitz* et al. (1980) into:

* quality features related to the *application*. These affect the appropriateness of the product for the intended application. These are correctness, reliability and user convenience.
* quality features related to the *maintenance*. These affect the capacity of the product for change and expansion of the program functions. These are readability, expandability and testability.
* quality features related to the *portability*. These affect the ability of the product to be adapted to other environments. These are portability and testability.

The quality features for *intermediate products* can be grouped according to *Bons* and *van Megen* (1982) and *Cavano* (1978) into:

* quality features related to the *transformation*. These affect the capacity of an intermediate product to be transformed into subsequent (higher level) products. These are correctness, readability and testability.
* quality features which affect the *quality of the final product*. These directly affect the quality of the final product and are correctness, readability and testability.

2.3   The Interactions between Quality Features and their Effect on Cost and Time Parameters

The interactions between quality features and their effect on cost and time parameters are shown in illustration 2.2 (compare also *Bons* and *van Megen*, 1982). A positive effect is shown by a "+", a negative effect by a "-" little or no effect by a "0".

The information given in illustration 2.2 indicates that the task of satisfying a given quality requirement initiates measures in the development process which on the one hand may be connected with cost and time expenditures (for example increasing the correctness, reliability, user convenience, etc.), but on the other hand generally result in cost and time savings in the maintenance and operation of the software product (for example through better readability, testability and robustness). Then again some quality features are incompatible (for example reliability has a negative effect on efficiency).

Feature \ Affects	Correctness	Reliability	Adequacy	Learnability	Robustness	Readability	Changeability	Testability	Efficiency	Portability	Development Time	Lifetime	Development Costs	Operating Costs	Maintenance Costs	Transportation Costs
Correctness		+	0	0	+	0	0	0	0	0	-	+	-	+	+	0
Reliability	+		0	0	+	0	0	0	-	0	-	+	-	+	-	-
Adequacy	0	0		+	+	0	0	0	+	-	-	0	-	+	-	-
Learnability	0	0	0		0	0	0	0	-	0	-	0	-	+	0	0
Robustness	0	+	+	+		0	0	+	-	-	-	+	-	+	+	-
Readability	+	+	0	0	+		+	+	-	+	+	+	+	0	+	+
Changeability	+	+	+	0	+	0		+	-	+	-	+	+	0	+	+
Testability	+	+	0	0	+	0	+		-	+	+	+	+	0	+	+
Efficiency	-	-	+	-	-	-	-	-		-	-	+	-	+	-	-
Portability	0	0	-	0	0	+	+	0	-		-	+	-	-	+	+

Illustration 2.2 Interactions between Quality Features and their Effect on Cost and Time Parameters

Further Reading

Boehm, B.W., et al.: Quantitative Evaluation of Software Quality; Proc. of 2nd Internat. Conf. on Software Engineering; IEEE Comp.Soc. 1976.

Boehm, B.W.: Software Engineering; In: Classics in Software Engineering; Yourdon Press 1979.

Boehm, B.W.: Characteristics of Software Quality; North Holland 1978.

Bowen, J.B.: Are Current Approaches Sufficient for Measuring Software Quality; Proc. Software Quality Assurance Workshop, San Diego; 1978.

Jones, T.: Measuring Program Quality and Productivity; IBM Systems Journal, vol. 17(1); 1978.

Kopetz, H.: Software Reliability; Macmillan Press 1979.

Ramamoorthy, C.V., et al.: Techniques in Software Quality Assurance; Proc. of the German Chapter of the ACM, Vol.9; Teubner 1982.

3. The Choice of the Programming Language

From the point of view of software engineering it is, of course, interesting to ask whether, and in what way, the quality of a software product is influenced by the choice of the programming language. When programmers first started to formulate algorithms, in order to run them on a computer, the task of programming consisted quite literally in the translation of these algorithms into octal, or even into binary coded bit sequences. The programmers had to orient their programs according to the special properties of a particular computer. The prerequisite for this was an exact knowledge of the details of the machine on which the program was to be run. The program structure was influenced to a much larger extent by the architecture of the machine than by the nature of the problem. In this respect, *Wirth* (1978) writes: "The intentional orientation of algorithms to the strangest peculiarities of a particular computer was a poor application of the human intellect, and because of its strong adhesion to a particular computing system the programmer was not only enabled but even encouraged to devise all possible tricks in order to get a maximum out of the peculiarities of that computer." The code, which was unstructured and barely readable, made programming more difficult and was unsuited to represent complicated algorithms. Such programs could usually be adapted to new requirements only by the programmer himself, just because of their unreadability. Interchanging programs between different machines was completely impossible.

These deficiencies led to the development of so called "*higher programming languages.*" Such languages can--as *Wirth* expresses it--be considered command languages for ideal computers, which are oriented not to hardware architecture, but rather to the customs and capabilities of human beings in expressing their concepts. The availability of higher programming languages influenced the development of data and information processing immensely. The choice of the *right* programming language for the implementation of software products influences, to a much greater extent than is often assumed in practice, the quality of these software products. For this reason, this chapter is concerned with the importance of the programming language to a software project and with the *logical* and *pragmatic* criteria for the choice of a programming language.

3.1 The Relevance of the Programming Language

During implementation, the functions defined in a specification must be realized in such a way that they may be executed on a computer. The programming language is the tool for this transformation process. It is therefore clear that certain conditions be placed on this tool, and that this transformation process is decisively influenced by the degree to which these conditions are fulfilled. During the implementation of a program system it is necessary that the decomposition into modules, which is defined in the design phase, should be expressible in an algorithmic language, that the objects on which the specified functions operate should be representable in that language, and that the language should provide control structures which make it possible to formulate the specified functions.

From the standpoint of software design, these requirements are still not satisfactory. We know today that the costs as well as the quality of a software product depend strongly on testability and maintainability. Therefore the simplicity, the readability (that is the documental value) and the redundancy of the programming language have a large impact on the software product.

An inappropriate notation for the representation of a program system can detract considerably from the testing and maintenance of the system. In some cases it may even make them impossible. The choice of the right programming language minimizes these problems, reduces the test effort and is the prerequisite for economic program maintenance.

The engineer who works on a software project usually knows during the design phase of the algorithms in which programming language these will be implemented later. We know that there is a relationship between a natural language and the thinking of someone who uses it. This is also true of programming languages. Knowledge of the structure of a programming language influences the thinking of the programmer, his programming style and the amount of structure in the algorithms which he designs (compare *Goos* (1977) with this). This, however, means that the properties of a programming language also affect the phases of software production which come before the actual process of programming, assuming that the programmer knows the implementation language.

The choice of a programming language often determines even the way in which a problem is implemented on a computer. Programming languages usually contain concepts which support certain methods of solution. So somebody who uses Fortran will not easily arrive at the solution of a problem through the use of two parallel processes, or implement a syntax analyzer according to the principle of recursive descent, because Fortran neither supports the programming of parallel processes, nor allows recursive procedures. And the same is true of the data structures and data types which are permitted by a programming language. It will never occur to a Basic programmer to use abstract data types, whereby somebody who programs in Ada or Modula-2 may well consider this. Compare in this respect *Goos* (1977).

The considerations mentioned above make the relevancy of the programming language clear. Unfortunately the question as to which programming language is the right one for which software project is extremely difficult to answer. Not only are there an unlimited number of applications and hundreds of programming languages, but there are also many different opinions on the matter. It is not possible even to attempt to find an answer which is satisfactory to everyone. But we can discuss the most relevant logical and pragmatic decision factors and put the problem into the correct light.

3.2   Logical Criteria for the Choice of a Programming Language

In software engineering a number of criteria are known which are important for the choice of a programming language in general, as well as in connection with a particular application. The primary criteria are:

* the area of application,

* project size,
* simplicity and readability,
* the size of the language,
* program control structures,
* flow control structures,
* data structures,
* arithmetic,
* string processing,
* input/output support,
* the efficiency of the compiler,
* separate compilation,
* type checking.

Of these, the most important criteria for the choice of a programming language is the *area of application.* The distinction usually made between commercial and scientific-technical applications is certainly justified, but reality is much more complicated. Many applications in the technical or scientific field use functions which previously were associated with the commercial domain, and vice versa. In addition there are applications which cannot be associated with either of these fields. The trick is to start from the problem in order to extract the requirements which are to be put on the programming language and to incorporate these into the decision process according to their importance (once again relative to the application).

Requirements on the programming language may also be extracted from the *project size.* Mastering the complexity of a large program system is closely tied to the modularity and the degree of structure in the system. Module and flow structures should be representable in the implementation language.

Further criteria are the *simplicity* and *readability* of the programming language. The sizes of programming languages differ greatly. The size influences not only the simplicity and learnability but also the command over the language that a programmer has, and also the readability of the algorithms formulated in the language.

Small language size does not necessarily mean that the programs will be readable. Programming languages like Snobol or APL permit very abbreviated notation, but the programs are extremely difficult to read because of the the high semantic content of the symbols. *Medium sized languages* such as Pascal or Modula-2 are easy to learn and lend themselves well to the writing of readable programs. *Large programming languages,* for example PL/I or Ada, also have high documentary value but are difficult to learn because of their size.

Another very important criterion is the availability of *program control structures.* How well structure of the decomposition of a solution to a problem can be expressed in an algorithmic language is obviously important. The nature of the program control structures also influences the readability and the amount of structure of programs. Languages with procedure and modul concepts (for example Ada and Modula-2) encourage modular programming, whereas languages like Basic induce one to construct large, monolithic programs.

The *availability* of useable *flow control structures* is of major importance for the internal structure of programs. Flow control structures influence the readability and the amount of structure of programs. Languages without GOTO's (for example Modula-2) encourage structured programming, while languages which contain numbered IF's and GOTO's (for example Fortran) induce one to write unstructured programs.

The next criterion is the *availability of data structures*. Many programming languages only offer data structures of limited complexity; for example the most complex data structure offered by Fortran is the "array." If one requires more flexible data structures, such as "records," he must use a language such as Cobol or PL/I. If it is appropriate to the problem to define new data types (which extend beyond the standard types) one needs a language such as Pascal, Ada or Modula-2. For many applications it is useful if complex data structures (such as trees) can be dynamically generated.

The *arithmetic* which is supported by a programming language is also a criterion. For commercial applications one can seldom manage without real numbers and in scientific or technical applications one may not be able to forgo complex numbers.

A further criterion is the possibility of *string processing* in non-numeric tasks. Fortran is less adapted than PL/I or Cobol for such tasks, but Snobol was developed especially for this and is precisely adapted to tasks in this field of application.

Primarily for reasons of portability, *input/output support* is an important criterion. Portability depends especially on input/output handling in the language used. Here it is important that only trivial structures such as sequential files be supported because no generally accepted standards exist for more complex access types.

The *operating system (batch or dialog)* is a criterion which influences the choice of language. Modern programming languages like Ada and Modula-2, but also dialog languages like APL and Basic, are better adapted to dialog programming than, for example, Fortran, and in some cases the consideration of special dialog languages is called for.

The *Efficiency and size* of both the compiler and the code which the compiler generates are also decision factors. Computer systems with a small main storage area permit only compilers with minimum storage use. Compilers for PL/I, for example, use a large amount of storage and, in addition, often generate inefficient code. In spite of the rapid developments in hardware technology, run time and storage use are still critical factors.

Further criteria are *separate compilation* and *type checking*. The facility of separate compilation of program modules not only guarantees that the modular decomposition given in the design can be expressed in the programming language, but also saves much unnecessary compilation time during the test phase. Separate compilability is a necessary requirement for the implementation of complex programming languages. Just as important a requirement is the complete checking of types, which means that in expressions and assignments the type compatibility of the operands, and in procedure calls the type compatibility of the actual and formal parameters be checked by the compiler. Many programming errors can be exposed at compilation time, and thus many unpleasant and expensive run-time errors can be avoided. Modern programming languages such as Ada and Modula-2 admit complete type checking between separately compiled modules. This increases the security of the interface consistency between separately compiled modules.

Another important criterion determining the choice of language is the availability of *real-time functions*. Some languages are well adapted to this. Here it is wise to consider not just general programming languages like PL/I, Concurrent Pascal or Modula-2 for the availability of real-time functions, but also to take special languages such as RTL/2 or Coral66 into consideration.

Because of the high value of the implementation language in a software project, it may even be economically feasible, for large projects, to define a language specifically tailored to the task. Practical examples of this are the use of the programming language C for the implementation of the manufacturer independent operating system UNIX, and CHILL for the implementation of a telecommunications system.

3.3   Pragmatic Criteria for the Choice of Programming Language

In the previous section we discussed the most important *logical criteria* which affect the choice of programming language in a software project. In practice, however, we see that the choice of programming language is often determined by *pragmatic criteria.*

The most important criteria are (compare with *Sommerville*, 1985):

* the demands placed by the customer,
* the availability of compilers,
* the standardization of the language,
* the level of experience of the programming team,
* the implementation languages of earlier projects,
* the availability of facilities and tools.

Demands placed by the customer: The implementation language is often prespecified by the customer. He is often guided by market standards or by which implementation language was previously used in his organization.

The availability of compilers: Because a specific computer is usually given for the implementation of a software project, the choice of programming language also depends on the availability of acceptable (that is efficient and convenient) compilers for the machine.

The standardization (portability) of the language: If a software product is only to be used on a particular computer and only for a limited time, the question of portability is of little consequence. If a software product is to be developed for various users, however, then it should be guaranteed that the product can be run on different computers. The portability of software products is closely connected with the standardization of the implementation language. For languages such as Cobol or Fortran, for example, there exist internationally valid standards. Programs in these languages can therefore be transferred to almost any computer. Pascal--a much more modern, and in many respects a better language than Fortran or Cobol--although widespread, exists in many dialects. This greatly limits the portability of Pascal programs.

The level of experience of the programming team: Learning a programming language is in principle not very complicated. Still, much practice and experience are necessary for the secure handling of a language. This is often a reason for the nonacceptance of new languages. Although practice and experience with a programming language are certainly important criteria, nevertheless, for large software projects lack of experience of the programming team should not be grounds for nonacceptance a language which satisfies the logical requirements.

The implementation languages of earlier projects: The more different programming languages that are in use in an organization the higher the level of experience of the programming team must be. When a programmer works simultaneously with numerous programming languages, the number of coding errors increases because he confuses the syntax rules. For economical reasons, therefore, an attempt will be made to limit the number of programming languages. Another disadvantage is that standard modules (such as input/output modules, mask generators, etc.), which have already been implemented, are not necessarily useable when a new implementation language is introduced.

The availability of facilities and tools: Good software facilities and tools such as editors, test facilities, diagram generators, etc. assist immensely in reducing the development costs and time for a software project. Some tools, such as structure oriented editors, compilers, debuggers and data and program flow analyzers are tied to a particular programming language. The availability of these kinds of tools simplifies the implementation and validation of software products and therefore influences the choice of implementation language.

In summary (compare with *Meek* and *Heath,* 1980; *Sommerville,* 1985):

One of the most important decisions in the production of large software systems is the choice of the right implementation language. It influences the design and the implementation, reduces the test and maintenance effort and determines the amount of structure, readability, security and portability of a software product.

At the present there exist no programming languages which are equally well adapted for all imaginable applications, and which are acceptably standardized. Nor are there likely to in the future, because the requirements contradict each other. It is therefore recommended that when choosing a programming language, one start with the problem in deciding which requirements are to be placed on the language and how they are to be weighted, because it is practically impossible to find an already existent language which satisfies all requirements in equal measure. The criteria above serve as a guideline for determining the requirements for the implementation language. From the set of programming languages considered, the language which is the most appropriate on the basis of the system specification should be selected. Because of the importance of the programming language in a software project, every pragmatic criterion which speaks against choosing the most appropriate programming language for the task should be evaluated with utmost care.

Barry W. Boehm (1980) writes:

"Choosing a Higher Order Language, like choosing a wife, is hard to undo after getting involved, and is not to be taken lightly."

Further Reading

Boehm, B. W.: Software Engineering As It Is; Academic Press 1980.

Hoare, C. A. R.: Prospects for a Better Programming Language; In: High level Languages, Infotech State of the Art Report 7; Infotech Ltd, Maidenhead, England 1972.

Hoare, C. A. R.: The High Cost of Programming Language; Software Systems Engineering, Online Conferences Ltd., Uxbridge England 1976.

Sommerville, I.: Choosing a Programming Language; In: Software Engineering; Addison-Wesley 1985.

4. Modula-2

This chapter is *not* an introduction to the programming language Modula-2; for this the reader is referred to the book by *N. Wirth* (1982). It is a complete description of Modula-2 which is organized to suit the present purpose. On the one hand this chapter serves as a preparation for the following chapters in which the elements of Modula-2 are used, and on the other hand it should serve the programmer as a manual.

The first section of this chapter explains the *lexical symbols* of Modula-2, in the second section the *syntactic structure* of programs is described. Programs always consist of two parts; the description of data objects, and the actions which use these objects. The third section is therefore concerned with the linguistic possibilities for describing *data* and *data types*. In the fourth section the rules for the construction of *expressions* are given, in the fifth section the rules for the *compatibility* of objects, and in the sixth section the *statements*. Modula-2 is distinguished from other programming languages primarily by the module concept and the possibility of dividing programs (or modules) into a specification and an implementation part. The *module concept* is described in the seventh section of this chapter. In the eighth section the *low level facilities* of Modula-2 are discussed and in the ninth section the *process concept* for the support of programming parallel processes is introduced. The tenth and last section describes the *standard procedures* defined in Modula-2. Because this book is concerned primarily with the aspects of applications programming, interrupt handling and the concept of module priority are not dealt with here. The interested reader is referred to appendix 1.

However, the intention is not to withhold *Wirth's* Modula-2 language definition from the reader. Appendix 1 therefore contains the Modula-2-Report (*Wirth*, 1982). After completion of the manuscript, *Wirth* published two changes and a few additions which are included in appendix 2 of this book. Appendix 3 contains a collection of all syntax rules including the alterations given in appendix 2.

To describe the syntax of Modula-2 *Wirth's* EBNF notation (extended Backus-Naur formalism) has been used. If x, y and z are arbitrary syntax symbols then the meaning of the following expressions are given below.

```
x y z               the concatenation of x, y and z
x | y | z           x or y or z
(x | y) z           xz or yz
[x] y               y or xy
{x} y               x occurs zero or more times (arbitrarily
                    often) in succession (y, xy, xxy, ...)
```

Every linguistic construction is described by a rule

```
Identifier = Expression.
```

where *Identifier* is a nonterminal symbol and *Expression* is an arbitrary expression of the above form which consists of terminal and nonterminal symbols.

Terminal symbols are those for which there are no rules for further decomposition (for example reserved words, identifiers or constants). *Nonterminal symbols* (such as programs or instructions) are those which may be further decomposed by certain rules.

For better legibility nonterminal symbols are capitalized and terminal symbols are written in lower case letters. Particular representatives of terminal symbols are given in quotation marks (for example "IF").

Example:

```
IfStatement  =  "IF" Expression "THEN" StatementSequence
                {"ELSIF" Expression "THEN" StatementSequence}
                ["ELSE" StatementSequence]  "END".
```

4.1 Lexical Symbols

The vocabulary of Modula-2 consists of identifiers, numbers (integers or real numbers), strings, operators, delimiters and comments. They are called symbols and consist of a sequence of characters. For a description of the structure of symbols the EBNF notation introduced above is used. The rules for the construction of these symbols are as follows:

(1) **Identifiers** consist of a sequence of letters and digits. The first character must be a letter.

```
ident = letter {letter | digit}.
```

A differentiation is made between capital and lower case letters.

Example:

```
Word  word   SymbolType    V24
```

Here "Word" and "word" are different.

In some cases, identifiers must be qualified in Modula-2 programs in order to indicate their origin or ownership. Qualified identifiers have the following form:

```
qualident = {ident "."} ident.
```

Example:

```
OutputModule.printpos    OutputModule.baserec.salary
```

(2) **Integers** ("IntConstants") are sequences of digits. For integers there is a difference between decimal, octal and hexadecimal numbers. Integers followed by a "C" represent the character corresponding to the ordinal expressed by the number.

Real numbers ("RealConstants") are sequences of digits which contain a decimal point and which may be followed by an exponential notation. The syntax rules are:

```
Number        = IntConstant | RealConstant.

IntConstant   = DecConstant | OctConstant | HexConstant
                | CharConstant.

DecConstant   = Digit {Digit}.

OctConstant   = OctDigit {OctDigit} "B".

HexConstant   = Digit {HexDigit} "H".

CharConstant  = OctDigit {OctDigit} "C".

OctDigit      = "0" | "1" | "2" | "3" | "4" | "5" | "6" | "7".

Digit         = OctDigit | "8" | "9".

HexDigit      = Digit | "A" | "B" | "C" | "D" | "E" | "F".

RealConstant  = Digit {Digit} "." {Digit} [ScaleFactor].

ScaleFactor   = "E" ["+" | "-"] Digit {Digit}.
```

Example:
```
1    1984   3.14159    4.0E3 (= 4000.)   33C    6BAH
OAH (=10 decimal)
```

(3) **Strings** are enclosed in quotation marks or apostrophes and may either not include quotation marks (when enclosed in quotation marks) or else apostrophes (when enclosed in apostrophes). Strings have the form:

```
String   = """ {character} """ | "'" {character} "'".
```

Example:
```
"arbitrary character sequence"
"Shakespeare's Hamlet"
'The "Lilith" of Niklaus Wirth'
```

(4) **Operators** and **delimiters** are the special characters, character pairs and reserved words listed below. Reserved words are written in capitals and may not be used as identifiers.

+	=	AND	FOR	QUALIFIED
-	#	ARRAY	FROM	RECORD
*	<	BEGIN	IF	REPEAT
/	>	BY	IMPLEMENTATION	RETURN
:=	<>	CASE	IMPORT	SET
&	<=	CONST	IN	THEN
.	>=	DEFINITION	LOOP	TO
,	..	DIV	MOD	TYPE
;	:	DO	MODULE	UNTIL
(	)	ELSE	NOT	VAR
[	]	ELSIF	OF	WHILE
{	}	END	OR	WITH
↑	|	EXIT	POINTER	
		EXPORT	PROCEDURE	

(5) **Comments** may be inserted in programs at any position between two symbols and are overread by the compiler. They are arbitrary sequences of characters which are enclosed in the comment brackets "(*" and "*)". Comments may be nested.

Example:

```
(* m is the number of lines of P*)
(* Next Symbol(sy) (*sy contains the type of the next source
   symbol*) i := i+1*)
```

Spaces may occur anywhere between, but not within, symbols (with the exception of strings). They are sometimes necessary in order to separate symbols (for example in "TYPE t=CHAR;"), but have no other importance.

In Modula-2 there are also **standard identifiers** which reference standard procedures, elementary data types, transfer functions and constant identifiers. They are not reserved words, which means they may be redefined.

ABS	EXCL	NIL
BITSET	FALSE	ODD
BOOLEAN	FLOAT	ORD
CAP	HALT	PROC
CARDINAL	HIGH	REAL
CHAR	INC	TRUE
CHR	INCL	TRUNC
DEC	INTEGER	VAL
DISPOSE	NEW	

4.2 Programs

A program is identified by a name and consists, in general, of a collection of data types, data (objects), modules and procedures, and instructions which manipulate the data and activate the procedures. The data, modules and procedures used must be declared. The syntax for Modula-2 programs is therefore:

```
ProgramModule = "MODULE" name ";" Block name ".".

Block = {Declaration} "BEGIN" StatementSequence "END".
```

* "name" is the name of the program, which may be chosen arbitrarily by the programmer.
* "Declaration" contains the declarations of data, modules and procedures used in the program (for details see sections 4.3 and 4.7).
* "StatementSequence" contains the program instructions (for details see section 4.6).

4.3 Declarations

Data are represented as values of variables or constants. Each variable which is used in the instruction section of a Modula-2 program must be declared, that is, its identifier must be associated with a data type. The data type defines the value domain which the variable can accept, and the operations which are permitted on this domain.

In general, the syntax rules for a declaration are:

```
Declaration = "TYPE" {TypeDeclaration ";"}
            | "VAR" {VariableDeclaration ";"}
            | "CONST" {ConstantDeclaration ";"}
            | ProcedureDeclaration
            | ModuleDeclaration.
```

The declaration of data types is first described. Thereafter it is possible to show how variables and constants are declared. Procedures and modules must be declared, like the data objects of a program. The rules for the declaration of procedures are contained in section 4.3.4, those of modules in section 4.7.

4.3.1 Declaration of Data Types

Data types can be either standard data types (such as INTEGER, REAL, BOOLEAN) or data types explicitly declared by the programmer.

4.3.1.1 Standard Data Types

In Modula-2 there are six *standard data types*:

INTEGER, CARDINAL, REAL, BOOLEAN, CHAR and BITSET.

The data type *INTEGER* represents a set of integer values, expressed in the range $[-2^{w-1}, 2^{w-1}-1]$, where w is implementation dependent (usually the word length of the target machine).

For objects which may only take on positive values Modula-2 provides the type *CARDINAL*. It represents a set of positive whole number values in the range $[0, 2^w-1]$.

Real numbers are represented by the type *REAL*. In the computer a real number is represented by a pair of values consisting of a mantissa and an exponent. Because these values can be represented in the computer only up to a certain number of places, rounding and truncation errors occur. Real numbers are therefore not exact representations of numerical values.

The data type *BOOLEAN* represents the truth values given by the two standard identifiers TRUE and FALSE.

The data type *CHAR* is used to represent characters. It represents a set of (printable) characters. Which characters belong to this set depends on the character set of the target machine. In general, however, it may be said that the data type CHAR includes all letters, the digits and special characters.

The data type *BITSET* represents the set of all sets that may be constructed from cardinal values between 0 and n-1, whereby n is once again implementation dependent (n is the word length of the target machine or a small multiple of it). Constants of this type are represented in the usual set notation, for example $\{2,4,6\}$ or $\{1..15\}$ or $\{\}$ (in which case the set is empty).

The data type of a variable determines the domain of its values, and also the operations which are defined on this domain. The operations can be divided into *arithmetic operations, comparison operations, logical operations* and *set operations*. The table shown in illustration 4.1 shows which operations are defined on which data types. The symbols given in parentheses in the column for the operations indicate the corresponding Modula-2 operators.

Objects of a standard data type admit also standard functions (such as determining the absolute value of an integer object, or the numerical equivalent of a character value) and transfer functions. In a way, they represent operations also, but we do not handle them until section 4.10.

4.3.1.2 Declaration of Type Names

The *type* of an object in a Modula-2 program can be either a *standard data type* (see section 4.3.1.1) or a *data type explicitly defined* by a type declaration in the program.

The syntax of a type declaration is:

```
TypeDeclaration = typename "=" Type.
```

* "typename" is the name of a newly declared data type, which may be chosen at will by the programmer.
* "Type" describes the type.

Two kinds of data type are distinguished: the *unstructured* (simple) and the *structured* (composite) types:

```
Type =     SimpleType | Set Type          (1) unstructured
                                               data types
           | ArrayType | Record Type
           | PointerType                   (2) structured
           | ProcedureType.                    data types
```

Operation		Data Type					
		INT	CARD	REAL	BOOL	CHAR	BITSET
Arithmetic Operation	Result ▶	X	X	X			
Sign Change	(-)	X	X	X			
Addition	(+)	X	X	X			
Subtraction	(-)	X	X	X			
Multiplication	(*)	X	X	X			
Whole Number Division	(DIV)	X	X				
Real Division	(/)			X			
Modulus	(MOD)	X	X	X			
Comparison Operations	Result ▶				X		
Equality	(=)	X	X	X	X	X	X
Inequality	(# or <>)	X	X	X	X	X	X
Less Than	(<)	X	X	X	X	X	
Less Than or Equal	(<=)	X	X	X	X	X	X
Greater Than or Equal	(>=)	X	X	X	X	X	X
Greater Than	(>)	X	X	X	X	X	
Contained In	(IN)	X	X	X	X	X	X
Logical Operations	Result ▶				X		
Negation	(NOT)				X		
Conjunction	(AND or &)				X		
Disjunction	(OR)				X		
Set Operations	Result ▶						X
Union	(+)						X
Difference	(-)						X
Intersection	(*)						X
Symmetrical Difference	(/)						X

Illustration 4.1 Operations and Standard Data Types

4.3.1.3 Unstructured Data Types

The standard data types described in section 4.3.1.1 are unstructured data types. The *enumeration type*, the *subrange type* and the *set type* are also unstructured data types.

Syntax:

```
SimpleType   =   Enumeration | SubrangeType | qualident.

Enumeration  =   "(" enuident {"," enuident } ")".
```

```
SubrangeType    =    "[" ConstExpr ".." ConstExpr "]".

SetType         =    "SET" "OF" SimpleType.
```

"qualident" is the (qualified) identifier of a previously declared data type. The qualification of identifiers is explained in sections 4.4.1 and 4.7.

The enumeration type

* The domain of this type is defined by explicitly listing the values.
* Each element ("enuident") of such a list may occur only once (uniqueness) and corresponds syntactically to an identifier.
* In use, the order of the list is important. It determines the exact ordering which makes an enumeration of the list possible. The first element receives the ordinal 0.

Example:
```
TYPE Weekday  = (monday,  tuesday, wednesday, thursday,
                 friday,  saturday, sunday);
```

The subrange type

* The domain of values of this type is given by explicitly specifying the interval ["ConstExpr1".."ConstExpr2"].
* The bounds of the domain must be constant expressions. The syntax rules for "ConstExpr" are discussed in section 4.3.2. The value of the lower bound must be less than that of the upper bound.
* Every subrange type has a base type which is defined by the data type of the bounds of the domain.
* All operations which are permitted for the base type are permitted for the subrange type.
* The objects of a subrange type may receive values only in the domain specified in the type declaration.
* For numerical subrange types: when the lower bound is negative, INTEGER is accepted as the base type. When the upper bound is larger than $2^{w-1} - 1$, CARDINAL is accepted as the base type. Otherwise, either is accepted. No subrange type may be defined for the types REAL and BITSET.

Example:
```
TYPE S        = [1..N];
TYPE Workday  = [monday..friday];
TYPE Letter   = ["A".."Z"];
```

The set type

* The previously introduced data types all have the property that their elements can be enumerated (with the exception of the type REAL). The set type, as opposed to the enumeration type, does not represent an enumeration of particular elements, but rather it is an encompassing structure for the combinations of elements of a particular base type. The domain of a set type is therefore the set of all sets which may be constructed from the base type (= the power set of the base type).

* The base type must be either a subrange type of the data type CARDINAL or an enumeration type or a subrange type of an enumeration type. The domain of the base type is limited and dependent on the actual compiler implemented.
* All operations which may be used on the standard data type BITSET are allowed on the set type.

Example:

```
TYPE Day = SET OF Weekday;
```

The standard data type BITSET is defined as SET OF [0..w-1]. w is the word length of the target machine, or a small multiple thereof.

4.3.1.4 Structured Data Types

There are four possibilities in Modula-2 for constructing structured data types: *array types, record types, pointer types* and *procedure types*.

The array type

An array type collects a certain set of data of the same base type into a unit (an array). The elements of the unit all carry the name of the unit and are identified by an index.

Syntax:

```
ArrayType = "ARRAY" SimpleType {"," SimpleType} "OF" Type.
```

* "SimpleType" describes the type and domain of an index, is thus the index type and must be either one of the standard data types BOOLEAN, INTEGER, CARDINAL or CHAR or a subrange type of an already known (that is a previously declared) enumeration type.
* If an array declaration contains more than one index type that means that the elements of the array with the first index type are again arrays with the next index type. In this fashion multi-dimensional arrays can be constructed.
* When the element type given by "Type" is defined by a type name, this name must be previously declared as a type name.

Example:

```
TYPE Name      = ARRAY[1..20] OF CHAR;
TYPE Goboard   = ARRAY[1..19],[1..19] OF BOOLEAN;
TYPE Namelist  = ARRAY[1..1000] OF NAME;
TYPE Table     = ARRAY Weekday, BOOLEAN OF REAL;
```

The record type

Record types offer the possibility of collecting data of arbitrary (that is to say differing) data types into a unit (a record). The components of a record all have their own name but may be used in statements only when identified by the record and component names together, except inside a WITH-statement (see section 4.6.1).

Syntax:

```
RecordType          =    "RECORD" FieldListSequence "END".

FieldListSequence   =    FieldList {";" FieldList}.

FieldList           =    [ident {"," ident} ":" Type
                          | VariantList].
```

* The components of a record can, if they are all of the same type, be collected into lists (FieldList). Each of these lists contains the names of these components, separated by commas, and the data type which is associated with these components.
* There are no restrictions with regard to the data type of a FieldList, except that no names may be used to describe "Type" which are not already known.
* The names of all components must be distinct.

Example:

```
TYPE Address = RECORD
                  firstname, lastname : ARRAY[0..20] OF CHAR;
                  street, city : ARRAY[0..25] OF CHAR;
                  zip : [0000..9999];
                  housenumber : [1..999];
               END;
```

The declaration of a record type is indicated by the fact that not only the number, but also the types of the components are explicitly given.

Applications often occur in which not every component of a record is used. One would like, therefore, to declare records with *different variants*, dependent on certain criteria. As an aid to clarity, the description of variants and the selection criteria should be explicitly visible in the declaration. For reasons of efficiency one does not wish to reserve memory space for all variants, so the variants should be superposed in memory and only use as much memory space as the "largest" variant requires. To this end Modula-2 offers the capability of so called *variant records*. In the above syntax description the nonterminal symbol "VariantList" is used. The syntax for this is:

```
VariantList    =    "CASE" [ident ":"] qualident "OF" Variant
                     {"|" Variant} ["ELSE" FieldListSequence]
                     "END".

Variant        =    CaseLabels {"," CaseLabels} ":"
                             FieldListSequence.

CaseLabels     =    ConstExpr [".." ConstExpr].
```

* A "VariantList" consists of a selection criterion and one or more variants.
* The selection criterion is described either by the identifier of a so called discriminator ("ident") and its data type ("qualident"), or just by a data type. The data type must be previously declared.
* The variants themselves consist of one or more constants ("CaseLabels"), followed by one or more component lists ("FieldLists").
* The value ("CaseLabels") given to a variant must be either a constant or a subdomain of the data type determined by the selection criterion.
* The values given to all variants must be different and may not overlap.

If these preconditions are satisfied, the declaration of a variant record implies that the record type either includes the components of each variant, whose given value coincides with the value of the selection object (in case a selection object is provided in the selection criterion), or the components of the "ELSE" variant (see syntax) in case it is provided and none of the values coincide with the value of the selection object. If a selection object is not given and if only a data type is given as a selection criterion, then all variants of the record are available superposed, simultaneously in memory. At run time it is not possible to specify which components are represented by the record type. The programmer is responsible for correctly managing this problem himself.

Example:

```
TYPE Maritalstatus   =    (single, married, widowed,
                           separated,divorced);

TYPE Date            =    RECORD
                            day : [1..31];
                            month : [1..12];
                            year : [1900..2000];
                          END;

TYPE Person  =  RECORD
                  firstname, lastname: ARRAY[0..20] OF CHAR;
                  street, city:        ARRAY[0..25] OF CHAR;
                  zip:                 [0000..9999];
                  housenumber:         [1..999];
                  CASE status: Maritalstatus OF
                    single:
                  | married..separated: marriagedate: Date;
                  | divorced: marriagedate, divorcedate: Date;
                  END;
                END;
```

The pointer type

It is common to the data types already discussed that they describe static data. During the run time of a program the correspondence between identifiers and addresses is constant, all that changes is the value of the object.

In many applications, however, one needs data whose structure, as well as whose value, may be changed in the course of its existence. Typical applications are data structures such as trees and lists, whose size and structure change constantly. Such dynamically changeable data structures can be created and managed in Modula-2 by the use of pointer types.

The pointer type is based on the idea of viewing storage no longer as a collection of words, but rather as a collection of values of a certain data type. Objects of the type pointer are then used to point to values of certain other data types in storage. Pointers also have a value. Their domain (data type) includes all possible storage addresses. Pointers themselves possess no structure, and are discussed here only because they are used in general to create and manage arbitrarily structured data objects.

It has already been mentioned that pointers have a value. This value can change during the life of the pointer. It goes without saying that pointers can occur as components of other objects. In this way it is possible to connect objects with each other, to decouple these objects, and in this fashion to create objects of arbitrary complexity dynamically.

Syntactically the declaration of a pointer is as follows:

```
PointerType = "POINTER" "TO" Type.
```

* Every pointer is connected to a certain data type (indicated by the nonterminal symbol "Type").
* There are no limitations on this data type. The declaration of the data type need *not yet be known* at the time of the pointer type declaration.
* The data type of each pointer includes also the value "NIL". The value NIL of a pointer expresses the fact that the pointer does not point to any particular storage location. NIL can be understood, in a way, as an address outside of storage.
* An object which is to be referenced by means of a pointer p has no name and is indicated by "p↑".

Example:

```
TYPE Famptr      = POINTER TO Familytreenode;

TYPE Familytreenode    = RECORD
                           firstname, lastname: ARRAY[0..20]
                                                 OF CHAR;
                           birthdate: Date;
                           father, mother: Famptr;
                         END;
```

The procedure type

Procedures consist in general--like programs--of a collection of data types and data (objects), and instructions which manipulate these data. If one now considers procedures as objects and allows the assignment of such objects to variables, then it must be possible to declare a data type whose "values" are procedures. For this purpose Modula-2 offers the concept of procedure types. A procedure type specifies the quantity and type of parameters for a procedure and, if a function procedure is involved, also the type of the result.

The syntax for this is:

```
ProcedureType   =   "PROCEDURE" [FormalTypeList].

FormalTypeList  =   "(" [["VAR"] FormalType
                    {"," ["VAR"] FormalType}] ")"
                    [":" FunctionType].

FormalType      =   ["ARRAY" "OF"] qualident.

FunctionType    =   qualident.
```

* "FormalTypeList" describes the quantity, kind and type ("FormalType") of the parameters and, if necessary, the type of the function result. The kind of parameter is expressed by the attribute VAR. If this attribute is missing, then a parameter is involved whose value is treated as a local object, that is the value of the actual parameter is copied into the procedure's local data area. For "VAR"-parameters on the other hand, it is not the value but rather the address of the parameter which is transferred. Each result or transfer parameter must therefore be a "VAR"-parameter.
* The type of a function result ("FunctionType"), expressed by a (qualified) type name, must be either an unstructured data type or a previously declared pointer type.
* The type of a parameter ("FormalType"), expressed by a (qualified) type name, must already be known, that is declared. It can also be an array of a given data type, which is expressed by the reserved words "ARRAY OF".
* The procedure type makes it possible to use procedures as parameters.
* Procedures which are assigned to a variable or are used as parameters, may not be declared internally as procedures (for procedure declarations see section 4.3.4).
* The standard name PROC (as type name) indicates a parameterless procedure type.

Example:
```
TYPE Anglefunction = PROCEDURE(REAL): REAL;
```

If there exist, for example, procedures for computing the sine and cosine (SIN,COS) of a given angle, both of which have a formal input parameter of type REAL and a result of type REAL, then a variable f can be given the data type Anglefunction (for variable declarations see section 4.3.3) and the assignment f:=SIN or f:=COS made. The variable f may then be used as a procedure.

4.3.2 Constant Declarations

Constants are objects which are represented either directly by their value or by a name (named constants) which stands for the value. The data type of a constant is not explicitly fixed, but rather is determined by the value of the constant itself. Its data type is that type in whose domain the constant lies. A special case are constants in the interval $[0,2^{w-1}]$. Based on their value they can be either of type INTEGER or of type CARDINAL and are compatible with both types.

In many cases it is helpful to work with named constants. On the one hand this improves the adaptability of a program, because a change in the value of a constant only affects one point in the program (the constant declaration), and on the other--for a reasonable choice of names--this increases the readability. The value and thus the data type of a named constant must be explicitly fixed in a constant declaration.

The syntax for a constant declaration is:

```
ConstDeclaration    =    constname "=" ConstExpr.

ConstExpr           =    SimpleConstExpr
                         [Relation SimpleConstExpr].

SimpleConstExpr     =    ["+" | "-"] ConstTerm
                         {AddOperator ConstTerm}.

ConstTerm           =    ConstFactor {MulOperator ConstFactor}.

ConstFactor         =    qualident | number | string | Set
                         | "(" ConstExpr ")"
                              | "NOT" ConstFactor.

Relation            =    "=" | "#" | "<>" | "<" | "<=" | ">"
                         | ">=" | "IN".

AddOperator         =    "+" | "-" | "OR".

MulOperator         =    "*" | "/" | "DIV" | "MOD" | "AND"
                         | "&".

Set                 =    [qualident] "{" [ConstExpr
                         [".." ConstExpr] {"," ConstExpr
                         [".." ConstExpr]}] "}".
```

* "constname" is the name of the constant which may be chosen arbitrarily by the programmer.
* The syntax of constant expressions ("ConstExpr") corresponds to the syntax for general expressions (see also section 4.4) and is explained there.
* A constant expression is an expression which may only contain constants, that is either constant values or names of previously declared constants.

Example:
(1) Named Constants

```
CONST maxindex = 20;        Data type: INTEGER,
                                       CARDINAL
      cr       = 15C;       Data type: CHAR
      empty    = {};        Data type: BITSET
      weekend  = Weekday{saturday, sunday};
                            Data type: SET OF Weekday
      name     = "PETER";   Data type: ARRAY[0..4]
                                       OF CHAR
      n        = -10;       Data type: INTEGER
      m        = n-1;       Data type: INTEGER
```

(2) Unnamed Constants

```
"A"                         Data type:  CHAR
3.14159                     Data type:  REAL
```

4.3.3 Variable Declarations

Variables always possess a name, type and a value, and must be declared in Modula-2 before they are used (except if they are imported, see section 4.7). Thus every variable must be associated with a data type which defines its domain.

The syntax for this is:

```
VariableDeclaration = ident {"," ident} ":" Type.
```

* The names ("ident") of variables of the same data type can be collected together into a list in the declaration.
* The data type ("Type") which corresponds to the name list must already be known.

Example:
```
TYPE Letter  = ["A".."Z"];
     Famptr  = POINTER TO Familytreenode;
     Weekday = (monday, tuesday, wednesday, thursday,
               friday, saturday, sunday);

VAR  i,j:         INTEGER;
     k:           CARDINAL;
     x,y,z:       REAL;
     ch:          CHAR;
     eof:         BOOLEAN;
     status:      BITSET;
     index:       [0..99];
     character:   Letter;
     vacationday: [monday..friday];
     goboard:     ARRAY[1..19],[1..19] OF BOOLEAN;
     father:      Famptr;
```

4.3.4 Procedure Declarations

It has already been mentioned that procedures are an important element for the software engineer for the structuring of programs. Procedures are independent objects of a program and exhibit in their structure great similarity with programs. Data objects represent values of a certain data type, procedure objects do not represent values, but rather instruction sequences which are activated by special instructions (procedure calls, see section 4.6.2). Obviously the instructions of a procedure also manipulate data. Because of the independence of procedures, it is useful that they too possess local data objects. Procedures consist therefore of a collection of local data (objects), a collection of instructions which manipulate these local data and perhaps a collection of parameters. *Data exchange* between procedures and the program unit which activates the procedure can occur by means of *global objects* and *parameters* and by the *result of a function.*

In this section the declaration of procedures are described first, then the concept of locality and lastly the various methods of data exchange between procedures and the calling program unit.

4.3.4.1 The Declaration of a Procedure

The syntax rules here are:

```
ProcedureDeclaration=     ProcedureHeading ";" Block procname.

ProcedureHeading    =     "PROCEDURE" procname
                          [FormalParameters].

Block               =     {Declaration}
                          ["BEGIN" StatementSequence] "END".

FormalParameters    =     "(" [FPSection {";" FPSection}] ")"
                          [":" FunctionType].

FPSection           =     ["VAR"] ident {"," ident} ":"
                          FormalType.

FormalType          =     ["ARRAY" "OF"] qualident.

FunctionType        =     qualident.
```

* "procname" is the name of the procedure, which may be chosen arbitrarily by the programmer.
* In procedures, the same objects and data types may be declared as in programs.
* The formal parameters of a procedure indicate either VAL-parameters (these are those whose value can be used in the procedure but not altered) or VAR-parameters (they are indicated explicitly by prefixing the standard identifier "VAR", and not its value but rather its address is transferred).
* For each formal parameter, its data type ("FormalType") must also be given.
* The data types of parameters ("FormalType") and in the case of a function procedure the function type (see data exchange between procedures and calling program units) must already be known.

Example:

```
    ...
TYPE Wordtype = ARRAY[1..30] OF CHAR;
    ...
PROCEDURE ReadWord(VAR word : WordType;
                   VAR wordlength : CARDINAL);

VAR symbol: CHAR;     (*declaration of local objects*)
    ...
BEGIN
    ...                (*statement sequence*)
END ReadWord;
```

4.3.4.2 Locality and Scope of Visibility of Identifiers

Because a procedure can contain further procedure declarations, procedures may also be nested. In each of these procedures data can be declared. Thus the question of the life span and the scope of visibility of data objects and their identifiers arises.

The *life span* of an object is extended to the procedure in which it was declared. This means that variables can receive a value only inside the procedure in which they were declared or in procedures contained within them. They cease to exist when the procedure in which they were declared is terminated and their values at the time the procedure is activated are undefined (exception: parameters).

Objects may be accessed only in the procedure in which they were declared, not in the surrounding blocks.

Although the life span guarantees, in any event, that an object exist during the execution of the procedure in which it was declared, this need not necessarily hold for the scope of visibility of an identifier.

The following rules hold for the *scope of visibility* of identifiers:

(1) The scope of visibility of identifiers extends from the declaration of the identifier until the end of the procedure in which it was declared and to all the procedures included in this procedure, on the condition that the identifier is not redeclared in them.

(2) If a procedure P contains a procedure Q and if a name i is declared in both procedures, then the inner declaration covers the outer one, that is, i in P and i in Q refer to different objects.

(3) The standard identifiers of Modula-2 (see section 4.1) are handled as if they had been declared in a program which surrounds the procedure. Standard identifiers may therefore be redeclared in procedures.

Illustration 4.2 shows the scope of visibility and the life span of identifiers.

	Scope of Visibility						Life Span					
	a	b	b'	c	c'	d	a	b	b'	c	c'	d
PROCEDURE P;	|	|					|	|				
VAR a,b: ...	|	|					|	|				
PROCEDURE Q;	|		|	|			|	|	|	|		
VAR b,c: ...	|		|	|			|	|	|	|		
PROCEDURE R;	|		|		|	|	|	|	|	|	|	|
VAR c,d: ...	|		|		|	|	|	|	|	|	|	|
END R;	|		|	|			|	|	|	|		
END Q;	|	|					|	|				
END P;	|	|					|	|				

Illustration 4.2   Scope of Visibility and Life Span of Identifiers

4.3.4.3 Data Exchange

As has been mentioned above, there are three possibilities for the *exchange of data* between a procedure and the calling program unit: *global variables, parameters* and *function values.*

The exchange of data by *global variables* is clear from the explanation of the life span and scope of visibility of identifiers (see illustration 4.2).

Data exchange by *parameters* demands that the formal parameters be declared in the procedure heading. The data type must be given here for each formal parameter. In this way it is possible at compilation time to check for type compatibility (see section 4.5.1) between actual and formal parameters.

Two kinds of formal parameters can be distinguished: parameters for the transfer of values from the calling program unit to the procedure--we call them "VAL" parameters--and parameters which also make possible the transfer of results from the procedure to the calling program unit--we call them "VAR" parameters. VAR parameters are distinguished from VAL parameters in that the standard identifier VAR is prefixed to them. If the formal parameter is a VAR parameter, the corresponding actual parameter must be a variable.

Because the data types of formal and actual parameters must correspond, it must be known at the time of compilation, if the parameter is to have the type array, how large the actual array given as a parameter in the procedure call is. This would be a large barrier in many applications. Modula-2 offers, therefore, the possibility of declaring formal parameters as *arrays with variable index bounds.* In the declaration of the formal (array) parameter, the identifier of the data type of the array elements--which must, of course, be compatible with the data type of the actual parameter--must be prefixed by the standard identifier "ARRAY OF".

Example:

```
PROCEDURE PrintWord(word: ARRAY OF CHAR);
```

This declaration makes possible the passing of character arrays with arbitrary index bounds. In the procedure, the lower index bound is assumed to be zero. The upper bound can be obtained at run time by using the standard function HIGH(word) (see section 4.10). The value of the function HIGH(x) is then equal to the number of elements of the array passed minus 1.

Data are also exchanged by the values of *function procedures*. A function procedure describes a value (dynamically) as well as an algorithm (statically) and thus must be associated with a definite data type. The declaration of a function procedure has the following syntax:

```
FunctionProc    =    "PROCEDURE" procname
                     ["(" [FPSection {";" FPSection}] ")" ]":"
                     FunctionType ";" {Declaration}
                     ["BEGIN" StatementSequence] "END" procname.

FunctionType    =    qualident.
```

The declaration of function procedures is distinguished from that of the usual procedure only in as much as it contains information about the data type of the value of the function ("FunctionType"). Which value is to be returned as a value of the function after execution of the procedure is determined in the body of the procedure ("StatementSequence") by a special statement (RETURN statement) (see section 4.6.10). Thus a function procedure represents a value and can therefore be used as an operand in expressions (see section 4.4.1). The data type of the function value must already be known and may not indicate a structured data type (except pointers) or set type.

4.4 Expressions

Expressions represent *values* and are composed of *operands* and *operators*. The value of an expression is the result of the effects of the individual operators and the order in which the operators are applied to the operands. Because expressions represent values, they also have a data type, which is determined by the data type of the operands.

The first part of this section explains which operands and operators are admissible and how the rules of syntax for the construction of expressions are given. The second part of this section gives the rules of priority for operators and the data types of expressions. A few examples should serve to illustrate these remarks.

4.4.1 Operands

Operands are *constants, variables, function calls* or *expressions*. Variables and named constants are indicated by so called "designators". Their form is given by the syntax rule:

```
Designator    =    qualident
                   {"." ident | "["Expression
                   {"," Expression} "]" | "↑"}.
```

* If the operand f is a component of a record R, then its name has the form R.f.

* If the operand is an object addressed by a pointer p, then its name has the form p↑.
* If the operand indicates an object whose export is qualified (see section 4.7.1), then its name must be qualified by a module name.
* If the operand is an array element the indices must also be given. The values of the indices are given once again by expressions. The designator for array elements has (as is shown by the syntax rule) either the form $A[Expr_1, Expr_2...Expr_n]$ or $A[Expr_1][Expr_2]...[Expr_n]$. The data types of the expressions $Expr_1,...Expr_n$ must be assignment compatible with the index types determined in the array definition (see section 4.5.3).

Example for the names of operands:
```
k    NamList.name    masterrec.balance    p↑.value    field[k,3]
pointer↑.value
```

Example for operands:
```
12                constant
maxsize           named constant
goboard[3,19]     variable
Sin(183)          function call
```

4.4.2 Operators

There are *four classes* of operators: *arithmetic, logical, comparison* and *set operators*. Illustrations 4.3 to 4.6 show the individual operators and the operator symbols used in Modula-2. One sees that the same operator symbols are used for different operations. The meaning of an operator symbol is therefore dependent on the data type of the operands to which it is applied.

Symbol		Operation
monadic	*+*	*no operation*
dyadic	*+*	*addition*
monadic	*-*	*sign inversion*
dyadic	*-*	*subtraction*
٭		*multiplication*
/		*real division*
DIV		*whole number division*
MOD		*modulus*

Illustration 4.3 Arithmetic Operations

Symbol	Operation
OR	*conjunction*
AND or &	*disjunction*
NOT	*negation*

Illustration 4.4 Logical Operations

Symbol	Operation
=	*equality*
<>	*inequality*
<	*less than*
<=	*less than or equal*
>	*greater than*
>=	*greater than or equal*

Illustration 4.5 Comparison Operations

Symbol	Operation
+	*union*
-	*difference*
*	*intersection*
/	*symmetrical difference*
IN	*contained in*

Illustration 4.6 Set Operations

The syntax rules for the construction of expressions are:

```
Expression        =    SimpleExpression [Relation
                       SimpleExpression].

SimpleExpression  =    ["+" | "-"] Term {AddOperator Term}.

Term              =    Factor {MulOperator Factor}.

Factor            =    number | string | Set | Designator
                       | [ActualParameters]
                       | "(" Expression ")"
                       | "NOT" Factor.

ActualParameters  =    "(" [Expression {"," Expression}] ")".
```

```
Relation        =    "=" | "#" | "<>" | "<" | "<="
                     | ">" | ">=" | "IN".

AddOperator     =    "+" | "-" | "OR".

MulOperator     =    "*" | "/" | "DIV" | "MOD"
                     | "AND" | "&".

Set             =    [qualident] "{" Element {","
                         Element]"}".

Element         =    ConstExpression [".." ConstExpression].
```

Example:

```
1984      a+b+c      NOT p OR q       e IN {0..10,20..30}
a[i]<=a[j]
```

If an expression contains more than one operator, then the order of the operators is determined either by the hierarchy of the operators (shown in illustration 4.7) or by the appropriate use of parentheses.

Priority	Operator
4	*NOT, +, -, as sign*
3	*∗, /, DIV, MOD, AND, &*
2	*+, -, OR*
1	*=, ◇, ⟨, ⟨=, ⟩, ⟩=, IN*

Illustration 4.7 Hierarchy of Operators

If two operators of the same priority have a common operand, then the operations are carried out from left to right.

The arithmetic operators (with the exception of DIV) can be applied to operands of the data type REAL or (with the exception of "/") to operands of the data type INTEGER, CARDINAL or subranges of these. The result also has the type REAL, INTEGER or CARDINAL.

The logical operators demand operands of the type BOOLEAN. The result has the type BOOLEAN.

The comparison operators can be applied to operands of the type INTEGER, REAL, CARDINAL, BOOLEAN, CHAR, enumeration type or subrange type. The result has the type BOOLEAN. The operators =, # and ◇ can also be applied to operands of set or pointer type.

The set operators demand operands of (arbitrary) set type. The result has the same data type as the operands. In an expression such as i IN s, s must be of the type SET OF T and T must be type compatible (see section 4.5.1) with the type of i.

The computation of boolean expressions ends (in contrast to Pascal) when the result is unique. In the expression NOT p AND q<10, the expression q<10 will not be computed if p=TRUE.

Examples of expressions:

```
VAR a,b,c:REAL;
p,q: BOOLEAN;
VAR e,i:INTEGER;
```

Expression	Type of the result
1984	CARDINAL
a+b+c	REAL
NOT p OR q	BOOLEAN
e IN {0..10,20..30}	BOOLEAN
i DIV 3	INTEGER

Incorrect expressions would be, for example:

```
a DIV b       i/3       i+a-b.
```

4.5 Rules of Compatibility

4.5.1 Type Compatibility

The concept of type compatibility of objects is frequently used in the following sections. It is therefore necessary to define what we mean by this. The following definition is taken from the "Context Conditions for Modula-2" (*Rechenberg*, 1982).

Two objects a (of type t1) and b (of type t2) are of the *same data type* if one of the following conditions holds:

(1) a and b are variables (or formal parameters) which occur in the same identifier list in a declaration, for example VAR a,b:[1..10].

(2) a and b are enumeration constants of the same enumeration type.

(3) t1 and t2 are given by the same name.

(4) t1 and t2 are given by type names and the name of the one is used for the declaration of the other, for example:

```
TYPE t1= ...;
t2 = t1;
```

4.5.2 Expression Compatibility

When an operator joins two operands, the operands must be *expression compatible*. This definition is taken from the "Context Conditions for Modula-2" (*Rechenberg*, 1982).

Two expressions with the data types t1 and t2 are called expression compatible if one of the following conditions holds:

(1) t1 and t2 are the same data type.

(2) t1 is a subrange type of t2 or t2 is a subrange type of t1 or t1 and t2 are both subrange types of the same (basis) data type.

(3) One expression has the data type INTEGER or CARDINAL and the other expression is a constant in the interval [0..maxint] where maxint is the greatest integer value.

(4) One of the expressions is the constant NIL and the data type of the other expression is an arbitrary pointer type.

(5) t1 and t2 are both procedure types; the procedures are either both function procedures with the same function type or else not function procedures; they have the same number of parameters, the corresponding parameters are both either VAL or VAR parameters and have the same (not just type compatible) data type.

(6) Both expressions are strings of the same length.

4.5.3 Assignment Compatibility

An object of data type t1 and an expression of type t2 are *assignment compatible* if:

(1) t1 and t2 are expression compatible (see section 4.5.2),
or
(2) One of the two data types is INTEGER or a subrange type thereof and the other is CARDINAL or a subrange type thereof,
or
(3) t1 is of type ARRAY[0..n1] OF CHAR, t2 is a constant of type ARRAY[0..n2] OF CHAR and n1>=n2.

4.6 Statements

The program bodies and procedures consist of sequences of statements, which are represented here by the nonterminal symbol "StatementSequence":

```
StatementSequence = Statement {";" Statement}.
```

Statements are separated by semicolons. The semicolon is used as a separator, not, as in some other programming languages (e.g. PL/I), as a terminator. But it can also be used as a terminator because a statement may be empty. Eleven kinds of statement can be distinguished:

```
Statement       =    [Assignment | ProcedureCall | IfStatement
                     | CaseStatement | WhileStatement
                     | RepeatStatement | LoopStatement
                     | ForStatement | WithStatement
                     | ExitStatement | ReturnStatement ].
```

4.6.1 The Assignment Statement

This replaces the value of a variable with a new value, which is given by an expression of the form:

```
Assignment = Designator ":=" Expression.
```

* "Designator" indicates the identifier of a variable of an arbitrary data type (the rules of syntax for the construction of a designator are included in section 4.4.1).
* The data type of the expression on the right-hand side of the assignment may be chosen arbitrarily. In this way, the assignment of structured objects is also possible. The variable on the left-hand side of the assignment must be assignment compatible with the expression on the right-hand side (see section 4.5.3).
* If a variable s with the type ARRAY[0..n-1] OF CHAR is assigned a string whose length is less than n, a zero character ("0C") is inserted after the last element of the string.

Example:
```
i := a+b
correct := z=x
set := {1,2,3,4,5}
a[i] := "A"
masterrec.balance := masterrec.balance+updrec.value
p↑.next := loc
```

4.6.2 The Procedure Call

This activates a procedure and has the form:

```
ProcedureCall = Designator [ActualParameters].

ActualParameters = "(" [Expression {"," Expression}] ")"
```

* "Designator" specifies the identifier of the procedure to be activated. The identifier must be a procedure name which is already known in the block, or indicate a standard procedure (see section 4.10).
* "ActualParameters" specifies the actual parameters (in case formal parameters are declared in the procedure which is to be activated).
* Actual and formal parameters must correspond in number and in the order in which they occur in the procedure declaration and call.
* In the declaration of the formal parameters a distinction is made between VAL and VAR parameters (see section4.3.4). For VAL parameters, the corresponding actual parameter can be an arbitrary expression. The evaluation of the expression is accomplished before the activation of the procedure. The result is assigned to the corresponding formal parameter (which represents a local variable of the procedure). For VAR parameters, the corresponding actual parameter must be a variable. Its identifier is specified by a "designator".

* Corresponding actual and formal parameters must be assignment compatible in the case of VAL parameters (see section 4.5.3), and of the same data type in the case of VAR parameters (see section 4.5.1).
* Procedure calls can also be recursive, that is a procedure may call itself (directly or indirectly).

Example:
```
Search(element,position)
Power(x,i+1)
Write("account list")
ClearStack
```

4.6.3 The IF Statement

This tests a condition and directs the further program flow contingent on the result. It has the form:

```
IfStatement  =  "IF" Expression "THEN" StatementSequence
                {"ELSIF" Expression "THEN" StatementSequence}
                ["ELSE" StatementSequence] "END".
```

* All expressions must be of the type BOOLEAN and are evaluated in the order in which they occur. The evaluation is continued until a result with the value TRUE is encountered. Then the statement sequence associated with this expression is executed. Thereafter execution is continued after the standard identifier END. When no expression yields the value TRUE, the ELSE clause (if present) is executed.

Example:
```
IF x<0 THEN i := 1 END;

IF x<0
  THEN i := 1
  ELSE i := 2
END;

IF (ch>="A") AND (ch<="Z")
  THEN ReadName(ch,name)
  ELSIF (ch>="0") AND (ch<="9")
    THEN ReadNumber(ch,number)
  ELSE Error
END;
```

4.6.4 The CASE Statement

This makes a selection from numerous statement sequences dependent on a condition. Its syntax has the form:

```
CaseStatement  =    "CASE" Expression "OF"
                    Case {"|" Case}
                    ["ELSE" StatementSequence]
                    "END".

Case           =    CaseLabels {"," CaseLabels} ":"
                    StatementSequence.
```

```
CaseLabels    =    ConstExpr [".." ConstExpr].
```

* The expression after the standard identifier CASE (CASE expression) is evaluated and that statement sequence is executed whose corresponding value list or domain contains the result of the evaluation of the expression. Thereafter execution is continued after the standard identifier END. If none of the value lists contains the result of the expression evaluation, the ELSE branch is executed. If no ELSE branch is given, the interpretation of the statement is not defined, which means it is dependent on the compiler in use.
* The data type of the CASE expression must be an unstructured data type, in fact it must be one of the predeclared data types or an enumeration type or a subrange type.
* "CaseLabels" must be constants or value domains and no value may occur twice, which means that the value domains may not intersect. Their data type must be expression compatible with the data type of the CASE expression.

Example:
```
TYPE Maritalstatus    = (single, married, widowed,
                              separated, divorced);
VAR status: Maritalstatus;
    age: ...;
    marriagedate, divorcedate: ...;

CASE status OF
  single:     Read(age)
| married..separated:     Read(marriagedate)
| divorced:     Read(divorcedate)
END;
```

4.6.5 The WHILE Statement

This repeats the execution of a sequence of statements that are contingent on a condition and has the form:

```
WhileStatement =    "WHILE" Expression "DO" StatementSequence
                    "END".
```

* The expression after WHILE ("loop condition") must be of the data type BOOLEAN.
* Before each execution of the statement sequence the loop condition is evaluated, and the statement sequence is repeated as long as the evaluation of the loop condition yields the result TRUE.

Example:
```
f := 0.0;
WHILE n>0.0 DO
  f := f+1.0/n;
  n := n-1.0
END
```

4.6.6 The REPEAT Statement

This, like the WHILE loop, repeats the execution of a sequence of statements that are contingent on a condition and has the form:

```
RepeatStatement     =    "REPEAT" StatementSequence
                         "UNTIL" Expression.
```

* The expression after UNTIL (loop condition) must be of the data type BOOLEAN.
* After each execution of the statement sequence the loop condition is evaluated and the sequence repeated, *until* the evaluation of the loop condition yields the result TRUE.

Example:

```
sum := 0; i := n;
REPEAT
  sum := sum+i;
  i := i-1
UNTIL i = 0
```

4.6.7 The FOR Statement

This defines inductive loops, that is the repeated execution of a sequence of statements with a fixed number of passes. The number of repetitions is governed by a control variable. The FOR statement has the form:

```
ForStatement    =    "FOR" ident ":=" Expression
                     "TO" Expression ["BY" ConstExpr]
                     "DO" StatementSequence "END".
```

* "ident" is the identifier of the control variable. The expression following the assignment symbol (:=) describes the initial value of the control variable, the expression following the symbol "TO" its final value. ConstExpr describes the increment (or, if negative, decrement) of the control variable.
* The expression for the initial value, final value and increment (decrement) are calculated before the first execution of the statement sequence and the initial value is assigned to the control variable. The loop is executed only if the initial value of the control variable is less (respectively greater) than the final value (otherwise the loop is empty). After execution of the statement sequence the value of the increment (decrement) is added to the control variable, and the statement sequence is repeated as long as the value of the control variable is smaller (respectively larger) than or equal to the final value.
* The identifier of the control variable must be previously declared and may not designate a component of a structured object, a real object, an imported identifier (see section 4.7) or a formal parameter.
* Both expressions must be assignment compatible with the control variable.
* "ConstExpr" must designate an expression of the data type INTEGER or CARDINAL.
* If the specification of an increment is absent, the value 1 is assumed.
* The value of the control variable is undefined after exiting the loop.

Example:
```
sum := 0;
FOR i := min+1 TO max-1 DO
  sum := sum+list[i]
END
```

4.6.8 The LOOP and EXIT Statements

The LOOP statement makes the repeated execution of statements possible. The repetition can be terminated with the EXIT statement. These statements have the form:

```
LoopStatement = "LOOP" StatementSequence "END".

ExitStatement = "EXIT".
```

* The EXIT statement may be used only within a sequence of statements which are enclosed between LOOP and END.
* If an EXIT statement is encountered during the execution of a sequence of statements enclosed between LOOP and END, then execution continues after the standard identifier END.

Example:
```
LOOP
  ReadChar(ch);
  IF ch=" " THEN EXIT END;
  i := i+1;
  s[i] := ch
END
```

4.6.9 The WITH Statement

This makes it possible to use record components without stating the record name. It has the form:

```
WithStatement =    "WITH" Designator "DO" StatementSequence
                   "END".
```

* "Designator" designates the identifier of a record variable. Within the statement sequence contained in "DO" and "END" the components of the record indicated by "Designator" may be written without prefixing the record name.

Example:
```
Type Masterrecord    = RECORD
                            accountno: CARDINAL;
                            balance: REAL
                       END;
VAR masterrec: Masterrecord;
WITH masterrec DO
 accountno := oldnum;
 balance := balance+updaterec.value
END
```

This is equivalent to:

```
masterrec.accno := oldnum;

masterrec.balance := masterrec.balance+updrec.value
```

4.6.10 The RETURN Statement

This causes a procedure to be terminated and permits the return of the function value in the case of a function procedure. It has the form:

```
ReturnStatement = "RETURN" [Expression].
```

* The RETURN statement can occur at any place in the body of a procedure and causes, on encounter, the return to the calling procedure unit.
* In function procedures, the RETURN statement must contain an expression; this represents the function value. The data type of the expression must be assignment compatible with the function type (see section 4.5.3).

4.7 Modules

For the structuring of program systems Modula-2--as opposed to many other programming languages--offers in addition to procedures, a further data and program control structure, the *module*.

A *module* is a collection of data types, data objects, procedures and statements. The module, in a way, constitutes a fence around the data, data types and procedures declared in it, and keeps these hidden from the outside world. Main programs themselves constitute a module (program module); this is expressed by the fact that they begin with the standard identifier MODULE. In accordance with the principle of abstraction, it can certainly be useful to distribute the data and procedures within a program module among various subsidiary modules, which all solve certain partial tasks. We call these *local* modules.

Modules must, in general, communicate with each other and with the outer world. For this it is necessary that the data and (or) procedures of a module be made accessible (visible) to other modules, and it can happen that a module needs data and (or) procedures from another module.

The communication between modules must be explicitly described in Modula-2. All objects (data types, data, procedures and local modules) which a module offers to the outside world must be exhibited in an *export list*, all objects which a module requires and are declared in other modules must be exhibited in an *import list*. This insures that only certain objects of a module can get outside, while the other objects are protected from unauthorized outside access.

4.7.1 Local Modules

For the formulation of *local modules*, the syntax rules for the declaration of a procedure in section 4.3.4 are extended in the following way:

```
Declarations      =    "TYPE" {TypeDeclaration ";"}
                       | ...
                       | ModuleDeclaration ";".

ModuleDeclaration =    "MODULE" modulename ";" {Import}
                       [Export] Block modulename.

Import            =    ["FROM" ident] "IMPORT"
                       ident {"," ident} ";".

Export            =    "EXPORT" ["QUALIFIED"]
                       ident {"," ident} ";".
```

* The syntax rules for "ProgramModule" (section 4.2) and for "Declarations" allow each program module to contain arbitrarily many local modules. Also a (local) procedure can contain local modules.

* "modulename" is the name of the module which may be chosen arbitrarily by the programmer.

* The statement sequence defined by "Block" (module body) is executed before the first statement of the program to which the module is local. If this program contains more than one module, the modules are executed in the order in which they are listed. The body of a module can therefore be used to initialize the data objects of the module. The modules which are contained in a procedure are executed each time the procedure is called before the first statement of the procedure.

* The identifiers given in the export list ("Export") must be declared in the module. Through their exportation they also become known in the block which contains the module, as if they had been declared there. Exported type and constant identifiers constitute an *exception:* they may be used only in declarations which occur statically after the local module.

* If the symbol QUALIFIED (*qualified export*) is written in the export list, then all identifiers occurring in the export list must be qualified with the module name outside the module, if one wishes to use them, for example:

```
...
MODULE OutMod;
EXPORT QUALIFIED Write;

...

END OutMod;

...

OutMod.Write(x);
```

By means of this construction a module can import various *different* objects which have the *same name*, and distinguish them by qualification.

* If a structured object (record) or a record type is exported, then the names of all its components are also exported.

* If an enumeration type is exported, then its constant names are also exported.

* Modules can be nested (as the syntax rules show). If the name of a module is exported, then all the objects which it exports are exported qualified.

* The identifiers given in the import list designate objects which have been declared outside the module, and which can be used in the module as if they had been declared there.
* Standard identifiers (see section 4.1) qualify as being automatically imported.
* Each module can have arbitrarily many import lists. If the standard identifier FROM followed by a module name is entered in the import list, then this expresses from which module the names given in this list were imported. The imported names can then be used *unqualified* within the module (without prefixing the module name) as if they had been exported unqualified.

Example:

```
MODULE MainProg;  (*
================  *)
  IMPORT Filesystem;

  MODULE AccountCatalog;  (*
  ======================  *)
    FROM Filesystem IMPORT OpenFile, File;
    EXPORT QUALIFIED ProcessAccCat, CloseAccCat, Accno,
      InitAccCat;
    TYPE Accno = CARDINAL;
    VAR Masterfile, Updatefile: File;
    PROCEDURE InitAccCat(VAR masteracc, updateacc: Accno);
      ...
    END InitAccCat;

    PROCEDURE ProcessAccCat(VAR masteracc, updateacc: Accno);
      ...
    END ProcessAccCat;

    PROCEDURE CloseAccCat;
      ...
    END CloseAccCat;
      ...
  BEGIN
    OpenFile(Masterfile); OpenFile(Updatefile);
  END AccountCatalog;

      ...

  MODULE FileWriter;  (*
  ==================  *)
    FROM AccountCatalog IMPORT Accno, InitAccCat,
                              ProcessAccCat, CloseAccCat;
    EXPORT AccountWriter,...;

    PROCEDURE AccountWriter;
      VAR macc, uacc: accno;
    BEGIN
      InitAccCat(macc, uacc);
      ProcessAccCat(macc, uacc);
      CloseAccCat;
    END AccountWriter;
      ...
  END FileWriter;
```

```
        ...
    BEGIN (*body of MainProg*)
      FileWriter.AccountWriter;
    END MainProg.
```

4.7.2 Compilation Units and Separate Compilation

If one decomposes a program system into modules--in order to master complexity and with an eye to ease of changeability and expandability--then it is necessary for efficiency reasons that the modules be separately compilable--especially if the individual modules are to be implemented by a number of people. The modules of a program system must--as for the local modules of a program--be able to communicate with each other. Separately compiled modules use the same import/export mechanism as local modules.

If one wishes to test at compilation time whether the operations applied to an object of a module are permissible, then the declarations of all objects, and thus also of imported objects, must be known at compilation time. This would mean that at the compilation time of a module, all modules from which objects are imported must already be completely coded and compiled, and that the compiler must have access to the results of these compilations.

In order to avoid this, in Modula-2 every compilation unit (separately compilable module) is divided into a definition and an implementation module. The *definition module* contains the export list of the module and the declarations of all exported objects. The *implementation module* contains the declarations of all non-exported objects and all details of the implementation. The definition module specifies the export interface and the implementation module describes the concrete realization of the module.

At the time of compilation of a module, the definition modules of all modules from which the compiled module imports objects must already be compiled and available to the compiler. Then for each object it can be tested during compilation whether it has been used correctly.

This technique has the advantage that the details of the implementation remain hidden from the user of a module. This coincides with the design principle of stepwise refinement for the formulation of solutions to problems which is given in section 5.3.

At the time of execution of a module it must be guaranteed that no definition module of a module from which objects have been imported is later altered. If this happens to be the case, it is no longer guaranteed that an imported object is used correctly (that is according to its data type). From this it follows that for a change in the definition module, all modules which import objects from this changed module must be re-compiled. If on the other hand only the implementation module is changed, no re-compilation is necessary for modules which import objects from the changed module (see also section 6.4). This is understandable, because nothing in the interface has changed.

Separate compilation, as it is described it here, is distinguished from the *independent compilation* of modules (in which no type checking of "external" objects is carried out) in that an exact compilation sequence must be observed in order to allow type checking (this is also explained in section 6.4).

The syntax rules for compilation units are:

```
CompilationUnit     =    DefinitionModule
                         | ImplementationModule
                         | ProgramModule.

DefinitionModule    =    "DEFINITION" "MODULE" modulename ";"
                         {Import} [Export] {Definition}
                         "END" modulename ".".

ImplementationModule=    "IMPLEMENTATION" ProgramModule.

ProgramModule       =    "MODULE" modulename ";" {Import}
                         Block modulename ".".

Definition          =    "CONST"{ConstantDeclaration ";"}
                         | "TYPE" {ident ["=" Type] ";"}
                         | "VAR" {VariableDeclaration ";"}
                         | ProcedureHeading ";".
```

* "modulename" is the name of the module which may be chosen arbitrarily by the programmer, and must be the same for associated definition and implementation modules.
* For the import and export of objects the same rules hold as for local modules. However, export must be qualified.
* The constants, data types and variables defined in the definition module may not be declared again in the implementation module (definition and implementation modules constitute a "logical" entity).
* The rule for the definition of data types in definition modules also permits the definition of a type name which is not associated with a concrete data type. This allows the export of so called *hidden types* (this is referred to as *opaque export*). The concrete type declaration is contained in the implementation module and thus remains hidden to the user. In this way only type names which are bound in the implementation module to objects which fit into a computer word may be exported. This, however, implies no limitation for the programmer of the implementation module, because pointer types (which are one word long) can be connected with any arbitrary data type. If an opaque type is imported, variables of this type can only be used in assignments and as actual parameters in procedure calls.
* The import list of a definition module need contain only those objects which are required for the declaration of the exported objects.

Example of a definition and an implementation module:

```
DEFINITION MODULE StackMod; (*modul for stack handling*)
   EXPORT QUALIFIED Push, Pop, empty, stackoverflow;
   VAR empty, stackoverflow: BOOLEAN;
```

```
PROCEDURE Push(x: CARDINAL);
   (*Stacks the object x. If x can no longer be stacked
     (stack full), stackoverflow=TRUE is set.*)

PROCEDURE Pop(VAR x: CARDINAL);
   (*Yields the top stack object x. If the stack is
     empty,empty=TRUE is set.*)

END StackMod.

IMPLEMENTATION MODULE StackMod; (*Module for stack handling*)
  CONST stacksize=50;
  VAR stack:ARRAY[1..stacksize] OF CARDINAL;
      top: [0..stacksize];


  PROCEDURE Push(x: CARDINAL);
  BEGIN
    IF top<stacksize
      THEN
        top:=top+1;
        stack[top]:=x;
      ELSE
        stackoverflow:=TRUE;
    END
  END Push;

  PROCEDURE Pop(VAR x: CARDINAL);
  BEGIN
    IF top=0
      THEN
        empty:=TRUE;
      ELSE
        x:=stack[top];
        top:=top-1;
    END
  END Pop;
BEGIN
  top:=0;
  empty:=TRUE;
  stackoverflow:=FALSE;
END StackMod.
```

4.8 Low Level Facilities of the Language

Modula-2 is a programming language which is adequate for *systems programming* as well as for *applications programming.* The systems programmer is forced in many cases to take into consideration the special properties of the computer on which a (systems) program is to run. It must be possible to address directly particular storage cells, registers or hardware interfaces or to interpret data placed in memory in a different way than is possible through the related type declarations (for example in the implementation of input/output or operating system modules). This is not possible with the language constructs discussed up until now. Modula-2 offers so called *low level facilities* for this.

Through these *low level facilities* the programmer has the opportunity to break through the strict type and abstraction concepts laid down by the language. It is clear that whoever utilizes these properties of the language must be completely aware of the consequences because in so doing he rejects the type and access checks offered by the language. Therefore the use of these properties of the language should be limited to a few special modules.

The low level facilities of Modula-2 relate to the provision of *computer specific data types* and *procedures, type transfer functions* and to the opportunity of declaring variables with *fixed addresses.*

There is a *module SYSTEM* (which is known to the compiler) for the provision of computer specific data types and procedures. The module SYSTEM exports the *data types WORD, ADDRESS, PROCESS* and the *procedures ADR, SIZE, TSIZE, NEWPROCESS, TRANSFER* and, dependent on special compiler implementations, possibly also other objects.

The *type WORD* represents a computer specific memory unit (a memory word). For objects of this type only the assignment operation is permitted. The type WORD can be used, for example, in procedures for the declaration of formal parameters, if one wishes that the corresponding actual parameter be an object of arbitrary data type, on the condition that the value of this object is representable in a memory word.

The *type ADDRESS* is defined as a pointer type and corresponds to the declaration "TYPE ADDRESS=POINTER TO WORD". Objects of this type are assignment compatible with objects of arbitrary pointer types and with objects of the type CARDINAL. For objects of this type, therefore, all arithmetic operations are permitted. Objects of the type ADDRESS are pointers to memory cells and are used to compute addresses of memory words.

The *function ADR* has an argument x (= name of a variable) and delivers as function value the address of x; the function type is ADDRESS.

The *function SIZE* also has an argument x (= name of a variable) and delivers as function value the number of memory words for the variable x, the function type being CARDINAL.

The *function TSIZE* has as argument a type name T and delivers as function value the number of memory words which are required for a variable of the type T, the function type being also CARDINAL.

The meanings of the *type PROCESS* and the *procedures NEWPROCESS* and *TRANSFER* are explained in section 4.9.

The *module SYSTEM* is a *fictive module* which is known to the compiler. Its definition module is to be interpreted as follows by the programmer:

```
DEFINITION MODULE SYSTEM;
   EXPORT QUALIFIED WORD, ADDRESS, PROCESS, (*exported types*)
     ADR, SIZE, TSIZE, NEWPROCESS, TRANSFER; (*exported
                                        procedures*)
```

```
(*Declaration of hidden data types, whose concrete
  implementation is compiler independent.*)
TYPE WORD;
     ADDRESS;
     PROCESS;

(*AnyType is a data type which is type compatible with
  every arbitrary data type.*)

PROCEDURE ADR(x:AnyType) : ADDRESS;
  (*Yields the address of the variable x.*)

PROCEDURE SIZE(x:AnyType) : CARDINAL;
  (*Yields the number of memory words required
    for the variable x.*)

PROCEDURE TSIZE(AnyType) : CARDINAL;
  (*Yields the number of memory words required
    for a variable of data type AnyType.*)

PROCEDURE NEWPROCESS(P:PROC; A:ADDRESS; n:CARDINAL;
                      VAR q:PROCESS);
  (*See section 4.9*)

PROCEDURE TRANSFER(VAR source, destination:PROCESS);
  (*See section 4.9*)

END SYSTEM.
```

Example:
```
FROM SYSTEM IMPORT ADDRESS;
  ...
PROCEDURE Copy(source,dest:ADDRESS; size:CARDINAL);
BEGIN
  REPEAT
    dest↑:=source↑;
    dest:=dest+1;
    source:=source+1;
    size:=size-1;
  UNTIL size=0
END Copy;
```

Modula-2 also permits the circumvention of the strict type checking by the provision of *type transfer functions.* To this end type names can be used as function names. The object (or the value of an expression) for which a type conversion is to be done is given as a parameter to the corresponding type transfer function.

Example:

1. x is a variable of type CARDINAL.
   INTEGER(x) implies then that the physical representation of x is to be interpreted as an INTEGER.

2. x is a variable of type CARDINAL.
    BITSET(x) implies then that the value of x is interpreted as the bit pattern of the set representing x.

The result of the type transfer functions is not defined by Modula-2, but rather is implementation dependent, that is the programmer who uses these functions must know the physical data representation of the computer.

For the systems programmer it is in many cases useful not to let the address of a variable be determined by the compiler, but rather to be able to determine it himself (for example in order to access operating system components with a fixed address). The *absolute addressing of variables* is possible in Modula-2 by giving the desired address in square brackets immediately behind the name of the variable in the declaration of the variable.

Example:

```
VAR TWS [177564B]: BITSET; (*status register*)
    TWBC[177566B]:   CHAR;   (*buffer register*)
```

4.9 Processes

Modula-2 permits the programming of parallel processes and offers the *"coroutine concept"* for this. Only parameterless procedures, which are not allowed to be contained in another procedure, are permitted as processes.

For the *generation of a new process*, the *procedure NEWPROCESS*, which is exported from the *module SYSTEM* (see section 4.8), is used:

```
PROCEDURE NEWPROCESS(P:PROC; a:ADDRESS; n:CARDINAL;
                          VAR p:PROCESS);
```

NEWPROCESS demands four parameters:

P: the name of the procedure which is to run as a process.

a: the start address of the memory area which is to be used by the process.

n: the size of the required memory area.

p: the generated process (output parameter).

Example:

```
VAR area[1..50] OF CARDINAL;
    keyboard: PROCESS;
    ...
PROCEDURE Driver;
    ...
END Driver;

NEWPROCESS(Driver, ADR(area), SIZE (area), keyboard);
```

By this call the process *keyboard* (behind which the procedure Driver is concealed) is *set up*, but not *executed*. The process is only executed when it is given control by a call of the *procedure TRANSFER. TRANSFER* is exported from the *module SYSTEM* and is defined as follows:

```
PROCEDURE TRANSFER(VAR old, new:PROCESS)
```

Example:
```
VAR main: PROCESS
...
TRANSFER (main, keyboard)
...
```

This call interrupts the *current process* and activates the *process keyboard*. The state of the current process is stored in *main*. The interrupted *process main* can be continued later by a call of *TRANSFER(. . .,main)*. A process is finally terminated when the (dynamic) end of the procedure corresponding to it is reached.

The *procedures NEWPROCESS* and *TRANSFER* as well as the *data type PROCESS* must be imported from the *module SYSTEM*.

The process concept of Modula-2 is defined at a very low level; it contains *no mechanisms for process synchronization or process communication*. It does allow, however, the implementation of higher concepts for managing parallel processes. The procedures which are necessary for this must be written by the programmer himself. Examples of this may be found in (*Wirth*, 1982).

4.10 Standard Procedures

Standard procedures are *predeclared procedures and* are denoted by *standard identifiers*. Standard identifiers qualify as automatically imported and can, therefore, only be redeclared in procedures.

In the following the concept of *ordinal number* is introduced. Ordinal numbers are of the data type CARDINAL and denote elements of the data types INTEGER, CARDINAL, CHAR and any arbitrary enumeration type. The following list shows the standard procedures of Modula-2 and their meaning.

ABS(x)
>The function is applicable to all objects of the types INTEGER, CARDINAL and REAL, or a subrange type of these. ABS(x) yields the absolute value of x. The data type of the result is the same as that of x.

CAP(ch)
>ch is an object of type CHAR. CAP(ch) yields the capital letter corresponding to ch.

CHR(x)
>x is an ordinal number. CHR(x) yields the symbol with the ordinal number x in the given physical data representation of the computer.

FLOAT(x)
>x is a number of type CARDINAL. FLOAT(x) yields the REAL value of x.

HIGH(a)
> a is an object of ARRAY type. HIGH(a) yields the number of elements -1 of a.

ODD(x)
> x is an object of type INTEGER or CARDINAL. ODD(x) yields the boolean value of x MOD 2<>0.

ORD(x)
> x is an object of type CHAR, INTEGER, CARDINAL or any arbitrary enumeration type. ORD(x) yields the ordinal number (of type CARDINAL) of x.

TRUNC(x)
> x is an object of type REAL. TRUNC(x) yields the integer part of x with the data type INTEGER.

VAL(T,x)
> T is one of the types CHAR, INTEGER or CARDINAL, or an arbitrary enumeration type, x is an ordinal number. VAL(T,x) yields the value of the ordinal x for the data type T. (VAL(T,ORD(x))=x).

HALT
> HALT interrupts the execution of a program.

INC(x)

INC(x,n)
> x is an object of type INTEGER, CARDINAL or CHAR, or of an arbitrary enumeration type. INC replaces the value of x with x+1 (INC(x)) or with x+n (INC(x,n)), if x is of type INTEGER or CARDINAL, otherwise with the successor (INC(x)) or the nth successor (INC(x,n)) of x.

DEC(x)

DEC(x,n)
> x is an object of type INTEGER, CARDINAL or CHAR, or of an arbitrary enumeration type. DEC replaces the value of x with x-1 (DEC(x)) or with x-n (DEC(x,n)), if x is of type INTEGER or CARDINAL, otherwise with the predecessor (DEC(x)) or the nth predecessor (DEC(x,n)) of x.

EXCL(s,i)
> The set operation s:=s-{i} is applied to the set s.

INCL(s,i)
> The set operation s:=s+{i} is applied to the set s.

NEW(p)
> p is an object of data type POINTER TO T. NEW generates an object of data type T and causes p to point to the newly generated object. The use of the standard procedure NEW assumes that the procedure ALLOCATE is available (for instance imported).

DISPOSE(p)

p is an object of data type POINTER TO T. DISPOSE frees the storage area, which is occupied by the object to which p points. The use of the standard procedure DISPOSE assumes that the procedure DEALLOCATE is available (for instance imported).

NEW(p,t_1,...,t_n)

DISPOSE(p,t_1,...,t_n)

p is an object of data type POINTER TO T, whereby T is a record type with variants, and t_1,...,t_n are constants for the selection of the corresponding variants, whereby t_1 refers to the outermost variant and t_n refers to the innermost variant. The functioning of NEW and DISPOSE is just as described above.

Further Reading

Ford, G.A. and Wiener, R.S.: Modula-2. A Software Development Approach; Wiley & Sons 1985.

Joyce, J.: Modula-2: A Seafarer's Manual and Shipyard Guide; Addison-Wesley 1985.

Knepley, E. and Platt, R.: Modula-2 Programming; Prentice-Hall 1985.

Wiener, R.S. and Sincovec, R.F.: Software Engineering with Modula-2 and Ada; Wiley & Sons 1984.

Wirth, N.: Programming in Modula-2; Springer Verlag,1982.

5. The Software Life Cycle

Like other large projects, software projects can be broken up into individual *project phases*. For this analysis the author has choosen the following divisions: *requirements analysis, requirements definition (specification), design, implementation, test, operation* and *maintenance*.

The purpose of the *analysis phase* is to determine and document which functions and steps are to be executed and what the nature of the interactions is for a problem area in which a software solution is sought.

The purpose of the *definition phase* is to arrive at a contract (requirements definition) between the customer and the software manufacturer which determines precisely what the planned software system should provide.

The purpose of the *design phase* is to determine how the requirements given by the specification will be realized.

The purpose of the *implementation phase* is to translate the concept determined in the design phase into a programming language.

The purpose of the *test phase* is to discover as many errors in the software product as possible and to guarantee that the implementation satisfies the specification.

After conclusion of the test phase, the software system is installed and released for use. The task of software *maintenance* is to eliminate errors which first appear during *operation,* and to implement system changes and expansions (from changing the specification to testing).

The phases cited above are collectively referred to as the *software life cycle* (see illustration 5.1).

The manufacture of software systems is an *iterative*, not a *linear* process. Past experience shows that the individual phases often entail consequences for the results of previous phases. Sometimes it is not clear until the design phase that the requirements definition is incomplete, or implementation and testing show where design errors were made. The sequence of phases in the software life cycle is interrupted repeatedly, and the process of development must occasionally be taken up in an earlier phase, or in the worst case even started all over again.

The following sections describe the subject and scope of the individual phases of the software life cycle, which problems can occur and how they can be overcome.

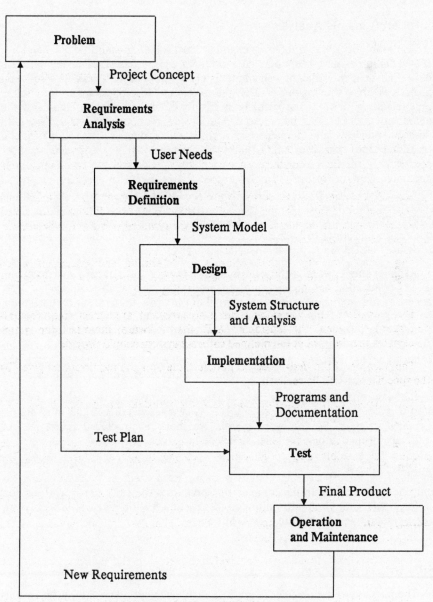

Illustration 5.1 The Software Life Cycle

5.1 Requirements Analysis

The problems which a software engineer must solve are manifold and complex. It is a common misconception that a problem can be described to the software developer in a way that he can immediately grasp. The first task in a software project is that the customer and the software developer come to a clear understanding about what actually needs to be done. The problem and the amount of service must be assessed. The objective of *requirements analysis* is to describe precisely the demands on a software product, taking all peripheral conditions into consideration. Usually the customer and the software engineer possess only minimal knowledge of each other's field, and the communications gap must first be bridged. In this respect, it is useful to discuss the project specification with as many people as possible: the *users*, the *project manager* and all other *people involved* in the project. This is the best way of ascertaining which "capabilities" the software product should have; occasionally it is helpful to stipulate what is not to be included. A detailed discussion of the most important activities involved in requirements analysis is given below.

As an example, when a software solution is sought for a particular department of an organization and no clear project specification is available, an *analysis of the current system configuration* must be carried out in order to determine what should be automated. During the analysis of the system configuration, therefore, the current (organizational) system and the affected operations should be analyzed and the user requirements compiled. For the analyst it is important in this connection to discover who the actual "customer" is; in many cases the requirements of the customer differ from the requirements of the future user.

Stepwise analysis of the current system configuration is advisable. The first step is *system delimitation*, the second step is *system analysis* and the third step is *system description*. By the word system we mean a structured interaction of mutually influential objects which satisfy certain rules.

Not every software project begins with requirements analysis. In many applications no pre-existing system is being automated, and thus there is no current system configuration to analyze. Sometimes the customer is in a position to formulate a requirements definition (see section 5.2) on his own, in which case this phase of the software life cycle is left out.

5.1.1 System Delimitation

The purpose of *system delimitation* is to decide which parts of the system are to be included in the analysis and which parts are to be excluded. This is not evident from the start. Usually the first project specification for a software project is kept very general. For example: "For the supervision of cost developments an accounting system is to be implemented." During system delimitation the amount of service concealed behind this vague formulation is to be clarified. For example, is only a billing system intended, or is an audit and a monthly profit/loss account also part of the system. A further goal of the systems delimitation phase is to work out which environmental factors are relevant for the project. In many projects the mistake is made of paying too little attention to system delimitation and the articulation of environmental factors. The result of this is that, at the introduction of the software product, extensive alterations and adjustments are necessary in wide areas of the environment. Only when it is clear what is to be automated and which functions are to be excluded, can the actual analysis of the current system configuration be started.

5.1.2 System Analysis

System analysis constitutes the essence of requirements analysis. On the one hand, the analysis of the current system configuration should concern itself only with those facets of the system which are already in existence. On the other, it must be remembered that the following situation often occurs in practice: a department in an organization seeks software support for a particular operation. The employees restrict their requests to a minimum, either for personal reasons or because they are not convinced of the feasibility of the project. Often, shortly after the final software product is introduced and the user has acquired a certain confidence in the use of the system, he starts to place new demands on the software product. The result is finally a program system in which the "appendages" far outweigh the original version. This results in a lessened quality of the software product, especially if the original version was poorly structured and not modularized. Therefore, it is necessary that the analyst always retain more problems in view than the user presents on his own. Taking into account later desires to expand the system at the time of systems analysis improves the design of a software product with respect to expandability. In view of this the analyst must closely examine the *weak points* of the current system in addition to the *problem area* and the *flow of information* during system analysis. To this end it is helpful to introduce a rough systemization and thus to separate the analysis task into the following seven main points:

(1) Structure Analysis
(2) Problem Analysis
(3) Communications Analysis
(4) Document Analysis
(5) Data Analysis
(6) Flow Analysis
(7) Weak Points Analysis

(1) Structure Analysis

The *purpose of structure analysis* is to obtain clarity about the infrastructure of the department for which a software solution is sought. This is important in order to be able to present the desired software concept to all those involved. Structure analysis should yield results about:

* the hierarchy of the department to be investigated
* the number and the qualifications of the employees
* the nature and scope of the interactions with other departments

As a means of representation organigrams, hierarchy diagrams and, for the description of employee qualifications, verbal job descriptions are suitable.

(2) Problem Analysis

The *purpose of problem analysis* is to compile information on the volume and nature of tasks (functions) occurring in the area in question, and on the particulars of the internal processes of the functions determined. Therefore the following must be determined:

* What is to be done, that is which functions fall in the area to be examined?
* Who carries out the various functions?
* When and how often are the functions executed?
* For what purpose is a function executed?

After this a description with the following content should be created for each function:

* data and information used (for example catalogs, documents, forms, instructions)
* data and information produced
* function flow (processing algorithms)

In the process it is important to become acquainted with all decision procedures according to which management and personnel make decisions in order to be able to decide whether and what functions can be automated. As a means of representation for the function processes, flowcharts are suitable. Everything else can be written in simple prose.

(3) Communications Analysis

Communications analysis is concerned, in contrast to flow analysis, with the informal relationships between the various functions. Of interest here are the form (for example by telephone, written, verbal), the type (for example discussions, conferences, access to catalogs or archives) and the frequency of communications between the various functional units. As a mode of representation a communications matrix is recommended which records for each function the form, type and frequency of its use.

(4) Document Analysis

The *purpose of this analysis* is to compile all documents which are used and produced in the area in question. The results of this analysis form the basis for the later specification of the format of input and output for the various functions. For each document, a description with the following content should be acquired:

* identification
* contents
* purpose (control form, work order, processing instructions, etc.)
* the degree of formality
* the distributor
* the storage method

In addition, an applications matrix (which states by function which document is required and which document is produced) should be acquired.

(5) Data Analysis

The *purpose of data analysis* is to obtain clarity about the volume and type of data to be processed. In particular the following should be ascertained:

* the volume of the data, separated according to file (for example master and update files in commercial applications) and individual data
* the value domains of the data
* the data carrier used
* the order structures, number systems, sort criteria
* the frequency of processing
* the frequency of updating
* the type of and requirements on data protection
* the time dependence (especially for the receipt of update data in the commercial sector)
* the growth of volume of the data

(6) Flow Analysis

Flow analysis yields information about the sequence in which the various functions must be executed and about the data flow between the functions. As a means of representation for the results of this analysis, hierarchy diagrams, flowcharts and data flowcharts are suitable.

(7) Weak Points Analysis

From the results of the previous steps, the problems, omissions and redundancies of the system can be determined. *Weak points analysis* is intended to investigate both the individual functions and the whole system in light of this in order to expose the weak points in the current system.

5.1.3 System Description

The *purpose of system description* is to order, structure and explain the results obtained in *system delimitation* and *analysis* (matrices, flowcharts, hierarchy diagrams and descriptions composed in prose) so that they can be represented in a *closed and complete description of the system*. The question of the scope and organization of system description cannot be answered in general and depends on the complexity and type of the system to be evaluated. It is important here, that the system be described *from the outside in*, that is first delimit the system and determine the effect of the system on the outside, and only then specify the individual functions and their interactions.

5.1.4 Analysis Techniques

So far there has been no success in developing techniques for the various phases of requirements analysis which are *methodical* and of general applicability. The reason for this is to be found in the variety of fields of application for which software products are developed.

The choice of an appropriate procedure for the analysis of the current system configuration depends on the type, size and goals of a project and also on the experience and qualifications of the analyst. There are several procedures to choose from.

One frequently used analysis technique is the *questionnaire*, whereby the analyst directs detailed questions at the employees of the department in question. The disadvantage here is that the analyst must already have a very precise knowledge of the area of application, in order to be able to provide meaningful and complete questionnaires. Simpler and more flexible, but difficult to process and document, are *individual and group interviews*.

One procedure often recommended is the so called *report method*. The specialists in the field are requested to provide reports for the analyst about their field together with all related facts. The advantage here is that in this way the specialists are forced to be more exacting, and to work more constructively in the analysis phase. However, formulating useable (that is well structured, clear and precisely formulated) reports requires a certain type of experience which specialists often lack.

Probably the most informative, but also the most involved, method of analyzing the system configuration is the *direct employment of the systems analyst* for a sufficient period of time in the appropriate field.

5.2 Requirements Definition (System Specification)

The *requirements definition* is the contract between the customer and the software manufacturer. Therefore it must be understood, and accepted as complete and consistent by both. Drafting a requirements definition which meets these criteria is one of the most difficult tasks in the development of large software systems. If requirements analysis has been carried out, its results form the basis for drafting the requirements definition. Before one makes a requirements definition the basis of a project, it is important to be sure of the technical and economic feasibility of the project.

5.2.1 Content and Scope of the Requirements Definition

The purpose of producing a requirements definition (it is often referred to in the following as a system specification) is to define the system functions and to determine the user interfaces.

Analysis of software errors shows that one-third to one-half of all errors are caused by an incomplete, inconsistent or erroneous system specification (see *Kopetz*, 1979 and *Boehm*, 1975).

Those system parts which are quickly and superficially specified contain the most logical errors. According to *Boehm* (1975), a given extra effort during system specification yields more than double the savings in effort during implementation and testing.

As is mentioned above, the system specification represents the contract between the customer and the programmer and must therefore be understood by both sides. It should thus be free of computer jargon and presented in a clear and lucid manner. The following structure is suggested:

(1) initial situation and goals

(2) system operation and environment

(3) functional requirements

(4) nonfunctional requirements

(5) user interfaces

(6) error behavior

(7) documentation requirements

(8) acceptance criteria

(9) glossary and index

Paragraph (1) should contain a general description of the initial situation with reference to the analysis of the initial system (if it was carried out). In addition, the goals of the project should be described and the project should be delimited from the external system environment.

Paragraph (2) should describe the prerequisites which must be fulfilled for system operation. By this we understand the description of all information (data, records, etc.) that is required for system operation but is not part of the implementation (that is information which is provided from the outside). In addition this paragraph should contain facts about the number of users, the frequency of use and the jobs of the users.

Paragraph (3) should define the system functions expected by the user. A good specification of the system functions contains only the necessary facts about these functions. All additional information, for example about the solution algorithm, distracts the analyst from the actual task of specification and also limits the possibilities for the subsequent design phase. The definition of the functional requirements should also contain all necessary facts about the type, volume and expected precision of the data which are associated with a particular system function. In addition, facts about the expected volume of input data are very important for system development. Plausibility checks for discovering input errors are not possible until the domains of the data are exactly determined. *Liskov* (1975) and *Gibson* et.al. (1971) are of the opinion that in any case a formal notation of the functional specification is to be sought, because it constitutes the prerequisite for any potential mechanical processing of the system specification. The notation which is to be used for this is described in section 5.2.3.

Paragraph (4) should specify all nonfunctional requirements, for example failure security, reliability requirements, portability requirements and desired response and execution time. In view of the feasibility studies (see section 5.2.2) it is necessary to weight these requirements and to substantiate them in detail.

Paragraph (5) should contain one of the most important points of system specification. It should describe the manner and means by which the users communicate with the system. The communication should be as exactly portrayed in the form of screen overlays, printing formats and examples of man-machine communication as the user later encounters it. The acceptability of the software product is dependent on the quality of this paragraph. The content and structure of this paragraph is extensively covered in section 5.6.1.1.

Paragraph (6) should discuss the effects of the various types of error and the desired system behavior upon their occurrence. Designing a reliable system means, according to *Kopetz* (1979), thinking over the possibilities for error in each phase of the development and taking appropriate measures for preventing and weakening the effects of errors. Measures for handling errors should therefore already be covered in the specification phase (as far as possible).

Paragraph (7) should fix the scope and type of the documentation. The documentation of a system is on the one hand the prerequisite for the correct application of the software product (user manual) and on the other the basis for the maintenance of the system. The various user types should be taken into consideration during the layout of the user manuals (see section 5.6.1.1). When the user is a computer layman who uses the computer as an aid for his job, other means of representation are called for than if the user is a computer specialist. The scope and amount of detail of the system documentation depends also on the expected system changes and expansions and is described in detail in section 5.6.2.

Paragraph (8) should specify the acceptance criteria. They relate to the functional as well as to the nonfunctional requirements. It is recommended that the acceptance criteria for each individual requirement on the system be fixed here. If it is not possible to fix a quantitative acceptance criterion for some requirement, then it is reasonable to assume that the user is not clear about the meaning and value of this requirement (*Heninger,* 1980).

Paragraph (9) should reflect the fact that the requirements definition is a document which is the basis of all phases of a software project and which contains the preliminary considerations for the entire software life cycle. Therefore it must be easy to handle, and the author, along with *Heniger* (1980), supports the opinion that the requirements definition should be a reference document for all those involved in the project. It is therefore useful to include also a glossary covering the concepts used and an extensive index.

5.2.2 Feasibility Studies

Before the requirements definition can be made into a contract between the customer and the software manufacturer, it must be assured that it is complete and correct and that the requirements are also technically and economically feasible. The *validation* of the requirements definition embraces, therefore:

(1) Testing for the completeness of the requirements.
The customer must confirm that all functional and nonfunctional requirements, restrictions and peripheral factors are included.

(2) Testing the consistency of the requirements.
The analyst must assure that the requirements do not contradict each other.

(3) Testing the technical feasibility.
The technical feasibility depends on the availability of appropriate hardware and on the availability of an appropriate software technology which allows the desired service to be provided. It also depends, however, on whether the information expected by the system from its environment can be provided in the desired quantity and precision.

(4) Investigation of the requirements on personnel.
It must be assured that personnel with appropriate qualifications are available for production as well as for operation.

(5) Economical justification.
Obviously it must be determined in a cost effectiveness analysis whether the project can be realized with economically justifiable means.

5.2.3 Specification Aids and Methods of Representation

It has been shown how important, but also how difficult and costly it is to prepare a correct and complete system specification (*Congar,* 1973 reports that approximately 15-20% of the total expenditure falls on the phase of the requirements definition). Natural languages are only partially suitable for a clear, unambiguous description of the requirements definition. The inexactitude and ambiguity of natural languages and the volume and complexity of requirements definitions ordinarily make it difficult, if not impossible, to test this type of description for completeness and consistency. The length and ponderousness of prose descriptions increase the probability of an erroneous interpretation. Program designs which are constructed on such specifications often do not comply with the actual requirements.

It is therefore obvious that the discipline of software engineering must attempt to provide methodical aids. These aids should provide clear notation, help find errors early, guarantee completeness and admit a structure which assists implementation, cost estimation and time and personnel planning. One must be able to represent processes (that is algorithms), states (that is data and situations), data flow, hierarchical relationships and abstractions.

Until now it has not been possible to develop a method which satisfies all these desires. For this reason available specification aids are not described in detail. Instead, elementary and special aids are simply listed, and the reader is referred to the literature.

5.2.3.1 Elementary Aids

Flowcharts are diagrams which show the flow of system functions by the use of graphic symbols (see illustration 5.2). Flowcharts are unambiguous, there is no confusion about their interpretation. They are, however, difficult to test for completeness and lead to poor structure if used without discipline.

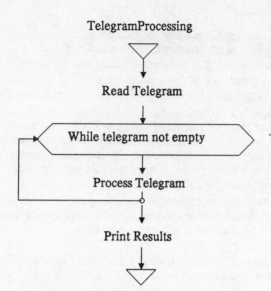

Illustration 5.2 Example of a Flowchart

Data flowcharts are diagrams which show the flow of data in a system (see illustration 5.3). They describe the interfaces between the functional components and give a survey of the information flow in the planned system (compare also *Kimm* et al., 1979 and *Wedekind*, 1973).

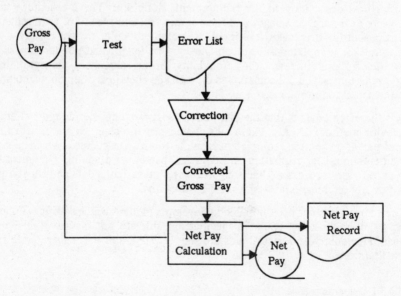

Illustration 5.3 Example of a Data Flowchart (Source *Wedekind*, 1973)

Decision tables are recommended when the execution of actions depends on a number of conditions in a complex manner (see illustration 5.4). The advantage here is that decision tables can be easily tested for contradictions, redundancies and completeness. Examples of this technique can be found in *Elben* (1973), *Erbesdobler* (1976) and *Strunz* (1970).

	1	2	3	4	5
Type	A	A	B	G	G
Ordered	Y	N	-	N	N
In Stock	Y	N	-	Y	N
Acceptable	-	Y	-	-	Y
Bill		X	X		
Return	X				
Dispose					X
Partial Acceptance		X	X		X

Illustration 5.4 Example of a Decision Table

5.2.3.2 Special Aids

Several special aids have been developed for the description of requirements definitions:

The *SADT Method* (Structured Analysis and Design Technique) is topdown and problem oriented, and admits the representation of function and data aspects but not the representation of flow control. It is not only a means of representation but also contains instructions as to how a system should be investigated. It is extensively described in *Schoman* and *Ross* (1977) and *SADT* (1976).

The *PSL/PSA Method* (Problem Statement Language/Problem Statement Analyser) is based on the model of a general system which, by the process of restriction, can accommodate certain classes of systems, especially information systems. The model assumes that a system can be described by objects and relations between these objects. The descriptions can be stored in a data base, and various completeness and consistency tests can be performed. This method was developed at the University of Michigan and is covered in *Teichrow* and *Hersley* (1977) and *Teichrow* et al. (1974). A similar model, RSL, is described in *Bell* et al. (1977).

The *HIPO Method* (Hierarchy Input Process Output, developed by IBM) can also be employed as a specification aid. It is characterized by a clear distinction between data and function notation, and by a tree oriented, hierarchical means of representation. A description of this technique can be found in *IBM* (1975).

All the special methods mentioned above emphasize only certain facets of specification. They are inflexible and tailored only to particular types of problem. For this reason they are not described here in greater detail and the reader is rather referred to the appropriate literature. That a generally acceptable method is missing shows how underdeveloped specification technique still is, and that specification, like programming, is a creative task which cannot be replaced by rules and methodology.

5.3 Design

The art of programming starts with design. The quality of a software product is especially influenced by the quality of the design. The design phase therefore takes on an important position in the software life cycle. The purpose of design is to determine the *architecture* of a software system, with the goal of achieving the most economical implementation which satisfies the quality requirements. It is clear that designing software is a creative process, but meaningful guidelines for it can still be given.

In this section techniques for mastering the complexity of software systems are discussed, that is techniques for decomposing systems into subsystems, as well as questions of the internal structure of program systems. First a rough overview of the various design techniques is given. Then a special design technique, stepwise refinement, is described in detail. In addition, concepts such as data capsules, abstract data types and attributed grammars as tools for modularization are discussed, together with a verification technique which helps to verify design decisions.

5.3.1 Design Techniques

One of the most important principles for mastering complexity is the *principle of abstraction*. The term abstraction is used when the solution of a task is considered without knowledge of all the details of the realization. The basic idea behind *abstracting topdown design*, which goes back to *Dijkstra* (1969) and *Wirth* (1971), postulates that the act of design should start with the analysis of the system specification and should ignore the details of the implementation. Starting with the system specification, a task is decomposed, topdown, into subtasks until functions are available which can easily be formulated as algorithms. *Topdown design* is a matter of successive realization from abstractly described solution concepts. Abstraction is the only possibility for getting an overview of complex systems. One deals only with those aspects of the system which are necessary for either a single step of understanding, or for solving the problem.

Another design technique is the so called *bottomup design*. Here one proceeds in the opposite direction. One begins with the design not at the level of the system specification but rather at the level on which the system is to be realized. The basic idea here is that the hardware and each overlying level of a software product can be considered as abstract machines. By an abstract machine we understand, according to *Gewald* et al. (1977), a set of fundamental operations in which one can express the total operation of a system or a subsystem at any one of the levels of abstraction. In bottomup design one starts with the properties of the concrete machine and designs one abstract machine after the other by successive additions of necessary properties until one arrives at the machine which is necessary for the functions desired by the user.

Both techniques have their advantages and disadvantages. A discussion of the subject may be found in *Schulz* (1982). For a new conceptualization of a software system, the topdown method is more suitable (see also section 5.3.2), whereas for the adaptation of an existing system to changed goals, usually both bottomup and topdown procedures are used.

These techniques are *problem oriented design techniques*, which means that the design strategy originates with the task to be solved. Based on the principle of stepwise topdown design with problem oriented design strategy, special design methods were developed, such as the *Constantine Method* (Brown, 1972 and *Stevens, Myers, Constantine*, 1974), the *SADT Method* (*Schoman, Ross* 1977) and the *Litos Method* (*Schulz* 1982). They are extensively described in the literature cited and are compared in *Schulz* (1982) and *Hesse* (1981). They are therefore not discussed here.

As opposed to problem oriented design techniques, we are also aware of *data oriented design techniques*. The design strategy here does not originate with the task to be solved, but rather with the data structures which are required for the solution. Certainly the best known technique of this type is the *Jackson Method* (*Jackson*, 1975). *Jackson* postulates the following maxim for the design of software systems:

"Program structures should be based on data structures."

His reason for this is that a computer can communicate with its environment only through data and its structures. According to this, every design step is based on two phases:

(1) the analysis and design of the data structures of a task and
(2) the 1:1 mapping of the data structures designed in phase (1) onto a program structure.

Further data oriented design techniques are the *LCP Method* developed by Warnier (*Warnier*, 1974) (Logical Construction of Programs) and the *HIPO Method* developed by IBM (*IBM*, 1975) (Hierarchy Input Process Output). These data oriented design procedures are extensively discussed in the literature cited. The interested reader is advised to consult this literature.

Special design techniques, like Jackson, LCP, Litos Method etc., usually emphasize only certain facets of design and are tailored to particular task types.

The author is of the opinion that the technique of *task oriented stepwise refinement* is the most general and reasonable design concept, because it is a *production technique* as well as a *design technique* and seems to be--from the viewpoint of the practitioner as well as from that of the theoretician--the most promising concept for the future. On the one hand, it is very general and equally suited for all areas of application, and on the other, it is practically self explanatory and does not require a great deal of formalism. Therefore, this technique is detailed in the following section.

5.3.2 The Method of Stepwise Refinement

The *purpose of designing,* in the sense of software engineering, is to develop an algorithmic solution for a specified problem. *Goos* (1973a) writes in this connection: "The design of a software system starts from a description of the problem to be solved and the available host system." We may assume that the requirements analysis and the drafting of the requirements definition is already accomplished. The question arises, how should one proceed if a problem is given and an algorithm for its solution is sought.

For this *Wirth* advances the general principle:

(1) Decompose the task into subtasks.
(2) Consider each subtask on its own and decompose it again into subtasks, until they have become so simple, that they can be formulated algorithmically.

Wirth (1971) calls this principle the *method of stepwise refinement.* The principle states that, for a complex task, one does not immediately jump to the handling of details, but rather should first attempt to decompose the task into its major components. The subtasks which result from this are in any event less complex than the original system, and are therefore easier to solve. The consistent application of this practice leads step by step to an ever more precise solution of the original problem. The process is finished when all the details are clarified.

It can become apparent, however, in the solution of subtasks, that the chosen decomposition was not the most appropriate and leads to difficulties in further refinement. This cannot be avoided from the start, and one may have to backtrack, or in the worst case even start all over again. The process of decomposition is iterative.

It is not feasible to demonstrate this design technique on a comprehensive problem which corresponds to one encountered in practice because that itself would fill half a book. It is, however, feasible to demonstrate this principle and the procedure on a less extensive problem. In addition the following literature is recommended: *Dijkstra* (1972b), *Rechenberg* (1974) and *Wirth* (1970).

Consider the following problem:

A stream of incoming telegrams is to be processed. Each telegram is terminated by the string "ZZZZ". The telegram stream is ended when an empty telegram, followed by the string "ZZZZ", arrives. The telegrams are read and then transmitted linewise with 60 to 80 characters per line. The words of a telegram are to be counted. The recorded number, together with a remark about how many words in the text are longer than twelve characters, is to be printed after each telegram. Unnecessary spaces should be eliminated for printing. The longest allowable word has 20 characters, longer words are to be truncated.

For the description of the solution a notation is used which, without further explanation, should be just as understandable as a flowchart or Nassi/Schneiderman diagram.

The description of an algorithm consists of a header and a body. The header contains its name, and possibly parameters, that is it describes the interface with the environment. The actions in the body can be sentences in prose or Modula-2 statements, according to the desired degree of abstraction. This notation is very similar to that of programming languages. It is distinguished from programming languages--without loss of precision--by a great deal of freedom in the formulation of actions and by not being constrained by syntactic exactitude. For better readability it is agreed that statements for flow control, as in Modula-2, are to be written in capitals. Names of variables are to be written in lower-case letters. Input, output and transition parameters are indicated by arrows ($\uparrow$, $\downarrow$, $\updownarrow$) and comments by the prefix "--". Prose and the names of algorithms are written with the usual capital and lower-case letters.

Let us now begin the design according to the principle of stepwise refinement.

In the roughest view, a telegram stream consists of zero or more telegram texts T followed by an empty telegram E (T...TE). This structure suggests a loop. It is therefore possible to deliniate the following rough scheme:

```
TelegramProcessing:
  REPEAT
    Process Telegram(↑empty)                    (1)
  UNTIL empty
END TelegramProcessing.
```

The task has thus already become much simpler. The action "Process Telegram" returns the information whether the processed telegram was empty or not. Following the principle of stepwise refinement, the action "Process Telegram" must now be refined; it is already much less complex than the original problem.

"Process Telegram" reads zero or more words of text W and an end word "ZZZZ" (WW..."ZZZZ"), counts them, prints them and the results of counting and yields the information as to whether or not the telegram just processed was empty (that is contained no words of text). The following structure results:

```
Process Telegram(↑empty):
  Initialize Word Counter(↑wordnum ↑longwordnum)
  REPEAT
    Read Word(↑word ↑wordlength)
    IF word<>"ZZZZ"                             (2)
      THEN
        Count Words(↓wordlength ↕wordnum ↕longwordnum)
        Print Word(↓word ↓wordlength)
    END
```

```
UNTIL word="ZZZZ"
IF wordnum=0
  THEN empty:=TRUE
  ELSE
    empty:=FALSE
    Print Results(↓wordnum ↓longwordnum)
END
END Process Telegram.
```

Once again, according to the specification of "Process Telegram", only the basic structure of the algorithm has been given, and the task has been decomposed into the subtasks "Initialize Word Counter", "Read Word", "Count Words", "Print Word" and " Print Results".

The values given and (necessary for further processing) sought for these subtasks have been introduced as parameters. Their meaning need not be further explained; it is expressed in their names. The type of parameter has been fixed by arrows (↑: input parameter, ↓: output parameter, ↕: transition parameter). It is not intended, at this time, to make any statements about their data type.

The action "Initialize Word Counter" is trivial, it must only take care that *wordnum* and *longwordnum* are initialized with zero.

The action "Read Word" must overread any potential leading spaces, read characters and construct a word, until the first space is recognized after a word. To this end the task can be decomposed further and the following algorithm results:

```
Read Word(↑word ↑wordlength):
  Overread Spaces(↑character)                    (3.1)
  Build Word(↓character ↑word ↑wordlength)
END Read Word.
```

The action "Count Words" must increment the number of words and, if the word length is greater than twelve, also increment the number of long words. It is assumed that the word counters are correctly initialized. The action is easily refined as:

```
Count Words(↓wordlength ↕wordnum ↕longwordnum):
  wordnum:=wordnum+1
  IF wordlength>12                               (3.2)
    THEN longwordnum:=longwordnum+1
  END
END Count Words.
```

Next the action "Print Word" is refined. For the control of the print format (according to specification) a memory variable (*printpos*) is required which informs us how full the line to be printed is. It must be initialized before the processing of a telegram. The next step is therefore to expand the basic structure of "TelegramProcessing".

```
TelegramProcessing:
  REPEAT
    Initialize Printposition
    Process Telegram(↑empty)                    (1a)
  UNTIL empty
END TelegramProcessing.
```

The action "Initialize Printposition" is trivial and for "Print Word" it is now possible to give the following structure:

```
Print Word(↓word ↓wordlength):
  --printpos (memory variable) indicates how many
  --characters the last print line already contains
  IF printpos>60
    THEN Linefeed; printpos:=1 END              (3.3)
  Print(↓word ↓' ') --print word and a space after
  printpos:=printpos+wordlength+1
END Print Word.
```

The action "Print Results" is easily refined, as follows:

```
Print Results(↓wordnum ↓longwordnum):
  Linefeed
  Print(↓"Number of words =" ↓wordnum)         (3.4)
  Linefeed
  Print(↓"Number of long words =" ↓longwordnum)
  Linefeed
END Print Results.
```

Now the actions "Overread Spaces" and "Build Word" must be refined:

```
Overread Spaces(↑character):
  REPEAT
  Read(↑character) --Reads next character
                   --from input medium         (4.1)
  UNTIL character<>' '
END Overread Spaces.
```

The action "Build Word" reads characters and counts them until a space is encountered. The character last read by "Overread Spaces" together with the string read by "Build Word", with the exception of the last space, constitute a word. The number of characters belonging to a word is the word length. If a word is longer than 20 characters the remainder of the word is overread and the word length is given as 20.

```
Build Word(↓character ↑word ↑wordlength):
  word:=empty
  wordlength:=0
  WHILE character<>' ' DO
    IF wordlength<20
      THEN                                          (4.2)
        Append character on word
        wordlength:=wordlength+1
    END
    Read(↑character)
  END
END Build Word.
```

With that, the refinement process is finished and the design of the solution is completed.

For the demonstration of the method the refinement process has been carried so far that the design is already represented as a practically finished program. In practice, one will usually not go so far as to further refine actions such as "Overread Spaces". These will just be specified; the refinement will then be dealt with during implementation.

One can of course object that an experienced software engineer could have immediately given a (perhaps better) solution to this simple problem, even without the principle of stepwise refinement. For simple problems this is certainly correct. For the design of larger program systems, however, the task is to master complexity, and the key is the principle of stepwise refinement. Practical experience shows that even for simple tasks, a systematic, stepwise design strategy reduces the number of design errors and leads to better program structures.

The solution of the telegram problem given above can be comfortably implemented in Modula-2 as a modular program system. The actions determined during the refinement process describe either the *reading* or *printing* or the *processing* of data. We implement the actions as procedures and organize them, according to their tasks, into the modules "ReadTelegram", "PrintTelegram" and "ProcessTelegram". This results in the hierarchy diagram given in illustration 5.5 (boxes indicate modules, ellipses indicate procedures).

The modules "ReadTelegram" and "PrintTelegram" contain procedures which, however, are not all to be made available to the module "ProcessTelegram". For example the procedure "ConstructWord" is a local procedure to the module "ReadTelegram" and it should not be used by any other module. Therefore the export interfaces of the two modules "ReadTelegram" and "PrintTelegram" must be determined and for this the concept of definition module from Modula-2 is used (see section 4.7.1):

```
DEFINITION MODULE ReadTelegram; (*input module
  This module contains procedures for reading the telegrams.*)
  EXPORT QUALIFIED ReadWord;
```

```
Procedure ReadWord(VAR word:ARRAY OF CHAR;
                   VAR wordlength:CARDINAL);
    (*Yields the first telegram word not yet processed
     and its length(wordlength).*)

END ReadTelegram.
```

The procedures "ConstructWord" and "OverreadSpaces" are hidden and are therefore missing in the definition module.

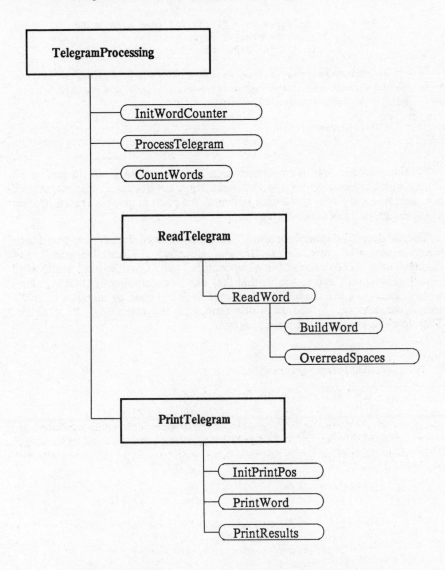

Illustration 5.5 Hierarchy Diagram for the Telegram Problem

```
DEFINITION MODULE PrintTelegram;(*Output module:
This module contains procedures for controlling
the printing of telegrams*)

EXPORT QUALIFIED InitPrintPos, PrintWord, PrintResults;

PROCEDURE InitPrintPos;
  (*Initializes the present print position in an
    output line with one.*)

PROCEDURE PrintWord(word: ARRAY OF CHAR;
                    wordlength: CARDINAL):
  (*Prints a telegram word (word) followed by a space,
    beginning at the present print position, and updates
    the print position based on the word length.*)

PROCEDURE PrintResults(wordnum, longwordnum: CARDINAL);
  (*Prints the number of words (wordnum) and the number
    of long words (longwordnum).*)

END TelegramPrinting.
```

All the prerequisites for implementation have now been given. In section 5.4 all the questions concerning the implementation are discussed. For the sake of completeness and clarity the author wishes at this point to give the transformation of the design into a Modula-2 program.

The module "TelegramProcessing" contains, in accordance with the design given above, the procedures "InitWordCounter", "ProcessTelegram" and "CountWords". The actions "InitWordCounter" and "CountWords" are local to "ProcessTelegram", and so simple that they can be coded directly (that is in line) without impairing the readability. This module is not used by any other module and it contains the procedure which represents the essence of the problem. Therefore it is chosen as the main program.

```
MODULE TelegramProcessing;

FROM ReadTelegram IMPORT ReadWord;
FROM PrintTelegram IMPORT PrintWord, PrintResults,
                         InitPrintPos;
VAR empty: BOOLEAN;

PROCEDURE ProcessTelegram(VAR empty: BOOLEAN);
  CONST longword=12;
  VAR word: ARRAY [1..20] OF CHAR;
      wordlength, wordnum, longwordnum: CARDINAL;

  PROCEDURE EndWord(word: ARRAY OF CHAR; wl: CARDINAL):
                   BOOLEAN;
    (*Tests whether a word is an end word*)
    CONST lendword=4;
    VAR i: CARDINAL;
```

```
    BEGIN
      IF wl<>lendword THEN RETURN FALSE; END;
      i := 0;
      LOOP
        IF word(i)<>'Z' THEN RETURN FALSE; END;
        IF i>=lendword-1
          THEN RETURN TRUE;
          ELSE i := i+1;
        END;
      END;
    END EndWord;

  BEGIN (*The action of ProcessTelegram*)
    (*Initialize word counter*)
    wordnum := 0;
    longwordnum := 0;
    REPEAT
      ReadWord(word,wordlength);
      IF NOT EndWord(word,wordlength)
        THEN (*Count words*)
          wordnum := wordnum+1;
          IF wordlength > longword
            THEN longwordnum := longwordnum+1;
          END;
          PrintWord(word,wordlength);
      END;
    UNTIL EndWord;
    IF wordnum=0
      THEN empty := TRUE; (*Empty telegram recognized*)
      ELSE (*Correct telegram recognized*)
        empty := FALSE;
        PrintResults(wordnum,longwordnum);
    END;
  END ProcessTelegram;

BEGIN (*Body of TelegramProcessing*)
  REPEAT (*For all telegrams*)
    InitPrintPos;
    ProcessTelegram(empty);
  UNTIL empty;
END TelegramProcessing.
```

The implementation modules for "ReadTelegram" and "PrintTelegram" can also be derived directly from the design:

```
IMPLEMENTATION MODULE ReadTelegram; (*Input module:
  This module contains procedures for reading telegrams*)

FROM InOut IMPORT ReadChar;
VAR character: CHAR;
PROCEDURE ReadWord(VAR word: ARRAY OR CHAR;
                   VAR wl: CARDINAL);
```

```
      BEGIN
        OverreadSpaces(character);
        BuildWord(character,word,wl);
      END ReadWord;

    PROCEDURE OverreadSpaces(VAR character: CHAR);
      BEGIN
        REPEAT
          ReadChar(character);
        UNTIL character<>' ';
      END OverreadSpaces;

    PROCEDURE BuildWord(character: CHAR;
                        VAR word: ARRAY OF CHAR;
                        VAR wl: CARDINAL);
      CONST maxwl=20; (*Maximal word length*)
      VAR i [1..20]; (*Word counter*)
      BEGIN
        wl := 0; i := 0; (*initialize word length*)
        WHILE character <>' ' DO
          IF wl<maxwl
            THEN (*build word*)
              INC(wl); word[i] := character; INC(i);
          END;
          ReadChar(character);
        END;
        word[i] := 0C;
      END BuildWord;

  END ReadTelegram.

  IMPLEMENTATION MODULE PrintTelegram (*Output module:
    This module contains procedures for printing
    telegrams*)

    FROM InOut IMPORT WriteLine,WriteString,WriteChar,WriteCard;
    VAR printpos: [1..81];

    PROCEDURE InitPrintPos;
    BEGIN
      printpos := 1;
    END InitPrintPos;

    PROCEDURE PrintWord(word: ARRAY OF CHAR; wl: CARDINAL);
    BEGIN
      IF printpos>60
        THEN (*begin new line*)
          WriteLine;
          printpos :=1;
      END;
      WriteString(word); WriteChar(' ')';
      printpos := printpos+wl+1;
    END PrintWord;
```

```
PROCEDURE PrintResults(wordnum, longwordnum: CARDINAL);
BEGIN
  WriteLine;
  WriteString('Number of words="); WriteCard(wordnum,3);
  WriteLine;
  WriteString('The number of long words=');
  WriteCard(longwordnum,3);
  WriteLine;
END PrintResults;

END PrintTelegram.
```

The example given above should show what is meant by the principle of stepwise refinement, how it is to be used and how one transforms the result into a Modula-2 program. Certainly many software engineers would handle the refinement differently and would therefore arrive at a different (perhaps even better) solution.

It should have become apparent that designing is a creative process. The principle of stepwise refinement does not free the software engineer from the necessity of intuitively grasping the problem nor of finding the correct decomposition, but it helps in the design of a large program system which is to be distinguished by good structure and solidly thought out to the last detail.

5.3.3 Structuring of Flow Control

In the previous section it has been shown how one can decompose a task into subtasks until the subtasks are so simple that one can solve them algorithmically. Nothing has been said, however, about the construction of flow control in the algorithmic formulation of a task.

A well accepted modern method for the construction of flow control in algorithms is structured programming. The principles of this method go back to *Dijkstra* (1969), *Wirth* (1973), *Dahl* (1972), *Hoare* (1969), *Böhm* and *Jacopini* (1966) and *Floyd* (1967).

The basic idea here is to insure a *correspondence* between the *static notation* of an algorithm and its *dynamic execution behavior* in order to keep the flow control clear, to reduce the succeptibility to error and to simplify verification of the algorithm (see section 5.3.8). The most important point here is to avoid unbounded flow structures which result from the undisciplined use of GOTO statements. Unbounded flow structures lead to a quadratic growth of paths in the flow control of an algorithm. In the process, the correspondence between static and dynamic control structures is lost.

Böhm and *Jacopini* (1966) and also *Mills* (1972) have shown that the algorithmic solution of any arbitrary task can be described by a combination of the units *sequence*, *selection* and *repetition*. Each of these units has only one entry and only one exit.

The *sequence* is a series of statements which are executed in order, it is also called a block. The *selection* is the condition dependent choice between two or more blocks and again represents a statement. The *repetition* is a block which is executed repeatedly, as long as a condition holds, and also represents a statement.

The statements available in programming languages which support these concepts are:

* assignment
* procedure call
* IF-THEN-ELSE statement
* CASE statement
* WHILE statement
* LOOP statement
* FOR statement

For the above mentioned reasons only these basic units should be used in formulating the flow control. This suggests setting the concept *structured programming* equal to *GOTO less programming*. Can, and should, one completely reject GOTO statements? This question is answered by two well known computer scientists.

Dijkstra (1968b) writes in this connection:

"For a number of years I have been familiar with the observation that the quality of programmers is a decreasing function of the density of **go to** statements in the programs they produce. More recently I discovered why the use of the **go to** statement has such disastrous effects, and I became convinced that the **go to** statement should be abolished from all 'higher level' programming languages (i.e. everything except, perhaps, plain machine code)."

Knuth (1974), on the other hand, writes:

"The new morality that I propose may perhaps be stated thus: 'Certain **go to** statements which arise in connection with well understood transformations are acceptable, provided that the program documentation explains what the transformation was.' The use of four letter words like **goto** can occasionally be justified even in the best of company."

5.3.4 Guidelines for Module Construction

Modularization is one of the most important principles of the design phase. In modular programming, system flexibility, that is ease of alteration, is the prime consideration, rather than system efficiency, as is the case in small programs.

As we saw in the previous section, following the process of stepwise refinement, a large program system is divided into a number of smaller units. But what do the interfaces between these new program units look like? How are the units related? By which criteria should they be incorporated into modules? In order to answer these questions, we first need to know what is meant by a (program) module and then which criteria should be considered in module construction in order to obtain a satisfactory decomposition of the system.

By a *module* we mean, as in *Goos* (1973b), a program segment with the properties that it communicates with the outside world only through a well defined interface, its integration into a larger program unit may be accomplished without knowledge of its inner mechanisms and its correctness may be determined without consideration of its embedding into larger systems (see also Dennis, 1973).

This definition expresses what is meant by a module, but not which criteria must be considered in the decomposition into modules. The way in which a program system is decomposed into segments has an effect on all criteria which affect the quality of the system, and so it is crucial to the quality of the software product. The conditions which must be considered in such a decomposition process are enumerated below.

Module Closure. Every module should realize a task which forms a closed entity. The functions which are included in a module should constitute a logical unit (for example they should operate on the same data structure). It is dangerous, and therefore undesirable, when a particular design decision (algorithm or data structure) gets divided among various modules.

Interface Minimality and Visibility. The interface between two modules is the set of all assumptions which they make about each other (*Parnas*, 1972) for example name, meaning and type of data. Every program system should be decomposed so that the interfaces between modules are as simple as possible (that is there should be few parameters, and where possible no transient parameters) and can be explicitly specified.

Testability. Each module should be constructed so that its correctness can be determined simply by consideration of the interfaces without knowledge of how it is embedded in the completed system.

Freedom from Interference. The decomposition should guarantee that modules do not exert any internal influence upon one another and that each module may be replaced by another which respects the original interface with no effect on the completed system.

Module Size. Each module should be concise. This cannot be defined in terms of the number of lines or pages of source code, as is often claimed in the literature. The rule "not longer than one page" leads to the misunderstanding that the complexity of a program is determined by its length. Well structured programs may certainly comprise a number of pages but nevertheless be concise and understandable. No general statement can be made about module size, and its importance in connection with modularization is often over emphasized.

Module Coupling. One important objective of modularization is to create largely independent (that is loosely coupled) modules. The fewer connections there are between modules the less the danger of error propagation. This also reduces the danger that changes initiated by the user will affect a number of modules, or that changes in one module will implicate changes in a number of others. Because modules communicate with one another, there must be some module coupling.

However, this should be accomplished exclusively through procedures, and with a minimum of parameters. Modules which do not communicate through parameters but rather access a common data domain, are closely coupled, and the search for errors is thereby impeded. The result is poor modularization. But parameters too, when misused, can lead to a close module coupling. When a parameter is used to influence the internal flow, that is to say the logic, of a called module, the calling module must know how the logic of the called module is constructed. Such "control parameters" also indicate poor decomposition.

Module Cohesion. This is a measure of the interrelatedness of the functions of a module. Good, or reasonable, modularization should strive for strong module cohesion. What is meant by strong module cohesion? We mean a functional, a data oriented or a sequential relationship (see also *Stevens,* 1974 and *Haney,* 1972).

A *functionally connected module* consists of functions which are all necessary and sufficient to solve a particular task. Functional connectedness, therefore, can be directly derived from the process of stepwise refinement.

A *data oriented module* consists of functions which all access the same data structures.

A *sequentially connected module* consists of functions which must be carried out successively, and whose results are the prerequisite for the functions which follow.

The Import Number of a Module. This is the number of modules imported by a module. A large import number is a possible indication that the module has to perceive too many co-ordination and decision tasks. There are too few levels of abstraction. A small import number is perhaps an occassion for checking whether or not the module should be further decomposed.

The Utilization Number of a Module. This is the number of modules by which a module is imported. The larger the utilization numbers of the modules in a program system, the greater the ease of maintenance, because only a small number of similar components must be processed during system service. But it must be guaranteed that such modules have strong module cohesion. It is no trick to create a module with a large utilization number if that module is just a collection of arbitrary functions.

Module Hierarchy. Experience shows that the inner structures of a large number of program systems have a similar construction regardless of size or application. Looking at the finished design, four hierarchical levels of modules can be destinguished.

Modules of the lowest level define data structures, data types and access operations on individual elements of these data structures. The overlying level includes modules whose functions manipulate groups of elements of a data structure. Thus both of these levels include functions which encapsule data oriented functions. Modules of the next level contain functions which combine elements of various data structures of types with one another, thus they encapsule problem oriented functions. The outermost modules contain control functions, which combine the functions of the lower levels in such a way that the (system) specification is satisfied.

The decomposition of a program system in practice, however, is not usually accomplished according to the above aspects, but generally according to the special features of the implementation language and the operating system under which the program system will eventually run. The result is that software products modularized according to conventional principles often consist of a series of individual components which communicate through more or less well defined interfaces but which do not satisfy the criteria above because of an unsystematic decomposition. The results are often detrimental for the long term life cycle. Therefore it is important to pay special attention to these modularization criteria.

5.3.5 Attributed Grammars as Tools for Modularization

This section shows that one can apply the method of *attributed grammars*, which were developed for language definition and compiler construction, as a tool for modularization in software engineering. This was discussed for the first time by *Rechenberg* (1980) in the article "Attributierte Grammatiken als Werkzeug der Softwaretechnik" (Attributed Grammars as a Tool of Software Engineering). This method is not suited to all areas of application, but it is applicable wherever a single stream of input data controls the program flow. It is not applicable for tasks with *many* co-ordinate input streams (for example merging master and update data) which is often the case for complex program systems.

The first part of this section is a short introduction to the method of attributed grammars and then the individual design steps are described in general terms. In order that the reader may be able to apply the method effectively, the telegram problem chosen in section 5.3.2 is again used as an example.

The reader should be aware that for the understanding of this section it is assumed that he is acquainted with the basic concepts of formal languages and compiler construction. An introduction to these basic concepts would exceed the limits of the book. The interested but uninitiated reader is therefore advised to acquire the appropriate knowledge before reading this section. The following literature is recommended for this: *Lewis* (1976), *McCarthy* (1962), *Hopfcroft* and *Ullman* (1969), *Aho* and *Ullman* (1972), *Gries* (1971) and *Wirth* (1977).

Attributed Grammars

Attributed grammars are used primarily for the definition of the static semantics of programming languages and, increasingly, also for the description of compilation processes. The definition and application of attributed grammars are described in *Knuth* (1968, 1971), *Lewis* (1976), *Marcotty* (1976), *Räihä* (1977), *Rechenberg* (1980), *Walt* (1977), *Pomberger* and *Blaschek* (1981)] among others. In the literature the attempt is repeatedly made to define the concept of an attributed grammar formally, but none of these definitions completely encompasses the concept of an attributed grammar. A formal definition is not given here, the properties and components of the grammar are merely described informally.

An attributed grammar consists of seven components:

(1) A *context free grammar*.

(2) A *set of attribute types*, which can be considered to be data types, and which define the values which an attribute can take on.

(3) The *attributed symbols of the grammar*. Each grammar symbol *v* corresponds to an ordered set of attributes *a*:

$$v_{\downarrow a_1 \downarrow a_2 \ldots \uparrow a_{n-1} \uparrow a_n}$$

The attributes can be divided into two classes, those that are inherited (indicated by $\downarrow$) and those that are synthesized (indicated by $\uparrow$). Attributes of symbols are values which are used (inherited attributes) or returned (synthesized attributes) for the recognition of symbols. Terminal symbols only have generated attributes.

(4) *Semantic actions* for the computation of attributes. For each synthesized attribute on the left hand side of a grammar rule and each inherited attribute on the right hand side there are semantic actions which compute the attribute from the synthesized attributes on the right hand side and the inherited attributes on the left hand side.

(5) *Context conditions*.

(6) Possibly actions for the *generation of output data*.

(7) The *attributed grammar* itself, which consists of:
   1. the rules of the context free grammar, whose symbols are replaced by the attributed symbols of the same name
   2. the context conditions which describe the relations between attributes
   3. semantic actions
   4. possibly also actions for the generation of output data.

Attributed grammars are *nonalgorithmic methods of description*. For their application as a means of design, however, it is useful to view them as *algorithmic*. For this, each grammar symbol is seen as a recognition process. The selection of one or more alternatives is to be understood as a branch; recursions in the grammar represent loops. When an alternative is selected, its components are processed from left to right.

The grammar must, moreover, be *one pass compilable*, which means that by strict processing of each rule from left to right, all inherited attributes have a value immediately after recognition of the symbol to which they correspond. The semantic actions and, where applicable, the checking of context conditions are executed only after the preceding symbol is recognized and before the recognition of the succeeding symbol is started.

With this, all the prerequisites which are necessary in order to apply attributed grammars as design tools have been described and we can move on to our example of the telegram problem from section 5.3.2.

The following notations are used for the formulation of the attributed grammar:

(1) The context free grammar is represented in Wirth's EBNF (as is described in chapter 4). Nonterminal symbols are capitalized and terminal symbols are written in lower-case letters.
(2) Semantic actions are written in pseudocode similar to Modula-2 and bracketed by the pair "sem" "endsem".

This method is now applied to the solution of the telegram problem in section 5.3.2 in the following way:

Terminal symbols:		Nonterminal symbols:
tword	Telegram word	Telegramsequence
eword	Endword (= ZZZZ)	Telegram

The grammar is trivial and reads:

```
Telegramsequence   =   {Telegram} eword.
Telegram           =   tword {tword} eword.
```

Because each grammar symbol is viewed as a recognition process, it is necessary to consider now which attributes correspond to the individual recognition processes (that is the grammar symbols). We can view the attributes as input or output parameters of the recognition processes.

The specification of the problem yields four attributes: w, the telegram word; wl, the length of the telegram word; n, the number of words in the telegram and lo, the number of long words:

Attribute	Data Type	Meaning
w	ARRAY OF CHAR	telegram word
wl	CARDINAL	word length
n	CARDINAL	number of words in a telegram
lo	CARDINAL	number of long words

We must assign the attributes to the corresponding grammar symbols:

$tword_{\uparrow w \uparrow wl}$

recognizes a telegram word and delivers its value w and its length wl. If the word is longer than 20 characters, it is truncated after the twentieth character, and wl receives the value 20.

$Telegram_{\uparrow n \uparrow lo}$

recognizes a telegram, writes it and delivers the number of words n and the number of long words lo.

`Telelgramsequence`

recognizes a sequence of telegrams and has no attributes.

`eword`

recognizes an endword ($=$ZZZZ) and has no attributes.

Because the grammar symbols are viewed as recognition processes, their description is algorithmically oriented.

Following the definition given above, it is necessary to consider which semantic actions and context checks must be executed for each grammar symbol (before and) after its recognition in order to compute the attributes.

It can be seen from the problem that the telegrams are to be formatted for printing. So a semantic action which handles the correct printer positioning before the recognition and printing of a telegram is needed. Further, semantic actions are needed for word counting, for printing a telegram word and for printing the count results, and, depending on the recognition process, it must be decided when these actions are to be executed and how they are to be specified. For this the attributed grammar and--in case a semantic action is expressed as a procedure--the corresponding specifications are formulated. The syntax symbols are separated from the semantic actions in the notation used and so we obtain:

```
Telegramsequence     = {                    sem InitPrintPos endsem
                         Telegram↑n↑lo

                                             sem PrintResults(↓n↓lo)
                                             endsem
                         }
                         eword.

   Telegram↑n↑lo      = tword↑w↑wl
                                     sem  n:=1
                                          IF wl>12
                                             THEN lo:=1
                                             ELSE lo:=0
                                          END
                                          PrintWord(↓w↓wl)
                                     endsem
                         {tword↑w↑wl
                                     sem  IF wl>12
                                             THEN lo:=lo+1
                                          END
                                          n:=n+1
                                          PrintWord(↓w↓wl)
                                     endsem
                         }
                         eword.
```

With that the semantic actions and their order are determined. The procedures used must of course be specified. This is done as follows:

InitPrintPos
: Initializes the output of a telegram (printpos=1).

PrintWord(↓w↓wl)
: Prints the word *w* (with length *wl*) under the conditions of the problem.

PrintResults(↓n↓lo)
: Prints the count results *n* and *lo* in a new line together with an explanatory text.

With that the design of the telegram problem is finished. The reading of telegrams is the task of a lexical analyzer, syntax and semantics handling are separated. The application of this technique leads in a certain respect automatically to an efficient decomposition of the problem.

As a module for the lexical analysis we can retain the module "ReadTelegram" given in section 5.3.2 practically unchanged, the only difference being that the procedure "ReadWord" for reading a word is called "NextSymbol".

```
DEFINITION MODULE ReadTelegram;
(*Lexical Analyzer for the Telegram Problem*)

EXPORT QUALIFIED NextSymbol, Symboltype;
TYPE Symboltype = (tword, eword);

PROCEDURE NextSymbol(VAR type: Symboltype; VAR w: ARRAY OF
CHAR;
                     VAR wl: CARDINAL);
  (*Reads the next symbol (word) of the input text and yields
     its type type, its value w and the length wl of the word
     read*)

END ReadTelegram.
```

If we use the *method of recursive descent* for the syntax analysis, the solution can immediately be written without difficulty in Modula-2. The *syntax module* controls the processing and is not used by any other module. This module is therefore made the main program and, by the rules for writing syntactic routines according to the method of recursive descent in *Pomberger* (1979), the following program is obtained in a straightforward manner from the attributed grammar given above:

```
MODULE TelegramAnalysis;
(*Syntax Analyzer for the Telegram Problem*)

FROM ReadTelegram  IMPORT NextSymbol, Symboltype;
FROM PrintTelegram IMPORT InitPrintPos, PrintWord,
                          PrintResults;
VAR n, lo: CARDINAL;         (*word counter*)
    wl: CARDINAL;            (*word length*)
    w: ARRAY[1..21] OF CHAR; (*telegram word*)
    type: Symboltype;
```

```
PROCEDURE Telegramsequence;
BEGIN
  WHILE type=tword DO
    InitPrintPos;
    Telegram(n,lo);
    PrintResults(n,lo);
  END;
END Telegramsequence;

PROCEDURE Telegram(VAR n,lo: CARDINAL);
BEGIN
  n:=1;
  IF wl>12
    THEN lo:=1;
    ELSE lo:=0;
  END;
  PrintWord(w,wl);
  NextSymbol(type, w, wl);
  WHILE type=tword DO
    IF wl>12 THEN lo:=lo+1 END;
    n:=n+1;
    PrintWord(w,wl);
    NextSymbol(type,w,wl);
  END;
  (*Assertion: endword recognized*)
  NextSymbol(type,w,wl);
END Telegram;

BEGIN
  NextSymbol(type,w,wl); (*Read first symbol of the input
stream*)
  Telegramsequence:
END TelegramAnalysis.
```

A comparison of the procedures in this module with the attributed grammar shows that this module realizes precisely the recognition processes determined by the attributed grammar. The implementation module for "ReadTelegram" reads:

```
IMPLEMENTATION MODULE ReadTelegram;


Procedure NextSymbol(VAR type: Symboltype;
                     VAR w: ARRAY OF CHAR;
                     VAR wl: CARDINAL);
  BEGIN
    ReadWord(w,wl);
    IF EndWord(w,wl);
      THEN type:=eword
      ELSE type:=tword
    END
  END NextSymbol;
  ...
  (*The procedures ReadWord, BuildWord, OverreadSpaces
    and EndWord can be taken directly from section 5.3.2.*)
  ...
END ReadTelegram.
```

The *semantic module* contains all output procedures and corresponds precisely to the module "PrintTelegram" from section 5.3.2.

The example above shows how one can apply attributed grammars as tools for modularization--the module structure is an automatic result--and that they represent a form of description at an intermediate level of abstraction. The attributed grammars are given in a form which represents a specification of the recognition process. Attributed grammars are therefore also suited as *tools for specification*. The method forces a separation of syntactic and semantic aspects of program design, and it supports the decomposition of a system into *data capsules* (see section 5.3.6.2). It is applicable when the program flow is controlled by one main stream of input data and fails for the case of many co-ordinate input streams.

The example also shows that *attributed grammars* are an excellent *means of documentation*. The form and structure of the documentation is given by the components of the grammar and is independent of the problem. The notation used is formal, and therefore short and precise. It permits the description of important details of the design but is still abstract enough to hide the details of the implementation.

Attributed grammars are a *powerful tool*, but their use requires much practice, and the software engineer who has never concerned himself with compiler construction will have difficulties in achieving an appropriate design with this method the first time around.

5.3.6 Modularization and the Choice of Data and Program Control Structures

The previous sections have demonstrated the great importance of data management within modules and of *data exchange between modules*. This leaves us with the question of which *data* and *program control structures* can be used to construct modules which satisfy the criteria given in section 5.3.4. Are the features available in conventional programming languages sufficient? What features do modern programming languages offer?

In this section the *relationships* between *data* and *program control structures* are considered, in view of their importance to the *modularization* of program systems. *Rechenberg* (1983b) presents a detailed discussion of this. He gives definitions of the concepts *data capsule*, *abstract data structure* and *abstract data type* together with a classification of data and program control structures which are well suited to our purposes. Borrowing from his discussion, first we shall examine the well known data and program control structures and their advantages and disadvantages for modular programming, and then data capsuling and the meaning of abstract data types will be discussed. These concepts are demonstrated by extensive examples.

5.3.6.1 Data and Program Control Structures

The oldest program control structure is the *procedure*. Just recently, due to the development of new programming languages--such as Simula (*Rohlfing*, 1973), Modula-2 (*Wirth*, 1982) and Ada (1981)-- *modules, coroutines* and *parallel* functioning sequential *processes* have been added. Illustration 5.6 (taken from

Rechenberg, 1983b) shows these program control structures and a few programming languages in which they are available.

Structure	Language						
Procedure	Cobol Fortran	Pascal	PL/1	Simula	Modula-2	Ada
Module	(Fortran)		(PL/1)	(Simula)	Modula-2	Ada
Coroutine				Simula	Modula-2	
Process			PL/1		(Modula-2)	Ada

Illustration 5.6 Programming Languages and their Program Control Structures

As opposed to program control structures, there exist no clear cut divisions for the types of data control structures. By data control structures we mean, along with *Rechenberg* (1983b), the mechanisms for the binding of names in a source program to values and addresses in the corresponding object program. These mechanisms are categorized by the scope of visibility of these names. In relation to data management in modules and data exchange between modules two kinds of scope of visibility can be distinguished:

(1) Global
(2) Local/Nonlocal

Global scope of visibility

Here only *global data* are available, which means that the scope of visibility of each name is the whole program. Even if a program system consists of many procedures (or modules), one requires no mechanism for data exchange between procedures. It is clear that this data control structure is completely unsuited for modular programming because it makes decoupling of the procedures, according to the guidelines for module construction, practically impossible.

Local/Nonlocal scope of visibility

The choice of a data control structure with both *local* and *nonlocal scopes of visibility* enables each program module in a program system (for example procedures) to have its own local data. Many possibilities exist for data exchange between program modules, contingent on the programming language. These possibilities are shown in illustration 5.7 and their importance for modular programming will now be discussed.

Data exchange by *implicitly declared nonlocal entities* works in such a way that all data which are used in a program control structure (for example procedures), but are not declared in it, are considered nonlocal. These data must be declared and embedded in a statically or dynamically encompassing program control structure.

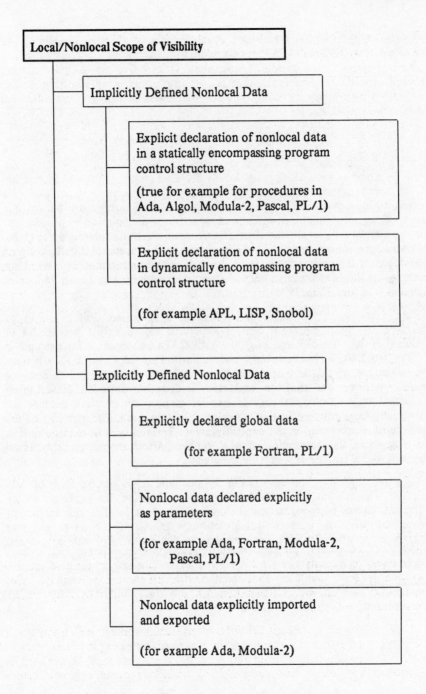

Illustration 5.7 Local and Nonlocal Scope of Visibility of Data Control Structures

The meaning of global data with a dynamic scope of visibility is given by the rule (*Rechenberg*, 1983b): "The use of a name which is not locally declared relates to the last dynamic declaration of the name." This implies also a close coupling between procedures. The procedures can be interpreted only according to the sequence in which they are called. For this reason this technique is not suited for modular programming.

We speak of statically encompassing program control structures when they can be nested, as in the case of block structured programming languages. The meaning of global data with a statically defined scope of visibility is given by the rule: the use of a name which is not locally declared relates to the last declaration of the name in one of the encompassing program control structures. This technique does permit a stepped nonlocality of data, achievable by nesting. However, it also permits unrestricted access rights to data objects by procedures; the explicit visibility of the interface of a program control structure is not given. This structure makes invisible coupling possible and leads to tightly coupled procedures. It is poorly suited for modular programming--although it was long perceived as the best program control structure (compare also *Liskov* and *Zilles*, 1974 and *Wulf* and *Shaw*, 1973).

Data exchange by *explicitly declared global data* means that data can be addressed by many program control structures (for example procedures or modules), if they are declared as global entities. This is posssible for example in PL/I by the EXTERNAL attribute, and in Fortran by the COMMON attribute. The advantage of this is that the scope of visibility of nonlocal data must be explicitly defined, and that the nonlocality is therefore bounded. Nevertheless this technique contradicts the guidelines for module construction because the individual procedures are in this way also tightly coupled. The visibility of the interface of a procedure is not explicitly given. Testability suffers through this, and changes in the declaration of nonlocal data affect the integrability of all program control structures which use these data.

Data exchange by *parameters* is the simplest and most elegant form of data exchange. The advantages of this data control structure are: the explicit visibility of the interface of a procedure and the decoupling of the local and global data of the procedures. This data control structure is excellently suited to modular programming, especially if it also permits the distinction of input, output and transient parameters through an appropriate notation. This technique was used in section 5.3.2 to demonstrate the principle of stepwise refinement by an example.

In programming languages which possess no module concept therefore, modules realized through procedures should communicate exclusively by parameters which satisfy the criteria of modular programming.

Programming languages which permit the description of *modules* (for example Ada and Modula-2) possess yet another possibility for the explicit determination of the scope of visibility of identifiers: the *import/export statements*. These data control structures permit an explicit description of which procedures, data and data types declared in each module are to be made visible to the environment, and which procedures, data and data types this module will import from other modules. Detailed examples of the use of these data and program control structures can be found in sections 5.3.2, 5.3.6.3 and chapter 6.

Modules with explicit interface description and parameter controlled data exchange between procedures are useful data and program control structures for the modularization of large program systems.

5.3.6.2 Data Capsules

By a program system we mean a collection of program modules and data on which the program modules operate. If *procedures* are used to structure large program systems, the consequence is that many procedures access global data stocks. Illustration 5.8 shows a schematic example of this situation.

In this example, the individual procedures access many data structures of the program system, which means that the data structures must be available to many procedures. If one implements this program system for example in Cobol as a collection of internal procedures, then the data structures are declared in the encompassing DATA-DIVISION and are known to all procedures; for an implementation in Fortran or PL/I (by separately compiled procedures) the data structures must be declared as common, respectively external, entities. This leads to:

(1) the data structures being difficult to alter--changing a data structure implies changes in all procedures which access it

(2) difficulties in testing such program systems--because the access rights to a data structure are spread over many procedures it is, in the case of an error, extremely difficult to discover the procedure which caused the error

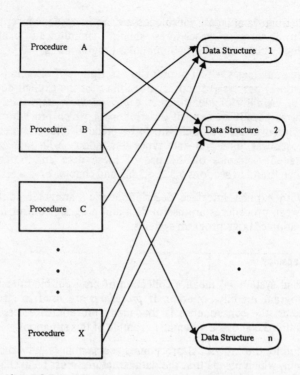

Illustration 5.8 Procedures and Data Structures of a Program System

In order to avoid these disadvantages, *Parnas* (1972) suggests keeping such data structures secret from their environment. One achieves this by collecting the data structures together with a series of access procedures into a module. All other modules which access these data structures can do so only by means of the access procedures. For this they provide--in a parameter list--those values which the access procedures are to enter, and retrieve those values from the data structure which they wish to use--also in a parameter list--by means of access procedures. The *access procedures* are the *connecting link* between the data and the program set of a program system. They decouple the procedures from the data structures on which they operate. This data and program control structure is called a *data capsule*, and, borrowing from *Rechenberg* (1983b) a data capsule can be defined:

A *data capsule* is a module which consists of the declaration of data and a collection of procedures which manage these data. Some of these procedures are available from the outside, they are called access procedures. Modules which access the data of the data capsule can achieve this only by means of the access procedures; the data itself and all procedures which are not access procedures are not available from the outside.

The general structure of a data capsule is shown in illustration 5.9:

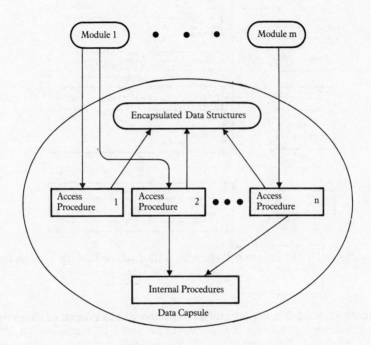

Illustration 5.9 Schematic Representation of a Data Capsule

Illustration 5.10 shows the structure of the program system from illustration 5.8 with encapsulated data. The procedures are to the left, the data structures are to the right and the access procedures are in the middle.

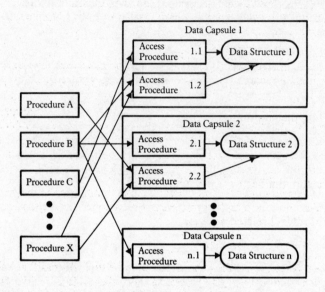

Illustration 5.10 The Program System from Illustration 5.8 with Encapsulated Data Structures

In order to illustrate the advantages and the disadvantages of the program system structures represented in illustrations 5.8 and 5.10, a concrete application will be developed, first according to conventional methods (represented in illustration 5.8) and then by the use of data encapsulation. A standard task of commercial data processing, the *updating of a master file, has been chosen* as an example. The specification of the task is discussed first, then a *"conventional"* solution is designed, next a *solution with data capsules* is designed and finally a comparison is made between the two.

(1) Specification

There is a sequential master file with one or more records. Each record contains two numerical data elements: *account number* and *balance*. All records have distinct account numbers in the master file.

There is a sequential update file with one or more records. Each record contains two numerical data elements: *account number* and *value*. The data element *value* can indicate a positive or negative value which is to be added to the *balance*. There may be more than one record with the same account number in the update file. Both files are sorted by increasing account number.

From the records of the master and update files, a new master file (whose records have the same structure as the old master file) is to be created according to the following procedure:

* Each master record, for which there is no update record, is taken into the new master file without change.

* If one or more update records with *values* v_i ($1 <= i <= n$; $n >= 1$) exist for a
  master record with *balance* k, the master record with the new balance
  $k + \Sigma v_i, (i = 1 \ldots n)$
  is taken into the new master file.
* If there is no master record corresponding to an *account number* for which
  there are update records with *values* v_i, a new master record with the balance
  $\Sigma v_i, (i = 1 \ldots n)$
  is taken into the new master file.

By the end all records of the old master file and the update file have been read
and processed. The new master file contains a record for each account number
which occurs in the old master file or the update file and is sorted according to
increasing account number.

The design method used is the principle of stepwise refinement and the design
notation is a Modula-2 related notation.

(2) Solution without data capsules

Each file processing operation can in principle be divided into three subtasks:
the *initialization*, the actual *file processing* and the *closing of the files*. The
initialization encompasses all jobs which need be executed only once, at the
beginning of processing; in our case this means opening the file and reading the
first master and update records. File processing takes care of the major part of the
task and after the files are processed only closing the files remains.

In agreement with the statements made in section 5.3.6.1 the stand point that
global data are unsuited for modular programming should be adopted as early as
the design phase, and data exchange between procedures should take place
strictly by parameters.

The design should be started--as is usually the case for conventional solutions
to data oriented problems (compare also *Schulz*, 1982)--with the rough
determination of the data structures involved. First the files are named:

> the old master file is called *masterfileold*
> the new masterfile is called *masterfilenew* and
> the update file is called *updatefile*.

A master record (*masterrec*) contains the master account number and the
balance, and for these write *masterrec.accountno* and *masterrec.balance;* an update
record (*updaterec*) contains the update account number and the value, and for
these write *updaterec.accountno* and *updaterec.value*.

The rough structure of the solution could be:

```
MODULE FileUpdate:
        IMPORT Initialize,ProcessFiles,CloseFiles
BEGIN
        Initialize(↑masterrec ↑updaterec)
        ProcessFiles(↓masterrec ↓updaterec)
        CloseFiles
END FileUpdate.
```

The action "*ProcessFiles*" can easily be refined on hand from the specification. As long as master records are present they must be processed with the corresponding update records. If there is no update record for a master record, it is taken into the new master file unchanged. If there exist no master records for update records, one (or more) new records must be created and inserted into the new master file. If there exist further records in the update file, they must be processed into new records in the master file. For this two new actions "*ProcessMasterRecord*" and "*BuildNewMasterRecord*" have to be introduced. We agree that the component *accountno* of the next master or update record shall yield the value *max* (a number larger than any account number), if the corresponding file has been completely processed.

```
PROCEDURE ProcessFiles(↓masterrec ↓updaterec):
    CONST max=a number larger than any account number
BEGIN
    WHILE masterrec.accountno<max DO
      (*old master file not yet completely processed*)
     ProcessMasterRecord(↕masterrec ↕updaterec)
    END
    WHILE updaterec.accountno<max DO
      (*update file not yet completely processed*)
      BuildNewMasterRecord(↕updaterec)
    END
END ProcessFiles.
```

The new action "*ProcessMasterRecord*" contains as input parameter the master record to be processed and the first not yet processed update record and yields the next master and update records to be processed. The action "*BuildNewMasterRecord*" receives as input parameter the next update record to be processed and yields as output parameter once again the (new) update record to be processed. The refinement of both of these actions causes no difficulties and could be as follows:

```
PROCEDURE ProcessMasterRecord(↕masterrec ↕updaterec):
BEGIN
    WHILE updaterec.accountno<masterrec.accountno DO
      (*there is an update record, for which there is no
      master record in the old master file*)
      BuildNewMasterRecord(↕updaterec)
    END
    WHILE updaterec.accountno=masterrec.accountno DO
      (*there is an update record for the master record to
        be processed*)
      (*accumulate updates*)
      masterrec.balance=masterrec.balance+updaterec.value
      ReadUpdateRec(↑updaterec)
    END;
    (*for the master record to be processed there exist no
      further update records*)
    Update(↓masterrec)
    ReadMasterRec(↑masterrec)
END ProcessMasterRecord.
```

```
PROCEDURE BuildNewMasterRecord(‡updaterec)
BEGIN
  (*initialize new master record*)
  masterrecnew.accountno:=updaterec.accountno
  (*accumulate all updates*)
  masterrecnew.balance:=updaterec.value
  ReadUpdateRec(↑updaterec)
  WHILE updaterec.accountno=masterrecnew.accountno DO
    (*accumulate all updates*)
    masterrecnew.balance:=masterrecnew.balance+updaterec.value
    ReadUpdateRec(↑updaterec)
  END
  Update(↓masterrecnew)
END BuildNewMasterRecord.
```

With this the basic structure of the solution has been acquired, and only the elementary actions remain to be refined.

```
PROCEDURE Initialize(↑masterrec ↑updaterec):
BEGIN
  Open masterfileold, masterfilenew, updatefile
  ReadMasterRec(↑masterrec)
  ReadUpdateRec(↑updaterec)
END Initialize.

PROCEDURE CloseFiles:
BEGIN
  Close masterfileold, masterfilenew, updatefile
END CloseFiles.

PROCEDURE ReadMasterRec(↑masterrec):
  CONST max=a number larger than any account number
BEGIN
  IF masterfileold still contains records
    THEN read masterrec from masterfileold
    ELSE masterrec.accountno:=max
END ReadMasterRec.

PROCEDURE ReadUpdateRec(↑updaterec):
  CONST max=a number larger than any account number
BEGIN
  IF updatefile still contains records
    THEN read updaterec from updatefile
    ELSE updaterec.accountno:=max
  END
END ReadUpdateRec.

PROCEDURE Update(↓record):
BEGIN
  write record to masterfilenew
END Update.
```

This completes the stepwise refinement. The solution is precise enough to be written in a programming language. Illustration 5.11 shows the four levels of hierarchy (they correspond to the guidelines given in section 5.3.4) and the call graphs of our solution. It can be seen that the overall solution is modular, the interfaces between the procedures are simply and explicitly described and the procedures are decoupled from each other. But the solution shows also that, with the exception of "*CloseFiles*", each procedure references the data structures "*masterrec*" and "*updaterec*". This implies that a change in these data structures affects large portions of the program, and is therefore extremely difficult to effect. Therefore this structuring is perhaps not optimal. In order to avoid this drawback a solution using data capsules is given which is better in this respect.

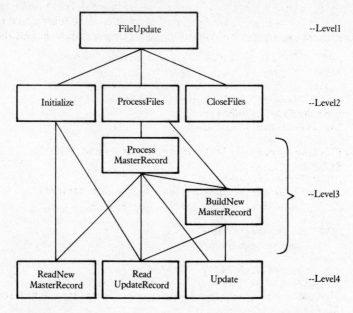

Illustration 5.11 Hierarchy Diagram for the File Update Program

(3) Solution with data capsules

Following the definition of "data capsule" given above, we can now proceed to decouple the program components from the data structures which compose the master and update records. This means that the components which represent the kernel of our solution (these are "*Initialize*", "*ProcessFiles*", "*ProcessMasterRecord*" and "*BuildNewMasterRecord*") will no longer access the data structures masterrec and updaterec directly, but rather only by means of access procedures.

For this the basic structure of these components need not be changed, it need only be insured that they have no knowledge of the nature of these data structures and receive the necessary elements only by means of the access routines of the data capsule (it is called "*DataManager*"). The components "*Initialize*", "*ProcessFiles*" and "*CloseFiles*" are collected into a module called "*FileProcessing*". In accordance with this the following structure is obtained:

```
MODULE FileUpdate:
  FROM DataManager IMPORT Accountno
  FROM FileProcessing IMPORT Initialize, ProcessFiles,
                                        CloseFiles
  VAR masteracc, updateacc: Accountno
BEGIN
  Initialize(↑masteracc ↑updateacc)
  ProcessFiles(↓masteracc ↓updateacc)
  CloseFiles
END FileUpdate.
```

It should be noted that the main module no longer has any knowledge of the structure of the master and update records and that the type of the account number has been imported (as this may also be altered later) from the data capsule in which the data structures are later encapsulated. In this fashion abstract and concrete data representations are decoupled. Further refinement yields:

```
PROCEDURE Initialize(↑masteracc,updateacc: Accno):
BEGIN
  Open masterfileold, masterfilenew, updatefile
  ReadMasterAcc(↑masteracc)
  ReadUpdateAcc(↑updateacc)
END Initialize.

PROCEDURE ProcessFiles(↓masteracc,updateacc: Accno):
BEGIN
  WHILE masteracc<max DO
    (*max=a number larger than any account number*)
    ProcessMasterRec(↕masteracc ↕updateacc)
  END
  WHILE updateacc<max DO
    BuildNewMasterRec(↕updateacc)
  END
END ProcessFiles.

PROCEDURE ProcessMasterRec(↕masteracc,updateacc: Accountno):
BEGIN
  WHILE updateacc<masteracc DO
    BuildNewMasterRec(↕updateacc)
  END
  WHILE updateacc=masteracc DO
    AccumulateUpdate
    ReadUpdateAcc(↑updateacc)
  END
  Update
  ReadMasterAcc(↑masteracc)
END ProcessMasterRec.
```

Observe that here the action of *accumulating* the update data has been replaced by an access procedure of the data capsule, in distinction to the conventional version.

```
PROCEDURE BuildNewMasterRec(↕updateacc: Accno):
BEGIN
  accountnew:=updateacc
  InitNewMasterRec
  ReadUpdateAcc(↑updateacc)
  WHILE updateacc=accountnew DO
    AccumulateUpdate
    ReadUpdateAcc(↑updateacc)
  END
  Update
END BuildNewMasterRec.
```

It should be noted here that the actions "*InitNewMasterRec*" and "*AccumulateUpdates*", which refer to the data structures, are formulated as access procedures.

The action "*CloseFiles*" can be taken unchanged from the conventional version. As previously indicated, the procedures given above can be combined into a module which exports the procedures "*Initialize*", "*ProcessFiles*" and "*CloseFiles*" (in order to make them available to the module "*FileUpdate*") and imports the modules "*ReadMasterAcc*", "*ReadUpdateAcc*", "*InitNewMasterRec*", "*AccumulateUpdate*" and "*Update*" from the module "*DataManager*".

Now only the data structures for the master and update records together with their access routines remain to be incorporated into the module "*DataManager*". The access procedures are:

```
ReadMasterAcc(↑masteracc)
ReadUpdateAcc(↑updateacc)
InitNewMasterRec
AccumulateUpdate
Update
```

Only the specification of the data capsule (that is the definition module) is given below as the implementation is trivial.

```
DEFINITION MODULE DataManager:
  EXPORT QUALIFIED ReadMasterAcc, ReadUpdateAcc,
                   InitNewMasterRec,
                   AccumulateUpdate, Update, Accno;
TYPE Accno=[1000..9999];

PROCEDURE ReadMasterAcc(VAR masteracc: Accountno);
  (*Reads the next master record from masterfileold, stores
    it and yields its account number (masteracc)*)

PROCEDURE ReadUpdateAcc(VAR updateacc: Accountno);
  (*Reads the next update record from updatefile, stores
    it and yields its account number (updateacc)*)

PROCEDURE AccumulateUpdate;
  (*Adds the value of the last read update record to
    the balance of the stored master record*)
```

```
PROCEDURE Update;
   (*Writes the stored master record in masterfilenew*)

PROCEDURE InitNewMasterRec;
   (*Saves the last read update record as a master record*)

END DataManager.
```

Note that even in the specification section of the data capsule no concrete representation of the encapsulated data is given. This is left to the programmer. In the present case he will certainly use the same data structures as in the conventional version.

(4) Evaluation of the two versions

* The algorithmic structure of both versions is the same (this need not, however, always be the case).

* The version with data capsules requires additional procedures for the decoupling of the processing algorithm from the concrete representation of the data structures and is thus somewhat less efficient than the conventional version.

* Changes in the data structures affect the entire program system in the conventional version, whereas in the version with data capsules only the module "*DataManager*" is affected. For an algorithmic change in the parts of the program system which are independent of the data structure, the data capsule remains as it is, in the conventional version however, this affects the entire program. The version with data capsules is therefore more flexible (more adaptable) than the conventional version.

* The access procedures are additional abstractions, the version with data capsules is therefore also more understandable.

Because of the brevity and simplicity of the example used, the advantages of data encapsulation are far less apparent here than for more complex tasks. Nevertheless, the example does exhibit many advantages of this technique. A change in the data structure would affect only the data capsule, leaving the processing algorithm untouched. Often, however, it is possible to effect algorithmic changes simply by a change in the data capsule. The reader should extend the example in a fashion similar to the presentations in *Dijkstra* (1976), *Dwyer* (1981), *Jeffords* (1982) and *Levy* (1982). Here, deletions of old master records are also possible. In addition, the update records contain an entry which can assume the values *insert*, *update* and *delete*. *Insert* means that a new master record is to be created from this update record, and that no old master record with the same account number is permitted to exist. *Update* is specified in our example. *Delete* means that an old master record with the same account number must exist, and that this master record is not to be transferred to the new master file. This extension of the problem would, in the conventional version, affect at least the procedures "*ProcessMasterRecord*" and "*BuildNewMasterRecord*", that is, it would affect the processing algorithm. In the version with data capsules, this extention can nevertheless be achieved merely by a change in the data capsules (for example by the introduction of a processing buffer), in spite of the fact that an algorithmic alteration is necessary in addition to the effect on the data structure.

Disadvantages of data encapsulation

* The sole disadvantage of data capsules is their dynamic and static *inefficiency*. Data capsules usually contain many short access procedures. Therefore program systems which work with data capsules almost always contain more procedures than conventional program systems. The task of an access procedure often consists only of delivering the value of a single variable. Calling such a procedure, including parameter handling, costs more time and storage than the simple accessing of the variable. The increased flexibility and security, however, outweigh this disadvantage.

Advantages of data encapsulation

* The data resources and their representation are not visible from the outside and are therefore protected from procedures which wish to access them directly. This limits the sources of error and facilitates testing and alterations in the representation of the data. Hiding the data structures agrees with the guidelines for modularization and Parnas' principle of information hiding given above.
* Data capsules eliminate the use of external entities and thus facilitate the decoupling of modules.
* Data capsules encourage the use of *abstract data structures* and *abstract data types* (see section 5.3.6.3) during program design. The decoupling effect of data capsules leads to easier decomposition of systems into independent subsystems, and in this way facilitates team program development.
* The use of data capsules encourages topdown design and protects against premature consideration of a particular data representation. This increases the readability and thus aids in the documentation.
* Data capsules can be considered as an implementation of abstract data structures or abstract data types. (The meaning of this is discussed in the next section.)
* Data encapsulation is a design technique--it leads to a particular decomposition--as well as an implementation technique--it protects data objects from uncontrolled access.

5.3.6.3 Abstract Data Structure and Abstract Data Type

In the design of large program systems, according to the principle of stepwise refinement, it is important not to consider prematurely any particular representation of data. This would, on the one hand, lead the designer into losing himself in details without having solved the basic problem, and on the other hand to the choice of a false or incomplete representation of the data due to an insufficient understanding of the problem. In the process of stepwise refinement, the chosen data structure would show itself to be unuseable or, even worse, the designer might attempt by all available means to fit his design decisions to the ill chosen data structure.

It is therefore useful, in the design of a software system, also to apply the principle of stepwise refinement in the design of the data structures on which the software system is to operate or, in other words, to use *abstract data structures*. A fitting definition of abstract data structures for our purposes reads:

An *abstract data structure* is a set of objects (its components) and a set of operations, which can be applied to the components or to the data structure as a whole.

If the definition of a data capsule is compared with an abstract data structure, it becomes clear that, in the implementation, the abstract data structures introduced can be realized most appropriately in the design of a software system by the use of data capsules.

In many cases it is desirable to generate a number of instances of a particular abstract data structure. This leads to the concept of an *abstract data type*, which can be defined:

An *abstract data type* defines a set of objects, which all have the same abstract data structure, by the operations applicable to them.

For better understanding of this, an example of an *abstract data structure* and an *abstract data type* is given. The example chosen is a search tree from the realm of text processing. The abstract data structure "*SearchTree*" is then defined by the data for the leaves (as the set of objects) of the tree and the operations:

NewTree
Generate an empty search tree.

Add(↓x)
Insert the object x into the search tree.

Search(↓x ↑found)
Search for the object x; return found=TRUE, if x is found; otherwise found=FALSE.

FirstObject(↑x ↑found)
Return the first lexicographic object x and found=TRUE; or found=FALSE, if the search tree is empty.

NextObject(↑x ↑found)
Return the next object x in lexicographic order after the last object processed (with FirstObject or NextObject) and found=TRUE; or found=FALSE, if all elements of the search tree have already been processed or if no object was previously processed.

If a number of search trees are needed in one of the algorithms of a software system, an abstract data type "*SearchTree*" is required. This is defined by the following operations:

NewTree(↑t)
Generate a new (empty) search tree with the name t.

Add(↓t ↓x)
Insert the object x into the search tree t.

Search(↓t ↓x ↑found)
Search for the object x in the search tree t; return found=TRUE, if x is found; otherwise found=FALSE.

FirstObject(↓t ↑x ↑found)

Return the first lexicographic object x in the search tree t and found=TRUE; or found=FALSE, if t is empty.

NextObject(↓t ↑x ↑found)

Return the next object x in lexicographic order after the last object processed (with FirstObject or NextObject) in the search tree t and found=TRUE; or found=FALSE, if all elements of t have already been processed or if no object was previously processed.

Note that in the definition of an abstract data *type*, as opposed to an abstract data *structure*, a variable t occurs as argument in each operation which indicates to which *search tree* the operation refers. This distinction between abstract data structure and abstract data type is often ignored.

In the example last given, "*SearchTree*" is an abstract *data type*, *t* is an *incarnation* of this type, and therefore an *abstract data structure*. In the present example "*SearchTree*" has been used as a *hidden* (nameless) abstract data structure.

The *implementation* of abstract data types presents no difficulties, data capsules are also suitable--as already indicated in section 5.3.6.2--for the implementation of abstract data types.

For the *specification* of abstract data types various methods are recommended. In our example, no special specification technique has been used, but rather the specification has simply been formulated in prose, with the drawback that the interfaces of the access procedures are not described precisely enough (the data types of the interface objects are missing) and the function specification can be ambiguous in some instances. Due to the concept of definition module and the opaque types, Modula-2 is well suited to the specification of abstract data types; one needs only to give the name of the abstract data type in the definition module (the concrete realization is undertaken in the implementation). The interfaces of the access procedures can be exactly specified but the description of the actions of the access procedures are (unfortunately) left to the discretion of the programmer.

Theoretical considerations yield a number of formal specification techniques (for example algebraic) by which an exact specification of the operations (access procedures) is possible. Good surveys of these are available in *Liskov* and *Zilles* (1975) and *Guttag* (1975, 1977).

Abstract data structures and *abstract data types* support the process of stepwise refinement. They represent--as the name indicates--an *abstract* description of the data structures used in a software system and thus increase *clarity* and *readability*; they also encourage the application of data capsules as early as the design phase and thereby lead to the *decoupling* of *data structures* and the *programs* which operate on them. *Abstract data structures* and *abstract data types* have thus become important concepts of software engineering.

5.3.7 Design Notation

In the examples discussed above the *designs* of solutions to problems have been formulated in a mixture of common language and elements of the programming language Modula-2, but nothing has been said about the *representation of design documents.* The *notation,* however, influences not only the *design decisions* but also the *readability, completeness* and the *verifiability* of the drafts of the design decisions. A technique which requires the representation of certain details demands of the user that he stipulate these details. But if it does not permit a differentiated representation of certain facts and objects, it reduces the precision of the design description. A design notation should be applied only for the purpose for which it is intended. No method of representation is universal. Therefore in this section a few common notations for the design phase are introduced and their advantages and disadvantages are discussed.

Natural language. It goes without saying that system or program designs can be formulated in natural language. The natural language description has the advantage that one can accommodate an arbitrary amount of text and has practically unlimited possibilities for expression. The drawbacks are its length, ambiguity and unclarity. It is therefore not suited for representing complex system designs. But it is suitable for getting down first ideas and for communication with people who are not well acquainted with the problem (for example from other fields of specialization).

Stylized prose. The description is a sequence of individually numbered actions. Each action starts with a key word which is a paraphrase of the action. The action itself is described in stylized prose. At the end of each action, the next action to be executed is given. If nothing is indicated then the next action to be executed is the one following it. For example:

action 5: *accumulate*: add value to masterrec.balance.

One finds this notation primarily in the books of *Knuth* (1968-1973). It has the advantage that, once again, in the description of each action one can accommodate an arbitrary amount of text. However, its disadvantages are again its length, the ambiguity of the text for the description of actions and also its unclarity. As opposed to the description with pure prose, the individual actions are more clear, but the overall structure is not expressed.

Design languages (pseudocode). Design languages are *semiformal* means of notation. They permit the description of algorithms and data structures, but without the syntactic precision required of programming languages. They manage with few constructs for the formulation of flow structures, leaving the user free to formulate everything else as desired. This notation is thus suitable for design descriptions on varying levels of abstraction. The algorithmic structure can be clearly expressed without distracting the reader with syntactic details. Often it is wise to base the formalism of the description language on a general purpose programming language. However, it need not always be bound to a particular language. This notation has been used elsewhere in this book (section 5.3 contains numerous examples). The advantages of design languages are obvious, which is why they are used more and more often in software engineering.

Attributed Grammars. These are a *formal* notation on an intermediate level of abstraction and are excellently suited to the documentation of system and program drafts. Their structure, advantages and disadvantages as a design notation are described in detail in section 5.3.5.

The design notations mentioned above are all *non graphic.* The most wide spread notations up to today for software design are, however, *graphic* or *semigraphic.* So in conclusion we wish to summarize the most important *graphic* design notations.

Flowcharts. The flowchart is a *semigraphic* notation. It consists of various (semi) graphic symbols which represent individual operations and arrows for representing the flow control. Illustration 5.12 shows some of the symbol types used in flowcharts.

Flowcharts show the structural properties of algorithms and the coherence of the solution pieces better than nongraphic notations. Remarks may also be included comfortably and specially emphasized. Disadvantages are that data structures may not be represented explicitly, and that the flow control can take on an arbitrary complexity because the use of arrows is not subject to constraints. Flowcharts are well suited to the description of the design, if one proceeds with discipline and circumspection.

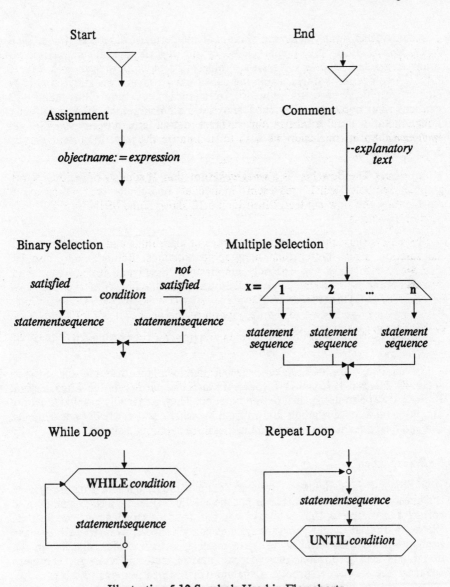

Illustration 5.12 Symbols Used in Flowcharts

Nassi Schneiderman diagrams. Nassi Schneiderman diagrams (*Nassi* and *Schneiderman*, 1973) are graphic aids for the design and documentation of program systems. In many ways they replace the older flowcharts and force a GOTO free design by encouraging the use of a few proven flow structures. They contain graphic symbols for sequence, selection and repetition. Illustration 5.13 contains an example. Just like flowcharts, they do not admit the representation of data structures. Besides this they are difficult to draw up and even more difficult to alter without machine support.

SORT (in: list, length; out: list)

FOR i: = 1 TO length − 1 DO

list(i + 1) < list(i) ?

yes   no

h: = list (i+1)

FOR j: = i DOWNTO 1 WHILE h<list(j) DO

list(j + 1) := list(j)

list(j + 1) := h

Illustration 5.13 Nassi-Schneiderman-Diagram for the Sorting Algorithm

Special design methods. Special design methods, for example the Jackson method (*Jackson*, 1975), SADT (*Schoman* and *Ross*, 1977) or the Litos method (*Schulz*, 1982) also use special design notation. They are usually graphic in nature and use a mixture of symbols known from flowcharts and newly defined symbols. The interested reader is referred to the literature mentioned above.

5.3.8 Verification

For the software engineer, after completion of the design of a program system, the question arises as to whether or not the solution which he has designed is also correct and complete, that is to say, whether or not it satisfies the specification. We know that all larger program systems contain errors, even when they have been produced by specialists who are masters of their trade. Mistakes in the design can lead to portions of a program system requiring redesign. The more advanced the production process is, the more difficult and expensive this is.

Methods that allow verification during design that an algorithm satisfies its specification are therefore needed. It is clear that this verification is hard to provide without formal and mathematical assistance. Mathematically oriented *verification techniques* can be found in the works of *Dijkstra* (1976), *Hoare* (1969), *Manna* (1969) and *McCarthy* (1962), among others. A survey of various methods of algorithm verification can be found in *Elspas* (1972).

The methods known at present can be used successfully for the verification of short, simple algorithms in most cases. But for large program systems the difficulties increase so rapidly that these methods are not practical. However, verification is discussed here because it is interesting for the software engineer in itself and because it helps to formulate program designs more carefully.

Here we consider *verification with the aid of inductive assertions*. This method is suited to the software engineer because it permits, in simple cases, a strictly formal, and in difficult cases a less strict and therefore practically justifiable verification of algorithms. It was developed by *Floyd* (1967) and *Naur* (1966), is described in *Knuth* (1968-1973) and is used extensively by *Wirth* (1978). Therefore a detailed introduction to verification is not given, but the most important rules are briefly described and their application is demonstrated by three examples.

The method

The principle of *verification* is the notation of general relations between the values of variables after each action of the algorithm to be verified. If an *algorithm* A exists, for which a *precondition* (input specification) V and a *postcondition* (output specification) N is given, then one can make the claim:

The precondition V can be converted to the postcondition N by formally promoting V according to the text of A. For this we write {V} A {N}. By verification we mean establishing the truth of this claim.

Two procedures can be identified. They are dependent on the direction of statement promotion: *forward* and *reverse verification*.

Forward verification. We consider A as a *sequence of instructions* $a_1 \, a_2 \dots a_n$. In the first step the *precondition* V is promoted by the individual instructions $a_1 \, a_2 \dots$ up to the *postcondition N'*. After each instruction a_i there is an intermediate condition Z_i, giving:

$$V = \{Z_i\} a_i \{Z_{i+1}\} a_{i+1} \{Z_{i+2}\} \dots a_n \{Z_{n+1}\} = N'$$

Z_i is that condition which results from Z_{i-1} if one considers that a_i has been executed in the meantime. The assertion before an action a is called the *precondition* on a, the one after a is called the *postcondition* on a. Thus we obtain {V} A {N'}.

N' is the *"strongest postcondition"* which results from V and A. (This method is therefore also known as the *"method of the strongest postcondition"*.) In the second step it is shown that N' implies N: $N' = >N$.

Reverse verification. Here we proceed in the opposite direction. In the first step we start with the given postcondition N and promote N by A backwards until we obtain the result V': {V'}A{N}.

V' is the *weakest precondition* which results from N and A. (This method is therefore also known as the *"method of the weakest precondition"*.) In the second step it is shown that V implies V': $V = >V'$.

The assertions, however, say nothing about whether the algorithm *ends*. In algorithms which contain loops this method yields therefore only the proof that a false result can never be produced from V by A; but the question whether any result at all will be produced under the precondition V remains open. The method must therefore also consider the verification of *termination*.

For the derivation of the postconditions from the preconditions and the action a few *elementary rules* (*promotion rules*) are given below and the assertions are written as comments indicated by square brackets in the design text. The application of these elementary rules to a number of examples is then described.

(1) Rules for assignment operations
    a) P does not depend on v

```
...
[V : P]
v:=x
[N : P∧(v=x)]
...
```

   b) P depends on x and v occurs in P only within x

```
...
[V : P(x)]
v:=x
[N : P(V)]
...
```

If the assertion $P(x)$ is valid before the assignment of the expression x to the variable v, then $P(v)$ is valid after the assignment operation.

(2) Rules for branch operations

```
...
[V : P]
IF B
   THEN
      [N1 : P∧B]
      ...
      [N1']
      ...
   ELSE
      [N2 : P∧¬B]
      ...
      [N2']
      ...
   END
[N : N1'∨N2']
...
```

If the assertion P is valid before a decision under the condition B, then after the branch operation the postcondition $(P∧B)$ or $(P∧¬B)$ is valid.

The determination of assertions in a sequence of actions generally does not present any problems. It goes without saying that either the first precondition or the last postcondition must be given, depending on whether a forward or reverse verification is to be conducted.

(3) Rules for loops

```
...
[V : P]
WHILE x DO
  [Q]
  ...
  [Q]
END
[N : R]
...
```

A loop is cut open before and after the body of the loop, and at the cuts an assertion (Q) is assumed as an hypothesis. The following procedure pertains for the verification of the loop:

Step 1:
State the pre- and postconditions.

Step 2:
Give an assertion Q intuitively before and after the body of the loop.

Step 3:
Show that if the precondition of the loop is valid, then Q is also valid for the first pass through the loop.

Step 4:
Show that if Q is valid for the nth pass through the loop, then it is also valid for the $(n+1)$st pass through the loop for arbitrary $n>=1$.

Step 5:
Show that the postcondition N follows from Q and NOT x.

Step 6:
Show that the loop terminates, which means find a quantity which is increased or decreased by a value $>=0$ on each passage through the loop for which there exists an upper or lower bound and for which the loop is left when this bound is reached or superseded.

We call Q the *loop invariant* because it represents an assertion which remains unchanged, that is invariant, regardless of the number of passes through the loop. Finding appropriate loop invariants is usually not easy (as is shown in the examples below) and requires experience and intuition.

(4) Rules for calling algorithms

```
...
[V : P(x)]
A(↓x ↑y)
[N : R(x,y)
...
```

Here we must have:

```
*  A(↓e ↑a)
   [P(e)]
   body of A
   [R(e,a)]
   end A
```

* In A only local objects or formal parameters are used.
* All formal parameters indicated by ↓ are used in A, all formal parameters indicated by ↑ receive a value in A.
* All actual output parameters are distinct.
* No actual output parameter is simultaneously an actual input parameter.

(5) Rules for recursive calls of algorithms

```
A:
  [V : P]
  IF B
    THEN
      [B∧P]
        A  --recursive call
      [R]
    ELSE
      [¬B∧P]
        a  --action sequence
      [R]
  END
  [N : R]
  END A
```

Before each recursive call the assertion (precondition) P is assumed, after each recursive call the assertion (postcondition) R is assumed. If it can be shown that {P}A{R} and {P}a{R} hold, then {P}A{R} also holds for recursive A.

The algorithm terminates when a status variable dependent on the depth of the recursion exists, which for a finite depth of recursion assumes a value such that the nonrecursive path a is taken.

The theoretical foundations of these elementary rules are omitted; the interested reader is referred to the appropriate passages in *Floyd* (1967) and *Naur* (1966).

To demonstrate the use of the rules given above three examples of the verification of algorithms are now given. The first example is from the field of systems programming, the second example is chosen from the field of applied mathematics. In both examples a strictly formal verification is given. In the third example, a sort algorithm, the verification is presented in a less formal, partially verbal notation.

(1) The design version of an algorithm

```
RealDiv(↓x ↓y ↓ε ↑z),
```

is given from *Elspas* (1972b), which is to compute the quotient z of the floating point values x and y $(0 \leq x \leq y)$ with an error less than ε. The first precondition V (input specification) reads: $(0 \leq x \langle y) \land (0 \langle \varepsilon)$, the last postcondition N (output specification) reads: $x/y - \varepsilon \langle z \leq x/y$.

```
RealDiv(↓x ↓y ↓ε ↑z):
  [(0<=x<y) ∧ (0<ε)]
  a:=0; b:=y/2; d:=1; z:=0;
  REPEAT
    [(a=yz ∧ (b=yd/2) ∧ (x-dy<zy<=x)]
    IF x-a-b>=0
      THEN
        [(a=yz) ∧ (b=yd/2) ∧ (x-dy<zy<=x-dy/2) ∧
        (a+b=y(z+d/2)) ∧ (x-dy/2<y(z+d/2)<=x)]
        z:=z+d/2;
        a:=a+b;
        [(a=yz) ∧ (b=yd/2) ∧ (x-dy/2<zy<=x)]
      ELSE
        [(a=yz) ∧ (b=yd/2) ∧ (x-dy/2<zy<=x)]
    END
    [(a=yz) ∧ (b=yd/2) ∧ (x-dy/2<zy<=x)]
    b:=b/2;
    d:=d/2;
    [(a=yz) ∧ (b=yd/2) ∧ (x-dy<zy<=x)]
  UNTIL d<ε
  [x/y-ε<z<=x/y]
END RealDiv.
```

The verification shows that the algorithm design satisfies the specification. The key to the solution lay in finding the loop invariant:

$(a=yz) \land (b=yd/2) \land (x-dy\langle zy \leq x)$

and in the idea of representing the condition x-a-b>0 in the following way:

x-a-b>0 $\langle=\rangle$ x>a+b $\langle=\rangle$ x>yz+yd/2 $\langle=\rangle$ yz<x-yd/2.

Because the algorithm contains a loop, it must also be shown that it terminates: For this the variable d is used; d runs through the values 2^{-k} for k=0,1,... and the termination term t=1/d. t is doubled for each pass through the loop starting with 1. With $1/\varepsilon$ an upper bound can be set such that the loop is exited when t>1/d holds.

(2) The following recursive algorithm is given:

```
Sum(↓n ↑f):
  IF n=1;
    THEN f:=1;
    ELSE
      Sum(↓n-1 ↑x);
      f:=x+n;
  END;
END Sum.
```

Precondition V: n>=1, where n is an integer.
Postcondition P: f=n(n+1)/2.

With the aid of assertions we can verify that the algorithm satisfies the specification, that is that for each n the value $n(n+1)/2$ is returned by the output parameter f.

```
Sum(↓n ↑f):
  [n>=1]
  IF n=1;
    THEN
      [n=1]
      f:=1;
      [f=n(n+1)/2]
    ELSE
      [n>1]
      Sum(↓n-1 ↑x);
      [x=(n-1)n/2]
      f:=x+n;
      [f=(n**2-n)/2+n=n(n+1)/2]
  END;
  [f=n(n+1)/2]
END Sum.
```

The verification shows that for the branch where n=1 $f=n(n+1)/2$ and for the branch where n>1: if $f=(n-1)n/2$ for an input parameter value of n-1, then $f=n(n+1)/2$ for an input parameter value of n. Therefore the algorithm yields the result $f=n(n+1)/2$ for all n>=1. For the calculation of f as a function of n, the calculation of f as a function of n-1 is used. The arguments n, n-1, n-2, ... constitute a monotonically decreasing sequence which ends with 1. The algorithm ends therefore after n-1 recursions.

(3) The design of an algorithm which sorts a list $L(1..n)$ with n>=0, containing positive and/or negative numbers is given such that all non-negative numbers are at the beginning of the list and all negative numbers are at the end of the list.

The precondition V reads:
  V: n>=0 ∧ ($L(1..n)$ is a list which contains n arbitrary real
      numbers).
The postcondition N reads:
  There exists a p with 1<=p<=n such that we have:
  $L(1..p-1)$ contains all non-negative and
  $L(p..n)$ contains all negative elements of the original list.

The algorithm is designed along the following lines:

Two running indices p and q scan the list, p starts at 1 and moves upwards, q starts at n and moves downwards. We always have p<=q. The indices divide the list into three sections: $L(1..p-1)$ contains only non-negative numbers, $L(q+1..n)$ contains only negative numbers from the segments 1 to p-1 and q+1 to n which have already been examined. The middle segment from p to q has not yet been examined. As soon as p equals q, all list elements have been examined and satisfy the postcondition.

```
Sort(⇕L(1..n) ↓n):
  [V]
  p:=1
  q:=n
  WHILE p<=q DO
    [S(p,q)]
    IF L(p)>=0
      THEN
        p:=p+1
        [S(p,q)]
      ELSE
        [S(p,q) ∧ L(p)<0]
        IF L(q)>=0
          THEN
            [S(p,q) ∧ L(p)<0 ∧ L(q)>=0]
            Exchange L(p) and L(q)
            p:=p+1
            [S(p,q-1)]
          ELSE
            [S(p,q-1)]
        END
        q:=q-1
        [S(p,q)]
    END
    [S(p,q)]
  END
  [N]
END Sort.
```

It is certainly appropriate to give the assertions less formally, but more understandably, in this case:

V: $n>=0 \wedge L(1..n)$ is a list which contains arbitrary real numbers.

S(p,q): L(1..p-1) and L(q+1..n) have been examined and are not changed in the future. L(1..p-1) contains all non-negative elements from L'(1..p-1) and L'(q+1..n), and L(q+1..n) contains all negative elements from L'(1..p-1) and L'(q+1..n), where L' represents the list as it was given before the execution of Sort.

N: L(1..p-1) contains all non-negative and L(p..n) all negative elements of L'(1..n). L' represents the list as it was given before the execution of Sort.

The application of this technique forces the software engineer to review all design decisions once again and thus helps in finding logical design errors. In the process, the aspect of actually *understanding* the algorithm is at least as important as the proof of correctness. *Verification* is an extremely useful technique for early recognition of design errors, and in addition supplements the design documentation. The verification itself, however, can be erroneous. It does not replace the testing of a software product. The larger a program system is, the more difficult it is to conduct a complete verification. *Gerhart* et al. (1976) write in this vein:

"Adopt a cautiously sceptical attitude toward proofs, as one of several possible means of persuasion, in which formalization and abstraction might provide some new insights and documentation. Keep in mind, however, that there are usually at least some parts of the program that are better explained informally, and it is pointless to attempt subverting these parts to fit a particular formalism. Formalism should supplement, definitely not replace, common sense and programming experience and intuition."

5.4 Implementation

By the phrase *"implementation of a program system"* we mean the transformation of the design into programs, which can be executed on a particular target machine.

Whereas the *developer* should make the design of a program system independent of the programming language in which the system will later be implemented, the choice of the programming language is of great importance for the *programmer*. Not all programming languages are equally well suited for the transformation of the design into programs. Languages such as Ada and Modula-2 offer features for modules and data type abstraction and they are better suited for the transformation process than assembler languages or older programming languages such as Cobol or Fortran.

The criteria for the choice of programming language are covered in chapter 3. In this section the criteria are considered briefly, from the view point of the programmer. But not only the aspects concerning the programming language are discussed here; many useful criteria concerning programming style and the preparation of the implementation for the test phase together with measures for increasing the portability of software products are also mentioned.

5.4.1 The Choice of the Implementation Language

For the phases of the software life cycle after implementation (test and maintenance), a good implementation should reflect good design decisions. In particular it is necessary that:

* the decomposition structures, data structures, identifiers and operations be reflected in the implementation,
* the levels of abstraction in the design (which affect the algorithms, data structures and data types) also be realized in the implementation,
* the interfaces between the modules of a program system be explicitly described,
* the consistency of interfaces and the type compatibility of objects and operations be tested at the time of compilation (prior to the actual testing of the modules).

The degree to which these demands are fulfilled depends on the choice of implementation language. At present, all these demands can be realized simultaneously only in a very few programming languages which are employed only to a modest extent in practice. The most important of these are Ada (*Ichbiah*, 1979), Chill (*Sammer* and *Schwärtzel*, 1982), Mesa (*Mitchell*, 1978), Modula-2 and some dialects of Pascal. The importance of the programming language for a software project and the criteria for the choice of a programming language are comprehensively discussed in chapter 3.

5.4.2 Programming Style

Program systems, after they have been implemented and tested, can only in the rarest cases be operated over a longer period of time without changes. Usually it is just the opposite, the requirements are changed or expanded after completion, and during operation previously unrecognized errors or deficiencies in the specification come to light. The implementation must be continually changed or expanded, and for this reason the source code must be read and understood again and again. Ideally, the function of a module should be understandable from the source code alone, without knowledge of the design documents. Source code is the only document which is always guaranteed to describe the present version of a module.

The readability of a program depends, on the one hand, on the programming language used, and on the other, on the *programming style* of the programmer. Writing readable programs is a difficult process. The programming style of the programmer influences the readability of a program much more than the programming language employed. A well written Fortran or Cobol program can be more readable than a poorly written Modula-2 or Ada program.

It is not possible to give foolproof methods for writing readable programs. However, one can state how good programming style is expressed: in the choice of names, in the use of data and program control structures, in the use of comments and in the representation of the algorithmic structure.

5.4.2.1 The Choice of Names

The documentation of programs starts with naming the functions and objects of the program in such a way that their names express what they mean. The choice of programming language influences this process also. In each programming language there are conventions for the lexical structure of names; several languages only permit capital letters and numbers (for example Basic, Fortran), others permit both capital and lower case letters (for example Ada, Modula-2), and yet others permit the use of certain special characters to enhance the power of expression (for example Ada, PL/I). The length of names is also limited in many languages.

Let us consider the following Basic program:

```
INPUT CS, CH, WB, WV
DA = ASIN((SIN(WB-CH)*WV)/CS)
PRINT DA
```

One can hardly see that this program computes the drift correction angle of an airplane from this text, if one does not happen to know the formula.

Taking a more reasonable choice of names into account the program can be reformulated in Modula-2 as follows:

```
MODULE DriftCorrectionAngleCalculation;
  FROM InOut IMPORT ReadReal, WriteReal;
  FROM Trigonometrics IMPORT ASIN,SIN;
  VAR calibairspeed, compassheading, winddirection,
      windvelocity, driftcorrectionangle: REAL;
BEGIN
  ReadReal(calibairspeed);  ReadReal(windvelocity);
  ReadReal(compassheading); ReadReal(winddirection);
  driftcorrectionangle:=
    ASIN((SIN(winddirection-compassheading)
    *windvelocity)/calibairspeed);
  WriteReal(calibairspeed);
END DriftCorrectionAngleCalculation.
```

It is pointless to discuss which of the two versions is more understandable. Of course one can object that names which are too long are tedious and compromise the readability of a program because they place everything else in the background (for example the control structures). This is a valid objection. Unnecessarily long names are sources of error, and the documentary value of a name is not proportional to its length.

Correctly chosen names are as short as possible, but nevertheless long enough to describe the function or the object they identify so that somebody who is acquainted with the problem has an idea of what they mean. Rarely used names may well be somewhat longer than frequently used names. The importance of global objects should be emphasized by a correspondingly long name, as should type names.

In programming languages which allow only short names, it is worthwhile for the programmer to invent particularly meaningful abbreviations, and in case of doubt to clarify the name with a comment.

5.4.2.2 Data Control and Flow Structures

The complexity and organization of the *data structures* to be employed is determined in the design. The designer normally has no set limits for the degree of abstraction in data structures. However, the programmer must adapt himself to the nature of the implementation language. How far the data abstraction can be depicted in the implementation depends again on the language to be employed. The use of abstract data types and abstract data structures increases the readability of programs.

In the implementation only those data control structures should be used which guarantee that the access rights to data objects laid down during design are not violated (see also section 5.3.6). Great importance should be attached to the locality of data objects. Global data compromise readability and increase susceptibility to error. All data objects should be explicitly declared, even when this is not required by the implementation language.

The *flow control structures* employed influence the readability and the testability of programs.

Unrestricted flow control structures--through the use of GOTO statements--can lead to quadratic growth in the number of program paths as a function of the number of instructions, and to the loss of correspondence between the static and dynamic program structure. Only those control structures should be used which have only *one* entry and *one* exit. The static and dynamic structure of programs which are composed only of elements of this type are identical. These basic components are:

* Sequence
* Selection (IF-THEN-ELSE and CASE instructions)
* Repetition (the REPEAT loop, the WHILE loop and the FOR loop)

Illustration 5.14 shows an example of a program for dialog application using GOTO statements. Although the program is simple, it is difficult to recognize that it contains a loop; it is even more difficult to determine how the loop terminates.

Illustration 5.15 shows how we can realize the same algorithm using only the basic components listed above. The program structure is clearly discernable and the effects of changes or extensions are substantially simpler to predict than in the solution given in illustration 5.14.

Good programming style is not distinguished solely by the absence of GOTO statements. Some (primarily the older) programming languages do not contain all the basic components mentioned above, and it is not possible to manage without GOTO statements. It would be foolish to condemn this (in some cases very useful) instruction indiscriminately. The structure of the program is the main consideration; the point is to avoid a programming style which makes programs unclear.

```
        TYPE Master=(user, program);
PROCEDURE DialogScheduler(master: Master);
        LABEL 1,2,3;
        VAR enddialog: BOOLEAN;
BEGIN
        IF master=user THEN GOTO 2;
1:      ProgramActions(enddialog);
        IF enddialog THEN GOTO 3;
2:      UserActions(enddialog);
        IF enddialog THEN GOTO 3;
        GOTO 1;
3:      CloseDialog;
END.
```

Illustration 5.14

```
    TYPE Master=(user, program);
    PROCEDURE DialogScheduler(master: Master);
      VAR enddialog: BOOLEAN;
    BEGIN
      REPEAT
        IF master=user
          THEN UserActions(enddialog); master=program;
          ELSE ProgramActions(enddialog); master=user;
        END;
      UNTIL enddialog;
      CloseDialog;
    END DialogScheduler.
```

Illustration 5.15

Good structure can also be expressed in Fortran or Cobol, or even in RPG or assembler language, although perhaps not as articulately and with somewhat more difficulty than in Ada or Modula-2. GOTO statements used with discipline, say for handling errors or exceptional conditions, do not compromise the readability of programs. *Knuth* (1974) gives a series of examples which demonstrate how to deal with GOTO statements.

The goal of the programmer must be to formulate programs so that they are understandable. He can do this, of course, much better if a clear structure is achieved during design.

5.4.2.3 Program Format

The *readability* of a program not only depends on the choice of data and control structures and the use of meaningful names, but also on the *layout* of the program. It has already been indicated that the programs (modules) of large software systems are, as a rule, written only once but read many times. Therefore readability takes on the higher priority.

The following example shows a well structured program whose structure, however, is not immediately clear to the reader because of the poor layout.

```
PROCEDURE TextCompression;
(*Reads text of arbitrary length from an input file, compresses
it (which means that redundant blanks are reduced to a single
blank) and writes the compressed text onto an output file.
-----------------------------------------------------------------*)
CONST blank = " ";
VAR char: CHAR;
predecessor: CHAR;
eof: BOOLEAN;
BEGIN
ReadChar(char, eof);(*Reads the first character*)
predecessor := "a";(*Initialize the state variable*)
WHILE NOT eof DO
IF predecessor<>blank OR char<>blank THEN
(*Character is not a blank or is an individual blank*)
WriteChar(char);
```

```
      predecessor := char;
      ELSE (*char is a redundant blank*) END;
      ReadChar(char, eof) END;
      END TextCompression.
```

The following version, on the other hand, clearly shows which structure is expressed by this program text:

```
      .....
      BEGIN
        ReadChar(char, eof);(*Reads the first character*)
        predecessor := "a";(*Initialize the state variable*)
        WHILE NOT eof DO
          IF predecessor <> blank OR char <> blank
            THEN (*Character is not a blank or is an
                     individual blank*)
              WriteChar(char);
              predecessor := char;
            ELSE(*char is a redundant blank*)
          END;
          ReadChar(char, eof)
        END;
      END TextCompression.
```

There are numerous suggestions based on practical experience for the *layout of programs*, but they are usually oriented toward a single application or to a particular programming language. The following general rules are a good guide:

* Organize the program modules according to a unified scheme into logical paragraphs of manageable size.
* Clearly separate the declaration from the algorithms and the procedures from the body of the module.
* Organize the declarations according to a unified scheme.
* Organize the description of the interfaces by separating the input and the output quantities.
* Make the program structure (nesting of statements) explicit through indentations.
* Use spaces and empty lines for structuring the program text, but pay attention to compact notation so that the program text does not get inflated by spaces.
* Separate comments from the rest of the program text so that the program structure remains distinctly visible.
* Choose an appropriate notation to distinguish between modules and procedures.

We intentionally say nothing about how the separation between the individual paragraphs, the organization of the declarations or the depth of the indentations of control structures should actually look. This is left to the skill (and to the aesthetic taste) of the programmer. It is only important that he adhere to the rules consistently, and that the rules chosen be the same for all components of the software system.

5.4.2.4 Comments

Good *programming style* appears also in the use of *comments*. Comments are useful and necessary aids for improving the readability of programs. They should be important program elements for the programmer. Their absence indicates a deficiency in program quality which is why the use of comments is possible in every (higher) programming language. A distinction can be made between comments that describe the *history*, the *version* or the *function* of a program--they are placed at the *head of the program*--and those which explicate the *objects*, *program sections* and *statements* or which are *assertions* at certain points of the program--they are used in the *declaration* and *instruction sections* of programs.

Correct *commenting* is an art which requires experience, fantasy and the ability to express essential factors briefly and precisely. There are no generally satisfactory rules as to how many comments a program should contain, what should and what should not be commented upon or how one inserts comments into the program text. This depends on the program size, the field of application, the complexity of the algorithms and the programming language used.

A *general principle* can be stated: Expend as much care during implementation in describing the decisions and details of the implementation with good comments as was expended in the design for the description of the design decisions.

Good comments are those which do not repeat what is written in the code, but rather give additional information, point out differences between the design and the implementation, clarify the meaning of objects and report on the status of the algorithm at the appropriate point. Ambiguous and *incorrect comments* are worse than none at all because they mislead the reader and make testing and the alteration of programs more difficult.

Each module must contain a comment which specifies who the author is, when and by whom the last alteration was carried out, to which program system the module belongs, what its task is, perhaps which files it accesses and how the interface to its environment is defined.

Each function (procedure) of a module should contain a comment which describes its function and the interface (if possible also its entry and termination status). Comments should be inserted in the program text in such a way that the visibility of the program structure is not lost.

It is important to consider and write down the comments at the time the module, the procedure, the declaration or the statement which is to be explicated is written down. Comments which are first appended after completion of the program, if not well thought out, are seldom good comments. They usually explain that which is already clear, because the programmer is so well acquainted with the problem by this time that he lacks the motivation for documenting the details.

We have already mentioned that comments are integral parts of a program. Therefore special care must be taken that *program changes* do not only extend to the declarations and statements, but also affect the *comments*.

The following example is given to illustrate the use of comments. It applies to a local module in a Modula-2 program.

```
MODULE EditFunctions:
(*====================
Version:05
Last Changed:11.12.83 by G. Pomberger
Author:G. Pomberger
Inspected by:G. Blaschek

This module is a component of the editor STRESS. It contains the
functions for the execution of the editor commands INSERT, COPY,
FIND and DELETE.*)

(*Import Interface: *)
  FROM FileSystem IMPORT ReadChar, WriteChar,...
...
(*Export Interface: *)
  EXPORT QUALIFIED ..., SearchPattern, ...
(*-----------------------------------------------------------------*)
...

  PROCEDURE SearchPattern(string, pattern: ARRAY OF CHAR;
                          VAR found: BOOLEAN;
                          VAR position: CARDINAL);
  (*Searches in the character string "string" for the pattern
    "pattern", furnishes the leftmost position "position" in
    which pattern starts in "string" and found=TRUE if
    successful, otherwise position=0 and found=FALSE.
  -----------------------------------------------------------------*)
  VAR strlen: CARDINAL;   (*length of the character string*)
      patlen: CARDINAL;   (*length of the pattern*)
      i,k:    CARDINAL;   (*loop indices*)
  BEGIN
    found := FALSE; position := 0;   (*pattern not yet found*)
    strlen := HIGH(string)+1;
    patlen := HIGH(pattern)+1;
    IF patlen>strlen
      THEN  (*pattern longer than string*)
        found := FALSE;  (*search ended*)
        RETURN;
    END;
    i := 1;
    WHILE (i<=strlen-patlen+1) & NOT found DO
      (*assert: pattern does not start at string(1..i-1)*)
      k := 1;
      WHILE (k<=patlen) & string(i+k-1)=pattern(k) DO
        (*assert: pattern(1..k-1)=string(i..i+k-1) and
          1<=k<=patlen*)
        k := k+1;
      END;
```

```
           IF k=patlen+1
             THEN (*string(i..i+patlen-1)=pattern(1..patlen)*)
               position := i;  (*pattern found*)
               found := TRUE;
             ELSE  (*pattern not contained in string(1..i)*)
               i := i+1
           END;
         END;
         (*assert: found=TRUE and
         string(position..position+patlen-1)=pattern(1..patlen)
         or found=FALSE and position=0*)
       END SearchPattern;
       ...
     END EditFunctions.
```

5.4.3 Test Preparation

The testing of program modules and their integration is a separate phase of the software life cycle (see section 5.5). However, measures can be taken at the time of implementation which affect testing.

In testing a program the point is to ascertain which errors the program contains. If an error is discovered, its source must be found and eliminated, in other words that point in the program which causes the error must be localized. In case of an error it is useful to know in which order the individual program units (modules, procedures) are executed, how often each unit was active--we call this the *program profile*--and in which unit the source of the error is hidden. So there must also be the opportunity for checking the status of the program before and after the execution of a program unit.

Modern programming environments (see chapter 7) provide tools (so called debuggers) which are suitable for furnishing the above information without manipulating the program. If no such tools are available--this, unfortunately, is still the usual case today--it is important to anticipate mechanisms during implementation with which the desired information can be obtained.

The statements for creating the program profile and for the registration of the program status can be systematically inserted by the programmer in the same way in each program unit as follows:

Let *Proc* be a procedure with the input quantities a and b and the output quantities p and q, and let *Mod* be the module which contains *Proc*. Then the implementation looks as follows:

```
MODULE Mod;
  ...
(*Import Interface: *)
  FROM DebugMod IMPORT debug, Debugkind, Debugunits;
  ...
(*---------------------------------------------*)
  ...
PROCEDURE Proc(a,b: Type1; VAR p,q: Type2);
  ...
BEGIN
  (*output of debug information*)
```

```
    IF debug[proc] >= trace THEN (*write trace information*)
      Write("Proc started"); WriteLine;
    END;
    IF debug[proc] >= interface THEN (*write the values of the
                                      input quantities*)
      Write("input: a=", a, "b=", b); WriteLine;
    END;
    (*end of debug information*)
    ...
    (*body of the procedure Proc*)
    ...
    (*output of debug information*)
    IF debug[proc] >= trace THEN (*write trace information*)
      Write("Proc ended"); WriteLine;
    END;
    IF debug[proc] >= interface THEN (*write the values of the
                                      output quantities*)
      Write("output: p=", p, "q=", q); WriteLine;
    END;


    ...
    BEGIN (*module body*)
    (*debug information*)

    IF debug[mod] >= trace THEN
      Write("Mod started"); WriteLine; (*write trace information*)
    END;

    (*end debug information*)
    ...
END Mod.
```

The module "*DebugMod*" for a program system then appears as follows:

```
DEFINITION MODULE DebugMod;
  (*Version01

    ...
    This module exports objects and functions for
    initializing and controlling the output of debug
    information for the program system ...*)

  (*Export Interface:*)
    EXPORT QUALIFIED InitDebug, Debugkind, Debugunits, debug;
(*----------------------------------------------------------------*)
  TYPE Debugkind=(nodebug, trace, interface);
       Debugunits=(mod,proc,...enumeration of all modules
                    and procedures for which the debug
                    information is desired);
  VAR debug: ARRAY Debugunits OF Debugkind;
  PROCEDURE InitDebug;
    (*Initializes the array debug. InitDebug expects the
      desired type of debug information (Debugkind) to be
      input by the user for each program unit listed in
      debugunits.*)
  ...
END DebugMod.
```

It goes without saying that the programmer can also anticipate the selective output of additional information in this way, if this seems appropriate to him.

In this way one has the opportunity prior to each execution of the program system--by calling *InitDebug* at the start of the program--to designate whether information concerning the status of the program run is to be furnished for the execution of a particular program unit, and what it should consist of.

To be sure, this technique reduces the efficiency and inflates the code, but it has the advantage that the scope and type of the debug "information" can be changed before each program run without altering the implementation, and that the program system can also be analyzed at any time during maintenance (that is after completion of the actual test phase) rapidly, comfortably and with differing degrees of abstraction. This advantage more than outweighs the loss in efficiency and, if run time requirements do not contradict this technique, it is very useful.

5.4.4 Portability Considerations

Because of the high development costs of software products and the rapid development of hardware, the quality feature *portability* is of increasing importance. The portability of a software product is fixed during implementation. It is clear that a program system which is to be run on a particular machine must respect the conventions which this machine imposes. The programmer must, however, insure that the parts adapted to the peculiarities of a particular machine are easy to localize and change, and that the basic structure of the program system is still preserved.

This process starts with the *choice of the programming language.* On no computer is there a compiler for every available programming language. Only for a handful of programming languages are there generally accepted standards. Unfortunately the programming languages which are most common today (for example *Cobol* and *Fortran*) are, from the point of view of software engineering, the least suitable for the production of high quality software products. The programming language *Pascal* is certainly much better for the realization of software technical concepts than the languages mentioned above. It is implemented on almost all computers, although in such varying dialects that Pascal programs are barely portable. We can assume though, that with *Ada* and *Modula-2* a new day in programming languages has dawned, and that these languages will prevail, enhancing the *portability* of programs also in the future.

But even *Ada* and *Modula-2* cannot do without low level facilities. To obtain a high degree of *portability* the programmer must insure that the system dependent units of the program system to be implemented are not dispersed over the entire program system, but rather are localized in a few modules. The module concept of *Modula-2* offers the linguistic prerequisites. It is thereby possible to isolate system dependent program components (for example input/output, access to individual memory words, registers or hardware ports) from the remaining program units. If one wishes to transport a program system from one machine to another, only these modules need to be rewritten, the remainder can be taken over as they are.

It goes without saying that techniques for increasing the degree of portability also exist for conventional programming languages. A detailed discussion would exceed the limits of this book. The reader is referred to the works of *Tanenbaum* (1978) and *Brown* (1977).

5.5 Test and Installation

The *quality* of a software product is distinguished by the measure in which the quality criteria *correctness* and *reliability* (see chapter 2) are satisfied, which means how many errors there are in all, and how many serious errors occur during the use of the software product. Each software product must therefore be carefully tested.

The *purpose of testing* is first to ascertain whether a program system satisfies the demands (that is the requirements definition) and second to discover as many errors as possible.

Past experience shows that the production of totally error free software products is in general not possible and so those test activities which point up as many errors as possible are the most useful. The effort and ambition of the test specialist should therefore be fired by the objective of finding as many errors as possible.

By *error* we mean every deviation from the behavior stipulated in the requirements definition. The *cause* of an error can be concealed in the *specification*, the *design* or in the *implementation*. It cannot--if the quality feature "robustness" is to be satisfied--lie in the erroneous choice of input values of a program system. Testing is therefore a measure which accompanies the entire project in the interests of quality assurance. It relates to the *requirements definition*, *design*, *implementation* and (for testing touch-ups) the *maintenance* phases and must also entail the checking of robustness. If one nevertheless speaks of a *test phase* in the software life cycle, it is because the testing of the final product is carried out after the conclusion of all preceding phases. In the following, however, test activities which are distributed over all phases of the software life cycle are discussed.

Closely connected with testing is so called "*debugging*". Whereas testing is an activity for uncovering errors, debugging is an activity for finding and removing *error sources*.

Various test methods are described in this section and ways in which *testing* and *debugging* should be carried out and documented are discussed. In conclusion, the measures that are necessary for the *installation* of a software product are listed.

5.5.1 Test Methods

Before one can discuss different *test methods*, that is before statements can be made about which activities are necessary for the systematic testing of a program system, it is necessary to ask *what* is to be tested.

The *system specification*, the individual *modules*, the *interactions between modules*, the integration of the modules into the *overall system* and the *acceptability* of the software product must be *tested*.

The tests mentioned above and those objectives which are to be followed in the process are described. After that various test methods and test strategies are discussed.

Testing the system specification

The system specification is the basis for planning and carrying out the program test. Understandability and clarity of the system specification are necessary prerequisites for testing a program system. The *goal of the specification test* is therefore to check the *completeness, clarity, consistency* and the *feasibility* of a system specification.

For the analysis of system specifications *Hughes* and *Michtom* (1976) suggest the technique of "*cause and effect*". *Causes* in this connection mean conditions or combinations of conditions which are given or which can occur, *effects* are results or activities. The specifications test should show whether causes (data or functions) are given for which no effects (functions or results) have been defined or, the other way round, whether effects are defined without their causes being given. The specifications test must always be carried out jointly with the system or module users.

Testing modules

Modules encapsule data structures and functions which operate on the data structures. The *object of module testing* is to reveal all discrepancies between the implementation and the module specification. In module testing the isolated functions are tested first, thereafter their interactions are tested. Modules are in general not executable programs. Their execution frequently presupposes the existence of other modules. Testing can only be accomplished if the "*environment*" of the module is available or can be simulated. A part of the effort during module testing consists of creating a suitable *test environment* which permits calling the module, examining the results of processing and simulating the effect of indispensable but non-implemented modules (see illustration 5.16). The problem here is to keep the test environment as simple as possible because the more complicated it is, the higher the probability that it contain errors itself.

Testing module interactions

The next step after module testing is the *testing of subsystems*. By a *subsystem* we mean the functional combination of individual (previously tested) modules. The *objective* here is to test the *interaction* between the individual modules of a subsystem. The test thus relates to checking the correctness of module communication and is hardly distinguished procedurally from module testing. Test environments must also be created for subsystems. After testing the many subsystems are combined into a hierarchically higher subsystem and the interactions between these subsystems are retested. This form of hierarchical testing is often referred to as an *integration test*.

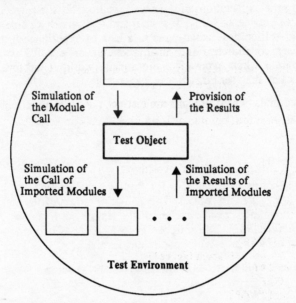

Illustration 5.16 Test Object and Test Environment

Testing the overall system

In testing the overall system, the *integration of all subsystems* is tested. The *objective* here is to discover all deviations of the system behavior from the system behavior prescribed by the requirements definition. Here it is important not only to check the completeness of the user requirements and the correctness of the results, but also to test whether the program system is reliable and robust against faulty input data. In this phase the observance of nonfunctional requirements (for example the required efficiency, see section 5.2) must be tested. The scope and number of tests vary from application to application, as do the choice of the appropriate *test data*. There is no universal recipe for testing program systems with the present level of technology. The effort put into testing the overall system will certainly depend on what damage the misconduct of the program system can cause.

Acceptance test

The development of a software product ends with the *acceptance test* by the user. In the *acceptance test* the software system is tested with *real data* under *real operating conditions*. The acceptance test has the purpose of discovering all errors which result, for example, from misunderstandings in conversation between the users and the software developers, from incorrect estimations of user dependent data volumes or from unrealistic assumptions about the real environment of the software system. It is this test which first shows whether the actual application corresponds to the requirements definition and whether the system behavior corresponds to the expectations of the user. It is precisely the correct arrangement of the interface between a software system and its users that causes the software engineer great difficulties--usually due to a lack of experience in the particular field. The user convenience (or inconvenience) of a software product first becomes apparent when exposed to the outside world. Therefore team testing using real cases by the user himself is indispensable.

Various methods which aid in conducting the tests mentioned above are described below.

5.5.1.1 Static Testing

Static testing consists of activities for finding errors which can be carried out without executing the test object. The activities in static testing relate to the *syntactic, structural* and *semantic analysis* of the test object (compare *Ramamoorthy,* 1974 and *Schmitz,* 1982). The purpose is to localize as early as possible those points in a test object suspected of containing errors.

The most important activities in static testing are:

* program verification
* code inspection
* complexity analysis
* structure analysis
* data flow analysis

The technique of *program verification* is discussed in section 5.3.8. There, verification is applied to checking the correctness of program designs. It is clear that in the transformation of a program design into a concrete implementation, errors can once again be made, and it is therefore desirable to verify the implementation by formal methods. The difficulties involved in formal verification are also discussed in section 5.3.8. The verification of the implementation of an algorithm is even more difficult than that of a program design, because the notation in certain programming languages (for example Fortran, Assembler, APL) complicates the verification, and because the description of the implementation is more complex and detailed than the design description.

In practice therefore, the technique of formal verification is applied at most to design verification. But even if the verification of the implementation is successful, this does not mean that the *dynamic testing* (testing by program execution) of programs can be skipped. Verification does not replace dynamic testing, both activities are necessary for quality assurance.

A very useful technique for finding design and implementation errors is *code inspection.* We know that many errors could easily be found, if one would only read his programs carefully enough. But unfortunately an individual is often not properly motivated.

The idea behind code inspection is that the author walks his programs through, step by step, with other software engineers. *Fagan* (1976) suggests a team of four consisting of:

(1) an experienced software engineer who is not involved in the project, as a moderator
(2) the designer of the test object
(3) the programmer responsible for the implementation
(4) the test specialist

In the process, each error discovered should be noted by the moderator and the inspection continued. The task of the inspection team is *to find, not to correct*, errors. Not until the inspection is completed are the designer and the programmer charged with the corrections.

The objective of *complexity analysis* is to examine what degree of complexity the program system exhibits. By this we mean the complexity measure of modules (for example according to *McCabe,* 1976 or *Halstead,* 1972), the depth of nesting of loops, the length of procedures and modules, the import and utilization numbers of modules (see section 5.3.4) and the complexity of the interfaces of procedures. The results of complexity analysis permit predictions concerning the quality of a software product and the localization of the error prone sections in the program system.

Structure analysis serves the purpose of discovering structural anomalies in a test object. It should, for example, yield information concerning whether all statements in a program can be reached from the start of the program, whether the end of the program can be reached from each statement, whether the program contains loops with multiple entries or whether the flow control contains illicit structures.

Data flow analysis should help to discover data flow anomalies. It yields information concerning whether a data object is assigned a value before it is used and whether a data object is used after it has received a value. Data flow analysis should be carried out for the body of a test object as well as for the interfaces between test objects.

Complexity, structure and *data flow analysis* require, for complex program systems, the availability of tools for obtaining the associated information. Chapter 7 describes which tools are suitable.

5.5.1.2 Dynamic Testing

In *dynamic testing* the test objects are executed or simulated. The activities in dynamic testing consist of

* the preparation of the test object for error localization (installation of aids for program and status tracking)
* the provision of a test environment
* the selection of appropriate test cases and data
* the execution and evaluation of the test

Dynamic testing is an indispensable process in the software life cycle. Each function, module and subsystem as well as the overall system must be dynamically tested, regardless of whether static tests or program verifications have been carried out. For this reason the dynamic test activities listed above are detailed in section 5.5.2 (test execution).

5.5.1.3 Black Box and White Box Testing

In principle each test object can be tested in one of *two ways*:

(1) By checking the input/output relationships without regard to the inner structure of the test object (interface test).

(2) By checking the input/output relationships with regard to the inner structres (interface and structure test).

The first test method is called a "black box", "functional" (*Kopetz*,1979) or "exterior" test (*Miller*, 1978), the second method is called a "white box", "structure" (*Kopetz*,1979) or "interior" test (*Miller*, 1978).

The *black box test* serves to check the interface behavior of a test object through its execution. In this way, the individual functions and combinations of functions of a test object can be checked. The selection of test cases is based on the specification of the test object without any knowledge of its inner structure. In the choice of test cases it is important also to construct test cases which show the response of the test object to incorrect input data.

Black box testing yields no information concerning whether all functions of the test object are actually used or whether data objects are manipulated which have no effect on the input/output behavior of the test object. Such indications of design and implementation errors are provided only by the white box test.

In the *white box test*, the test activities relate not only to the checking of the input/output relationships, but also to considerations of the inner structure of the test object. The objective here is to assess the behavior of the test object dependent on the input data for every possible control path through the test object. In this method the choice of test cases is based on the knowledge of the flow structure of the test object. The choice of test cases must take into account the following features:

* each module and each function of the test object is executed at least once,
* each branch is traversed at least once,
* as many control paths are traversed as possible.

It is important to insure that each branch is traversed. It is not sufficient only to assure that each statement is executed, because for binary branches--as the following example shows--errors are not found under certain circumstances.

One has written:

```
IF condition
   THEN
   action1
   action2
   END
```

instead of:

```
IF condition
  THEN action1
END
action2.
```

This error is not recognized if only the execution of all statements is tested using only one test case with condition = TRUE.

It is important to realize that it is practically impossible, even for well structured programs, to test all control paths (by this we mean all possible statement sequences of a program). The example depicted in illustration 5.17 of a simple program structure given by *Pressman* (1982) illustrates this point. It is practically impossible to test all program paths, even with automatic test data generation, because the execution time exceeds practical limits.

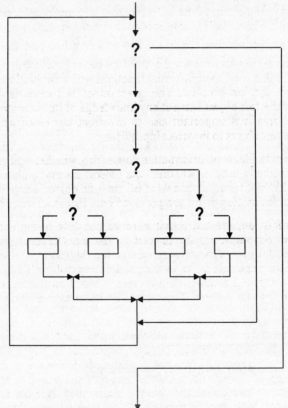

For a maximum of 20 passes of the loop, there are up to
10^{14} possible control paths.

Illustration 5.17 Flow Control Graph

The white box test is nevertheless one of the most important test methods. With it we can check the correct manipulation of the data structures and the input/output behavior of test objects for a limited number of control paths, which is usually sufficient in practice.

5.5.1.4 Topdown and Bottomup Testing

The test methods discussed above handle primarily questions of *module testing*. A strategy for testing *complete software systems* has not yet been given. Whereas program design is handled *topdown* (that is outside in), it is normally *the other way round* for testing. First the elementary units, the foundations of a program system, are tested, and then their integration. This procedure is known as *bottomup* testing. However, we can--according to the principle of stepwise refinement--also proceed in the other direction and gradually test a program system from the outside in. Then we speak of a *topdown* test. Both methods have their advantages and disadvantages and both are presently in practical use.

In *topdown testing* the main module is first implemented and also tested. In the process, the imported objects are represented by replacement objects (stubs). Replacement objects have the same interfaces as the imported objects and simulate their input/output behavior. After the test of the main module, all further modules of the program system are tested in the same fashion, that is their functions are represented by replacement procedures until the implementation has progressed to the point that the functions can be implemented and tested. In this case the test is carried out in step with the implementation. Implementation and test phase coincide. No integration testing of subsystems is necessary.

The application of this strategy has many *advantages*. Design errors are recognized at the earliest possible point in time, thereby saving development time and costs because corrections in module design can be carried out before their implementation. The characteristics of a software system reveal themselves from the start, which enables a simple checking of the stage of development and the acceptability to the user. The software system can be thoroughly tested from the start with authentic test cases.

This all sounds very convincing and almost as if one had found the philosopher's stone. Practical experience shows, however, that this method also has serious *drawbacks*. Strict topdown testing can turn out to be very difficult because the creation of useable replacement objects is often complicated, especially for complex functions. But the simpler the replacement objects are kept, the fewer test cases can be handled. Errors in lower levels are difficult to localize, but they can have effects on the design of the whole system. A further disadvantage is that in complex systems the results that are relevant for the user are not usually visible in the higher levels of the program system, but rather in the lower levels. The same is true of the control of Man-Machine dialog; the necessary functions can be dispersed throughout the whole hierarchy. It is difficult to provide useable replacement functions which are nevertheless simple to implement. Errors are difficult to localize because many modules are involved right from the start. It is also disadvantageous that the entire program system must always be loaded for testing the lower levels, and that the test cases for this are difficult to construct.

In *bottomup testing* one proceeds in the opposite direction to that of the topdown test. First those functions which require no other program units themselves are tested, and then the integration of these into a module is tested. After the module test, the integration of many (previously tested) modules into a subsystem is tested, until the integration of the subsystems, that is the overall system, can finally be tested.

The *advantages* of bottomup testing are the disadvantages of topdown testing, and vice versa.

The bottomup method is sound and reliable. The objects to be tested are known in all their details. It is easier to define relevant test cases and test data. The bottomup procedure is psychologically more satisfying because the test specialist has the assurance that the foundations of his test objects are already tested in all their particulars.

The *disadvantages* here are that the properties of the finished product are first known after the completion of implementation and testing, and design errors in the higher levels are recognized only very late. This can have devastating consequences because correcting these errors usually implies changes in lower levels and thus the repitition of all previous test activities. Testing the individual levels causes, in addition, high costs for the provision of suitable test environments.

One can not state conclusively which of the two methods is better. This problem is discussed extensively by *Yourdon* (1979) and *Zelkowitz* (1979). Subject to the application and to the individual tendencies of the software engineers involved, it is suggested that a combination of both strategies be chosen when the strategy is not fixed by the project organization.

5.5.2 Test Planning and Testing

Testing complex software systems is a difficult and costly process which requires the co-operation of all persons connected with the project. The *test strategy* selected can even influence the system design, so it is necessary to undertake preliminary *test planning* as early as possible--preferably as early on as system specification. The *testing* of software systems requires careful preparation of the *test objects* and *test cases*.

The test objects at the lowest level of software systems (modules) should be tested by the programmer himself, whereas their integration should be tested by associates who are not directly connected with the implementation. The most important activities of test planning and the actual testing are described below.

5.5.2.1 Test Planning

The purpose of *test planning* is to determine the objectives and strategies for testing.

Test planning should ascertain:

* the nature of the test strategy which is to be applied,
* the nature of the test documentation,
* the test objects and the quality requirements which are to be placed on them,
* the test criteria which must be satisfied (the number of test cases, the percentage of the program paths to be tested, etc.),
* the nature of the acceptance test for each individual test object,
* the test specialists to be employed,
* the test tools to be used.

The test plan forms the basis of quality assurance and is the prerequisite for the observation and control of the test execution by the project manager. The time expended in drafting a detailed test plan is therefore well invested.

5.5.2.2 Preparation of Test Objects for the Localization of Errors

Through the *execution* of a test object all errors should be exposed which remained unrecognized during static testing. But *error recognition* does not say much about the *sources of error*, and error diagnosis can be a very tedious process.

The *preparation of the test object for error localization* is therefore an important measure for the cost effective production of software products. There is no universal recipe, but a few useful techniques are mentioned below.

The easiest and most straightforward way to test a program is to trace the execution of a test object and its status and to observe the status of a test object at predetermined points. Today, modern programming environments offer tools for both. If these tools are missing it is advisable to equip the test object with switchable statements for program flow and status observation and for status surveillance (see section 5.4.3).

For *program flow tracing*, test points are useful which yield information about transferring control to labels, the passage of loops or the execution of particular statements.

For *status tracing* it must be possible at particular points of the test object to report the values of important status values (variables) and, for example, the minimum and maximum value which a variable takes on during execution.

Status observation relates to the indication of whether a variable exceeds or falls short of a predetermined bound, whether index boundaries are exceeded or whether assertions which must be satisfied at certain points in the test object are not kept.

One of the techniques for the preparation of test objects for error localization which allows the above information either to be made available or to be suppressed during test execution is extensively described in section 5.4.3.

5.5.2.3 The Choice of Test Cases and Test Data

It has already been indicated that *exhaustive testing* is generally impossible, even for simple test objects. The number of combinations of input data (test cases) is so large, even for simple test objects (see section 5.5.1.3), that such tests cannot be realized. The correct choice of test cases thus demands much experience and intuition on the part of the test specialist, if he is to succeed in discovering as many errors as possible within the given time/cost resources.

It is important to distinguish between the concepts "test data" and "test case". *Test data* are the input data with which a particular test object is to be tested. The description of a *test case* consists of specifying the test object and functions which are to be tested as well as the test data, and describing the results expected for these test data.

Because the selection of test cases for testing software products is a creative process, there is no methodology for it. But the most important criteria which must be taken into account are described below.

Testing of program units

Program units (modules, functions) must be subjected to a structure test (see section 5.5.1.3).

Here it is not sufficient to construct test cases which guarantee that each statement is executed at least once, as the following example given in *Kimm* et al. (1979) shows.

> "In a program segment for the calculation of the maximum of three numbers

```
IF x>=y THEN max:=x ELSE max:=y END;
IF z>=max THEN max:=z ELSE max:=y END;
```

> input data with the properties

```
z>=x>=y and y>x & y>z
```

> cause each statement to be executed once producing the correct results. It will not be recognized that input cases for which x is the maximum will lead to an error."

The weakest criterion which should be satisfied in the choice of test cases is that each program branch be executed at least once. But even this is in general not sufficient, as the example given above shows.

It is important to choose the test cases for a test object such that:

* a test is made to determine that all functional units and their interfaces satisfy the specifications,
* all branches of the functional units are traversed,
* the largest and smallest values of the input data are considered,
* each loop is checked with minimum and maximum loop count,

* all error exits of the test object are tested,
* the reaction of the test object to random input data is checked.

Testing the integration of program units

In testing the *integration of program units* it is assumed that all the units have been tested and can be considered to be correct. In the choice of test cases there is in principle no distinction from the testing of program units. Each program unit is viewed as a (complex) statement. The subsystem to be tested is considered to be composed of black boxes (program units) and the test cases are chosen such that the functions of each unit are exercised at least once. For reasons of clarity it is advisable that the connection between the test cases and the functions and program units affected be represented in a table such as that shown in illustration 5.18 (compare also *Kopetz*, 1979).

		Unit 1				Unit 2			
Function		1	2	3	4	5	6	7	8
Test Case	1	X	X						
	2		X						
	3						X	X	
	4				X				X

Illustration 5.18 Test Case Matrix

But in general it is not sufficient simply to construct enough test cases so that all functions are executed, especially if a number of functions operate on the same data stocks. It is usually necessary to construct test cases which test the combinations of functions also.

The *object in determining the test cases* is to determine the input combinations which are suited to the detection of as many errors as possible. Because complete reliability in selecting test cases is practically impossible, the quality of the test data is of paramount importance.

In determining the test cases, *task oriented criteria*--these depend on the specification of the test object, but do not presuppose any knowledge of the program text--as well as *structure oriented criteria*--these presuppose a knowledge of the program text--must be considered. The test cases should represent typical classes of data, but still characterize a variety of applications.

5.5.2.4 Organization of the Test Environment

Dynamic testing of modules or subsystems requires the preparation of a *test environment* for the simulation of actual operational conditions for a test object. The test environment (see also illustration 5.16) must contain all resources which are necessary for:

* (repeated) execution of the test object,
* preparation of the input data (data which are to be read),
* simulation of necessary, but not yet available external resources (for example imported modules, operating system components) and their results (for example values of results, interrupts, processes),
* indication or printing of the results of a test run.

The test environment should be kept as simple as possible in order to avoid the possibility of it itself containing errors. However, it must allow a sufficient number of tests to be executed.

5.5.2.5 Test Evaluation and Error Localization

After the execution of the tests, it is possible to determine whether the results of the test run coincide with the expected results and whether all fucntions listed in the test case description were also actually executed. However, if an error is detected nothing is yet known about its source.

How does one proceed when he wants to find the *source of an error*? The simplest way is to trace the run of a test object. For this the aids given in section 5.5.2.2 for program tracing and status observation can be used, and one can attempt to isolate the error in steps. The error search is much simpler if the test object has a modular construction with uniquely defined interfaces. Then it suffices in many cases to observe the data at the interfaces in order to isolate the defective section of the program. One can then attempt to localize the error within the defective module by finer flow control and status observation.

Once an error has been localized and its cause recognized it may be eliminated in a number of ways. Before a particular strategy is selected, the effects of the correction on other areas of the test object must be taken into account. For this it is useful to study not only the implementation of the test object, but above all the abstract design. *Error correction* requires extreme care, because new (perhaps worse) errors can be created in the process. *Wolverton* (1972) presents this graphically. Illustration 5.19 shows that the probability that a correction is successful in the first attempt is less than 50% (also in *Kopetz*, 1979).

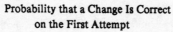

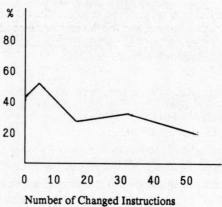

Illustration 5.19 Probability that a Correction is Right in the First Attempt, as a Function of the Number of Altered Commands (Source *Wolverton*, 1972)

After each correction, therefore, the test case which led to the discovery of the error and also all other test cases which the test object has already withstood must be repeated.

It is pointed out again that if no tools for program tracing and status observation are available, then the corresponding test output statements should not be removed after testing. It should be possible to reactivate them at any time.

5.5.2.6. Typical Errors

In practice it is seen that certain errors are made repeatedly. Knowledge of these error sources can be of great assistance in finding and correcting errors.

A few typical errors are listed below:

* ignoring special cases (for example division by zero)
* exceeding field boundaries
* iterative loops which do not terminate
* non initialized variables
* incorrect logical expressions in testing conditions (especially in connection with a negation operator)
* non-correspondence of parameter number and type in actual and formal parameter lists (this error is recognized by the compiler in languages with strong type checking and separate compilation)
* unauthorized access to common data areas (this error is avoided by the consistent use of data capsules)

5.5.3 Test Documentation

The *test documentation* is of great importance for carrying out the test phase economically, for quality control and for the maintenance phase. In team software production it also represents the basis of communication between the members of the team. The *test documentation* should contain:

* the test plan,
* the specification of the test cases,
* the description of the test environment used,
* the results of the individual test runs,
* the number and type of the errors detected,
* the description of the measures for error correction,
* information concerning the number of the required test runs for each test object.

Unfortunately the necessity of extensive test documentation is still accorded too little importance in practice. The necessity of the test document is obvious from the requirement that, after the correction of an error, all previously executed test runs of the altered test object must be repeated. This is also true of touch ups in the maintenance phase. In addition, the test documentation should also yield material for statistics concerning improved planning of future projects.

5.5.4 Acceptance Test and Installation

The object of the *acceptance test* is to show the customer that the newly completed software product complies with the requirements of the system specification. The acceptance test must therefore be carried out before the release of a software product for installation.

In the *acceptance test* the behavior of the product is tested from the view of the user under real environmental conditions. Only those *acceptance criteria* given in the requirements definition (and not the program text) serve as the basis for the selection of test cases. The determination of test cases for the acceptance test is a difficult task and should be undertaken by the user himself. He is the only one with a real understanding of the field of application. The acceptance test also includes the testing of the user manual (see section 5.6). If the customer notices differences between the operation instructions given in the user manual and the actual operating conditions, this can lead to changes in the implementation. The acceptance test should likewise be recorded in the test documentation.

The actual *installation* of the software product takes place after the conclusion of the test phase. In many areas of application (in particular for commercial applications) more or less large external data stocks are manipulated. If the software product to be installed accesses such data stocks (for example master files), the corresponding files must be initialized before the installation, assuming that this has not already been accomplished prior to the acceptance test. This *initialization of files* (for example compilation of master files) can be very costly, necessitating the implementation of large collection and test programs. The development of these programs must therefore be just as carefully planned, carried out and documented as the functional components of the software product, even if they are only needed at the time of installation.

After installation the user should run a *performance test*. The objective of the performance test is to check the *nonfunctional requirements* (such as utilization, response time for dialog systems,) and the *stability (reliability)* of the software product, that is its behavior over an extended period of time.

5.6 Documentation and Maintenance

Software products in general are not used by their developers, but rather by people who were neither involved in the implementation nor have knowledge of the field of software engineering. Also, software products must often be adapted to changing environmental conditions or expanded--we call this the *maintenance* of software products--and maintenance is also often conducted by persons not involved in the development. *Operation* and *maintenance* of software products therefore require--as do other industrial products--an extensive *documentation.*

This section is divided into two parts. The contents, structure and development of the documentation of software products are described in the first part, and the maintenance aspects of software systems is described in the second part.

5.6.1 The Documentation of Software Products

The *documentation* of software products should facilitate the communication between the people involved in the development phases, and after completion of the development phases it should support the operation and maintenance of the products. It should, in addition, document the project progress with the intent of assisting in the calculation of production costs and the better planning of future projects.

Documentation should yield information about:

* which purpose and which special characteristics the software system has,
* which measures are required for installation,
* how a user can apply the software system to the solution of his task,
* how the software system was implemented and how it was tested,
* how the production process and the development team were organized, which difficulties arose and what costs were incurred.

The readers of these documents can be divided into three groups:

(1) The *users* of the software product and *interested parties.*
(2) The *developers* of the software product and people who wish to undertake changes and expansions of the system.
(3) *Managers* of software projects.

In order to provide for the differing information requirements of these three groups, the documentation should be divided into three parts, each corresponding to the various groups. Here it is important to insure that each of these three parts contain only that information which is of interest to the corresponding circle of readers, and that everything else be excluded. The reader should not be burdened with information which has nothing to do with his tasks. The documentation should be easy to read, it should contain *as little information as possible*, but *as much information as necessary*. Accordingly the documentation of software products can be divided up in the following way:

(1) The *user documentation* should contain all information for those who wish to learn about the software system and for the user. It is, of course, also of interest to the system developers as it is the specification of the user interface.

(2) The *system documentation* should contain all details which are necessary for the understanding of the system structure and the system test. It serves as the communication between the system developers and supports those responsible for maintaining the system.

(3) The *project documentation* should contain all the details of the system development from an organizational and accounting point of view (project plan, project organization, project log, personnel, material and time expenditures). It serves project progress supervision and the calculation of the project costs and should yield information for future projects.

The contents and structure of these three types of document are described below.

5.6.1.1 User Documentation

The *user documentation* must guarantee that the software product can be used without the assistance of further information. In this document, the characteristics of the software product are first described generally, and then everything else which the user must know in order to apply the system is described. This includes:

(1) a general system description
(2) an installation and user manual
(3) an operator manual

Concerning (1)

The *general system description* should contain the systems characteristics, what it can do and what it cannot do. The general description should contain no details. The objective is to inform the reader what the purpose of the software system is, where its strengths and weaknesses lie and which prerequisites are necessary for operation. This part in particular should contain information about:

* the purpose of the software system,
* the necessary hardware and software resources,
* the form and structure of required input data,
* the content and form of the results produced,
* organizational and informational prerequisites,
* implementation dependent restrictions,
* the flexibility and portability of the software system.

Concerning (2)

The *installation and user manual* should contain everything that the user must know in order to apply the software system. Here the software system is viewed as a black box; only information concerning the user interface is given. This section should contain:

* information concerning how the system was installed, the prerequisites for installation (for example required files, technical resources) and how the system is embedded in the operating system,
* a complete and unambiguous description of all system functions and the user responses necessary for their use,
* extensive examples of applications for all system functions,
* information and explanations about the format of the input data,
* representation and explanations of the results, preferably through examples,
* a list of error messages with indications of error sources and measures for the elimination of errors.

Concerning (3)

The *operator manual* describes all messages which the software system relays to the operator console, which conditions caused which message and which reactions are expected from the operator. In many cases no operator messages are produced, in which case, of course, this part of the user documentation is left out.

The documentation is an *especially important component* of a software product. The *user convenience* of software products is influenced not only by the software furnishings of the user interface but also, very appreciably, by the contents, the structure and the form of the user documentation.

The user documentation should be *briefly* and *precisely* formulated, but not without redundancies. It should be so arranged that the reader is not forced to read the entire document in order to find out how the simplest functions are executed. It should be so structured that he can proceed from the general to the particular and thus slowly ingest all the details which the system has to offer.

For software systems which support a number of groups of users with differing user interfaces it is a good idea to draft separate user documents or to organize the document so that each user group is presented, in closed form, with the information necessary for them, without reference to the information of other groups.

The user documentation is a *reference work* and therefore should contain an extensive table of contents and an index.

Special importance is accorded to the *readability* of the user documentation. It must be understandable by the users. Therefore the choice of notation must be carefully considered. Many users have no experience with reading strictly formal descriptions, so it is not helpful, for example, to describe the syntax of an input language as a grammar in Backus-Naur-Form. If formalisms are necessary to make something more precise, then one must work on the assumption that these are not known to the user and that their meaning must be explained before they are used. The same thing is true for the use of technical jargon and graphic symbols from the field of software engineering. These are also not generally known and require an explanation.

An important criterion for the quality and acceptability of the documentation is the *style* in which the documentation is composed. Stylistic brilliancy is an ability which few possess, but the following of simple rules of style should be taken for granted. *Sommerville* (1985) gives the following guidelines:

(1) Use active rather than passive tenses when writing instruction manuals.

(2) Do not use long sentences which present a number of different facts. It is much better to use a number of shorter sentences.

(3) Do not refer to previously presented information by some reference number on its own. Instead, give the reference number and remind the reader what that reference covered.

(4) Itemize facts wherever possible rather than present them in the form of a sentence.

(5) If a description is complex, repeat yourself, presenting two or more differently phrased descriptions of the same thing. If the reader fails to completely understand one description, he may benefit from having the same thing said in a different way.

(6) Don't be verbose. If you can say something in 5 words do so, rather than use ten words so that the description might seem more profound. There is no merit in quantity of documentation--quality is much more important.

(7) Be precise and, if necessary, define the terms which you use. Computing terminology is very fluid and many terms have more than one meaning. Therefore, if such terms (such as module of process) are used, make sure that your definition is clear.

(8) Keep paragraphs short. As a general rule, no paragraph should be made up of more than seven sentences. This is because of short term memory limitations on the part of the reader.

(9) Make use of headings and subheadings. Always insure that a consistent numbering convention is used for these.

(10) Use grammatically correct constructs and spell words correctly. Avoid constructs such as split infinitives.

5.6.1.2 System Documentation

The *system documentation* describes all the details of the construction of a software system, the structure of the individual components and the test activities. It should contain all information which is necessary for the understanding of the overall implementation, for communication between the system developers, for error detection and for alterations and expansions of the system. It includes therefore all the documents written at the conclusion of each phase. The following arrangement of the contents is suggested:

(1) description of the task (requirements definition),

(2) description of the overall implementation,

(3) description of the implementation in detail,

(4) description of the files used,
(5) test report,
(6) tables and diagrams,
(7) listings of all programs.

Concerning (1)

It goes without saying that the *requirements definition* must be part of the system documentation. As the requirements definition is usually drafted as a contract between the customer and the software developer, it is useful to rework it for the system documentation into the form of a problem description.

Concerning (2)

The *description of the overall implementation* should clarify the conception and the structure of the software system--and as necessary also that of its components--to the extent that they can be understood by a software engineer who was not involved in the product development. It exhibits the chosen decomposition of the overall solution into partial solutions, and describes which algorithms were used in the solution of the problem and how their interfaces are defined. If the system design is carried out strictly according to the principle of stepwise refinement and the individual design steps are commented accordingly, this document virtually writes itself (during the design phase). It is important that *not just the results are documented;* the *development process* and indications of particular difficulties which arose or which could arise through system alterations must also be included. This document is the most difficult part of the entire system documentation; it may neither be too general nor too detailed. The reader must be able to gauge from this what consequences the alteration of an arbitrary part of the system would entail.

Concerning (3)

The *description of the implementation in detail* is, in general, easy to prepare. It contains the description of all system modules, preferably according to a unified scheme. If a programming language which provides separation of the definition and implementation modules (for example Modula-2) is used for the implimentation and if the conventions given in section 5.4.2.4 for commenting programs are observed, then the detailed description is already written. This has the advantage that the detailed description is always up to date, that the maintenance of this document poses no great difficulties and that the volume of documentation is reduced. For older programming languages which offer no module concept, no separation of definition and implementation modules, no possibility of formulating abstract data types and no explicit description of import/export interfaces, the program listing is not sufficient as documentation. Borrowing from *Rechenberg* (1981), the following outline for the documentation is suggested in this case:

Each module description consists of a header and a body with the following form:

Name:	The name of the module.
Keyword:	An acronym for the task of the module.
Import interface:	Entries for name, type and meaning of all imported objects and which module they belong to.
Export interface:	Entries for name, type and meaning of all exported objects.
Calls:	The calls of every exported procedure including parameters and parameter types. Here it is useful to distinguish input, output and transient parameters.

Task

Short description of the task of the module.

Abstract data structures

A description of the abstract data structures if the module is implemented as a data capsule. The properties of the data structures used are described here from the point of view of the module user and no statements are made which relate to the concrete implementation.

Exported procedures and internal procedures

Here the effects of the procedures in the module are described in detail. In case the procedure is dependent on its environment the *initial state* is first described. Then the *algorithm* is described in a form which corresponds to the complexity of the procedure. This is followed by the description of the *terminal state*, that is the state of the environment after the execution of the procedure. The procedure description must also contain all information which is relevant to the user concerning its *behavior in case of an error* as well as directions for the handling of exceptions.

Concrete data structure

A description of the concrete implementation of the abstract data structures (in case the module manipulates abstract data structures).

Module initialization

A description of the initializations effected in the module body. This point is excluded if a separate initialization procedure exists.

Concerning (4)

In case the software system operates on external files, it is necessary also to compile a *description of the files used*. For each file, the file description includes information about

* the file name,
* the contents,
* the record structure,
* the file organization,

* the (maximal) file size,
* the access rights and possible types of access,
* the form of the available read/write operations.

Concerning (5)

In the *test report* all measures for testing, the test data and the test results of the test cases examined are described.
The test report should contain:

* a test plan for the integration test and the acceptance test,
* a test plan for each module,
* a documentation of the test environment used for each separately tested module and each subsystem,
* a report of the test cases examined.

The completeness of the test report is of special importance for the repetition of test cases, for quality control purposes and after changes in the system. Unfortunately this is often underestimated in practice and the test report is often completely missing.

Concerning (6)

Tables and diagrams are important constituents of the system documentation. They offer a good overview of the complexity of a software system and help those who must maintain the system to recognize the dependencies between modules rapidly, to find the corresponding point in the program system in case of alterations and to understand the effects of such changes in other system components. Examples of such tables and diagrams are:

* a *module table*, which contains (in alphabetical order) all modules, their import/export interfaces and their storage requirements,
* a *table of all module functions*, which contains (in alphabetical order) all functions, their type (internal or export), to which module they belong and their interface description,
* a *table of all global data objects*, which contains (in alphabetical order) all data objects which are exported from modules, their data type, their meaning and information concerning the module in which they are declared, where the object is assigned a value and where it is used. This table is especially important for those who were not involved in the implementation because it is otherwise extremely difficult for them to maintain the system, especially in conjunction with errors involving global objects,
* a *hierarchy diagram*, which represents the module hierarchy graphically,
* an *import graph*, which represents the relation "imports" graphically. It shows the static dependency of the modules, how many compilation units belong to a program system, what their names are, how they are connected, whether there are any cycles and what the compilation sequence is for the program system.

The *system documentation* should, like the user documentation, be written *briefly* and *precisely. Schnupp* and *Floyd* (1976) mention that, as a rule, too much, not too little is documented. Extensive documentations are tedious to study and--a very important aspect--they often do not represent the present version of a software product because their management and maintenance is even more difficult than that of the software product.

As opposed to the user documentation, primarily *formal notation* should be used for the *system documentation*. But here it must be observed that the same formalisms and notations are applied by all those involved, so that the reader is confronted with a uniform style. The *stylistic guidelines* given in section 5.6.1.1 are also valid for the preparation of the system documentation.

The *system documentation* should under no circumstances first be written after the test phase. It should evolve gradually during the entire development process. The document (1) evolves in the specification phase, (2) in the design phase, (3), (4), (6) and (7) during the implementation phase and (5) during the specification and test phases.

After completion of the software product the documents which arose in the individual phases should only be checked, stylistically unified and, if necessary, corrected and amended.

5.6.1.3 Project Documentation

The *project documentation* contains information for project management and for project control. The *project management* requires a unified means of communication. This implies the prescribing of conventions and standards for all intermediate products manufactured in the course of system development. For *project progress control,* a project plan must exist and the system development process must also be clarified. *Quality control* also requires the definition of standards for intermediate products and the fixing of suitable check points in the software development process. For the purpose of *determining the production costs* of a software product, the expenditures on personnel, work time, machine time, etc. must be carefully documented.

In particular the following belong in the project documentation:

* a project plan which fixes the individual phases of realization and the time span which is planned for these,
* an organization plan which determines the allocation and supervision of personnel for the individual phases of realization,
* a statement concerning which results (documents) must be available after each phase of realization,
* the definition of project standards; here commitments are made, for example concerning which design methodology and which test strategy are to be used, conventions for the documentation and complexity limits for module design,
* an index of all documents which are part of the project; for each document, this index includes information about cataloging, the level of development (planned, in progress, released) and the access rights,

* an index of the work time used, machine time and other expenditures,
* a project log book for recording the discussions between project members; the project log provides information about the progress of the project, helps the project manager with progress checks and contains valuable information concerning decisions which were made much earlier and the reasons for which have already been forgotten by the members of the project.

In conclusion, it needs to be pointed out once again that *documentation* is an *integral part* of a software system. Documentation is *not assigned to its own phase* of the software life cycle, it is a part of each phase and is only reworked and expanded after the conclusion of implementation and testing. Each change in a software system implies a change in the documentation. Easy and efficient management of documentary material is a prerequisite for orderly documentation, and it is therefore advisable to use computer supported tools for documentation (see chapter 7).

5.6.2 The Maintenance of Software Products

The *maintenance of software products* includes all changes which are undertaken on the software product after the conclusion of the development stages. It is practically impossible to develop a software product which requires no maintenance. It has already been pointed out that it is not possible to demonstrate unambiguously the correctness of a software system through tests. Many errors are first recognized during actual use and can therefore be eliminated only after the development phases. Also, during operation new user demands are often added which imply system changes.

Software maintenance includes:

(1) *Touch ups of the user interface and optimizations*
   The operation of a software system with real data first exhibits the actual quality of the user interface, the utilization and the run time of the individual system components. Through calculated changes and optimizations, the run time behavior can be improved and the user interface can be adapted to the actual needs. One does not speak, in this case, of error correction, because the reason for maintenance is not a deviation of the system behavior from that specified in the requirements definition, but rather after the fact corrections requested by the customer. The development of new hardware technologies permit in many cases an improvement of the user interface (for example the use of screens and printers with graphics capability or the connection of a locator--mouse, joystick--as a useful input device). If one wishes to avail himself of these advantages, the software must also be reworked.

(2) *The correction of errors which were not detected by testing*
   Because it is impossible to test all program paths of a complex software system and all possible combinations of input data, errors are often first recognized during the operation of software products. They can therefore first be eliminated in the framework of software maintenance.

(3) *Changes due to new user requests*
The preparation of an exact requirements definition is successful in very few cases because the user himself is often not in a position to specify his own desires exactly. The actual use of a software product first shows how complete his requirements definition was and which additional functions are necessary.
A further reason for new user requirements is that, with increasing span of operation of a software system, new user desires always come up, the necessity or feasibility of which the user doubted at the begining. Also, organizational restructuring or other internal changes and the use of other software products in many cases imply new requirements on a software product.

Lientz and *Swanson* (1980) call these three types of maintenance *"perfective, corrective and adaptive maintenance"* and indicate that approximately 65% of the maintenance costs go on the the first, 17% on the second and 18% on the third type of maintenance.

A more or less precise estimation of the maintenance costs of a software product is practically impossible because the reasons for maintenance can hardly be assessed a priori and lie predominantly outside the sphere of influence of the software developer.

As a rule maintenance costs are underestimated. The investigation of *Lientz* and *Swanson* (1980) shows that the maintenance costs make up approximately 50% of the total costs and *Pressman* (1982) calculates the maintenance costs to be 40-60% of the total costs of a software product. It is therefore worthwhile to pay particular attention to the quality feature *maintainability* and to design software systems so that they are convenient to maintain.

Implementing a system which is *convenient to maintain* means guaranteeing modularity, good structure, readability and testability and checking each descision for the possibility and probability of its being changed, throughout the entire development process (compare *Kopetz*, 1979 with this).

The techniques of software development presented in the previous sections are especially designed to guarantee the maintainability of software products. The most important criteria for maintainability are (compare also *Kopetz* 1979, *Pressman* 1982, and *Sommerville* 1985):

(1) The *understandability*
By this we mean the clarity of the organization of the software system, the judiciousness of the decomposition of the overall system and the amount of structure of the system and its components. The principle of stepwise refinement supports the understandable and structured decomposition of a software system.

(2) *Module independence*
Program modules must be so constructed that changes have no effect on the environment. The guidelines for this are given in section 5.3.4.

(3) The *programming language employed*

Program systems which are implemented in an acceptable programming language from the stand point of software engineering (such as Modula-2) are easier to read (and therefore also easier to maintain) than program systems which are written in poor programming languages (such as Basic or RPG). The criteria for the choice of programming language are given in chapter 3.

(4) The *programming style*

The programming style determines the structure and the readability of the implementation. A software system is alterable if it is possible to find the point which is affected by the alteration, and if the program structure in question is so arranged that the consequences of the alteration are easily estimated. What we mean by good programming style is described in section 5.4.2.

(5) The *testability*

After each change the system must be tested again. It is therefore important that the preparation of the test objects for error detection, undertaken in the test phase, also be available for the maintenance phase. The same is true of the test environments of the individual components of a software system. One technique for error localization is described in the sections 5.4 and 5.5.

(6) The *expandability*

Software should be designed with an eye to the dimensioning of hardware and software resources, so that expansions are possible. It is therefore wise to set up data structures or files so that they can be easily expanded, to arrange the storage allocation as flexibly as possible and to consider the value domains of data objects with care.

(7) The *documentation*

The system documentation is the prerequisite for the maintainability of software products. The understandability of a software system is predominantly determined by the quality of the system documentation. Software maintenance without system documentation and with system specialists who were not involved in the development process is, as a rule, an expensive affair, in some cases even impossible. The data for tests which were undertaken after an alteration are also information which the system documentation should provide. The content and structure of the system documentation are described in section 5.6.1.2.

Further Reading

Software Engineering in General

Boehm, B.W.: Software Engineering Economics; Prentice-Hall 1981.

Gries, D.: Programming Methodology: A Collection of Articles by Members of IFIP WG 2.3; Springer-Verlag 1978.

Gries, D.: The Science of Programming; Springer-Verlag 1981.

Hoare,C. A. R.: Programing Is an Engineering Profession, Technical Monograph PRG-27 (1982); Programming Research Group, Oxford University 1982.

IEEE Standard Glossary of Software Engineering Terminology; IEEE Standard 729-1983.

Jensen, R.W. et al.: Software Engineering; Prentice-Hall 1979.

Ramamoorthy, et al.: Software Engineering: Problems and Perspectives. IEEE Transaction on Computer Vol. 17, No. 10; 1984.

Wiener, R.S., Sincovec, R.: Software Engineering with Modula-2 and Ada; Wiley & Sons 1984.

Shooman, M.: Software Engineering; McGraw Hill 1983.

Sommerville, I.: Software Engineering; Addison-Wesley 1982.

Requirements Analysis and Specification

Hays, I.J.: Applying Formal Specifications to Software Development in Industry; IEEE Transactions on Software Engineering; 1985.

Heninger, K.L.: Specifying Software Requirements for Complex Systems; New Techniques and Their Application; IEEE Transactions on Software Engineering, SE-6; 1980.

IEEE Trans. Software Engineering, Special Issue on Requirements Analysis, Vol. SE 3(1); 1977.

Yeh, R.T. and Zave, P.: Specifying Software Requirements; Proc. IEEE, 68(9); 1980.

Design and Verification

Alagic, S., Arbib, M.A.: The Design of Well-structured and Correct Programs; Springer-Verlag 1978.

Berg, K.K. et al.: Formal Methods of Program Verification and Specification; Prentice-Hall 1982.

Dijkstra, E.W.: A Discipline of Programming; Prentice-Hall 1976.

Dromey, R.G.: How to Solve it by Computer; Prentice-Hall 1982.

Floyd, R.W.: Assigning Meanings to Programs; Mathematical Aspects of Computer Science Vol.19; 1967.

Jackson, M.: System Design; Prentice-Hall 1983.

Parnas, D.: On the Criteria to be Used in Decomposing Systems into Modules; Comm. of the ACM, Vol. 15(12); 1972.

Wirth, N.: Program Development by Stepwise Refinement; Comm. of the ACM, Vol. 14(4); 1971.

Wirth, N.: Algorithms + Data Structures = Programs; Prentice-Hall 1976.

Welsh, J., Elder. J., Bustard, D.: Sequential Program Structures; Prentice-Hall 1984.

Yourdon, E., Constantine, L.: Structured Design: Fundamentals of a Discipline of Computer Program and System Design; Prentice-Hall 1979.

Testing and Debugging

Miller, E.: Program Testing Techniques; IEEE Computer Society Press 1977.

Myers, G.: The Art of Software Testing; Wiley & Sons 1979.

Roth, J.: Computer Logic, Testing and Verification; Computer Society Press 1980.

Documentation and Maintenance

Glass, R.L.: Software Maintenance Guidebook; Prentice-Hall 1981.

Mashey, J.R., Smith, D.W.: Documentation Tools and Techniques; Proc. of the 2nd Int. Conf. of Software Eng IEEE; 1976.

Miller, J. and Parikh, G. ed.: Techniques of Program and System Maintenance; Winthrop Publishers 1981.

Sommerville, I.: Documentation and Maintenance, in Software Engineering; Addison-Wesley 1985.

6. The Realization of Software Engineering Concepts in Modula-2

One important tool for the transformation of the software concepts described in chapter 5, such as stepwise refinement, modularization, interface specification, structuring the flow of control, implementation of data capsules and abstract data types is the available programming language. The syntactic and semantic capabilities of the programming language are important factors in the realization of the concepts mentioned above. This chapter describes the way in which these concepts are supported by Modula-2.

6.1 Stepwise Refinement

In designing a software system the problem is decomposed into subproblems according to the principle of stepwise refinement. For the subproblems, only the task is initially determined, not how it is to be realized. Each subsolution is considered an algorithm, for which only the name and parameters are defined. The procedure concept is sufficient for this technique. The procedures which arise through this are then associated with certain modules according to the guidelines for modularization (see sections 5.3.2 and 5.3.4). An algorithmic solution is not immediately designed for these procedures (module functions). Only the precise description of their tasks and interfaces are given.

Modula-2 offers, through the concept of definition module (see section 4.7.2), the possibility of describing the export interfaces of the system components (modules) exactly enough, but, as is desired for the design, also abstractly enough.

The principle of stepwise refinement as a design technique is independent of the language, and the designer should also make his design decisions independently of the language in which the system will later be implemented. The concept of defining the export interfaces of system components, as Modula-2 offers it, however, corresponds exactly to the requirements which are placed on a precise interface description. This concept can therefore be applied in the design phase, even if the program system is to be implemented in a different programming language. If Modula-2 is later used for the implementation, the designer has the advantage of prescribing the interface description for the programmer in the design phase.

This type of interface description is excellently suited for the design documentation and can even be used by the programmer unaltered. The implementation of inconsistent interfaces is broadly eliminated in this way.

The facility of separate compilation with interface checking for separately compiled modules (as described in section 4.7), additionally, enhances stepwise implementation.

To illustrate what has been said above the design and implementation of the file updating problem given in section 5.3.6.2 are reiterated here.

In the first step of the design it was pointed out that all data structures (for master and update records) and their access operations should be encapsulated in a module called "*DataManager*", and that the processing algorithms for both files (master and update files) should be combined into a module called "*DataProcessing*". The rough outline for updating the file is as follows (see section 5.3.6.2 solution with data capsules):

```
MODULE FileUpdate;
  FROM DataManager IMPORT Accountno;
  FROM FileProcessing IMPORT Initialize,
    ProcessFiles, CloseFiles;
  VAR masteracc, updateacc: Accountno;
BEGIN
  Initialize(↑masteracc ↑updateacc);
  ProcessFiles(↓masteracc ↓updateacc);
  CloseFiles
END FileUpdate.
```

In accordance with the principle of stepwise refinement, it is necessary to specify in the next step which functions and objects the modules "*FileProcessing*" and "*DataManager*" should provide and how their interfaces are defined. The module "*FileProcessing*" contains the functions "*Initialize*", "*ProcessFiles*" and "*CloseFiles*". For the description of the function interfaces the data type "*Accountno*", which is to be defined in the module "*DataManager*", is required. It will not be known at this point which other data structures and procedures the module "*DataManager*" must also include, and therefore the complete export interface cannot be given.

For the specification of the interfaces the concept of the definition module is used:

```
DEFINITION MODULE FileProcessing;
  FROM DataManager IMPORT Accountno;
  EXPORT QUALIFIED Initiailize, ProcessFiles, CloseFiles;

  PROCEDURE Initialize(VAR masteracc, updateacc: Accountno);
    (*Opens masterfileold, masterfilenew and updatefile, reads
    the first record of each masterfileold and updatefile and
    provides the corresponding account numbers masteracc and
    updateacc*)

  PROCEDURE ProcessFiles(masteracc, updateacc: Accountno);
    (*Processes masterfileold (the first record of which is
    already read and has the account number masteracc) and
    updatefile (the first record of which is already read
    and has the account number updateacc) and writes the
    results onto masterfilenew.*)

  PROCEDURE CloseFiles;
    (*Closes masterfileold, masterfilenew and updatefile*)

END FileProcessing.
```

```
DEFINITION MODULE DataManager;
    EXPORT QUALIFIED Accountno;
    TYPE Accountno = [1000..9999];
        (*Remaining data types, data structures and procedures
         not yet known.*)
END DataManager.
```

In this way the designer is forced to describe formally the interfaces chosen during the decomposition. However, the example does show that the degree of abstraction in the formalism is well suited to the documentation of the design. In addition it is possible at this point to write a Modula-2 program for each completely refined system component algorithm, for which the compiler can check the consistency of the interfaces with other system components although these system components are not yet implemented and perhaps not even designed.

6.2 Structured Programming

The object of structuring the flow control of algorithms is to provide a correspondence between the static notation of an algorithm and its dynamic behavior, thereby reducing the susceptibility to error and enabling verification of the algorithm (see section 5.3.3).

The most important measure for this is the avoidance of unbounded flow structures which occur through the undisciplined use of GOTO statements. Accordingly the complete renunciation of the use of GOTO's is often seen as a basic requirement of structured programming. For structuring the flow control the restriction is placed of using only those units which have only *one* entry and *one* exit.

Modula-2 satisfies this requirement completely. The language definition contains no GOTO. For formulating the control flow the following constructs are offered (see also section 4.6):

* assignment
* procedure call
* IF-THEN-ELSE-(ELSIF) statement (binary selection)
* CASE statement (multiple selection)
* WHILE statement (iterative loop)
* REPEAT statement (iterative loop)
* LOOP and EXIT statement (iterative loop)
* FOR statement (inductive loop)

Modula-2 belongs, therefore, to those programming languages which enforce GOTO-less programming. It is much more suitable for structured programming than older languages (for example Fortran), but it must be strressed that the absence of GOTO's in a program alone does not by any means indicate that the program is well structured. Good structuring of the flow control requires of the designer not only intuition and experience, but also discipline. Modula-2 offers the opportunity of clearly expressing the structure of the flow control in the implementation also.

6.3 Modular Programming and Interface Technique

The object of modular programming is the decomposition of a program system into a hierarchy of abstractions (see section 5.3). *Wirth* (1982) writes in this connection: "The principle motivation behind the partitioning of a program into modules is--besides the use of modules provided by other programmers--the establishment of a hierarchy of abstractions." This principle of abstraction is also expressed in the definition of a module given in section 5.3:

By a module we mean a collection of functions and data for the realization of a closed task, with the property that its communication with the outside world proceeds only via a precisely specified interface, for whose integration in a program system no knowledge of its inner working is required and whose correctness may be verified without knowledge of its embedding in a program system.

The realization of this concept of a module is well supported by Modula-2. We can view the module structure of Modula-2 as a fence which encloses objects (data structures and procedures) and seals them off from the environment. This fence can be broken through for the communication of the module with its environment. The programmer must, however, explicitly determine which objects are to be made known outside (that is exported) and which objects the module requires from its environment (that is wants to import). The requirement of explicit interface description is thereby fulfilled.

From the stand point of the principle of abstraction we can view the export interface of a module as its specification. It contains all the information concerning *what* the module performs (that is which objects and functions it offers) and hides all details of the implementation. It is therefore expedient also to separate the module specification and the description of the implementation textually. In Modula-2 this is realized by the division of a module into a definition and an implementation part.

The definition module describes only the export interface which implies that that part of the import interface which is required for the definition of the export interface also be described. The implementation module on the other hand contains all the details of the implementation and in particular that part of the import interface which is required for the implementation. These observations are depicted in illustration 6.1.

The realization of a module in Modula-2 can be demonstrated by an example of the implementation of a stack handling module. The programming of the stack module begins with the description of the export interface (that is the module specification):

```
DEFINITION MODULE StackMod;
  (*Module for the handling of a stack of INTEGER objects.*)
  EXPORT QUALIFIED Push, Pop, IsEmpty;


PROCEDURE Push(elem: INTEGER; VAR done: BOOLEAN);
  (*Places elem on the stack, done=FALSE if stack full,
    otherwise done=TRUE*)
```

```
PROCEDURE Pop(VAR elem: INTEGER; VAR done: BOOLEAN);
(*Yields the last element elem pushed on the stack, and
done=TRUE.
    If the stack is empty: done=FALSE*)

PROCEDURE IsEmpty(): BOOLEAN;
(*Yields the function value TRUE if the stack is empty,
   otherwise the value FALSE*)

END StackMod.
```

With this the module *StackMod* is completely specified. The details of the implementation are separated textually from the specification and are held in the so called "IMPLEMENTATION MODULE". The specification and implementation sections of a module form a logical unit, but are compiled separately. Once the specification (that is the definition module) of a module has been compiled, the compiler can check the agreement of the interfaces for each module which uses one of the exported objects. This concept supports and eases the testing of the module interactions (see section 5.5) and is discussed in detail in section 6.4.

One possible implementation of the stack handling module is:

```
IMPLEMENTATION MODULE StackMod;
(*Implementation of the module for the handling of
   a stack of integer objects*)
CONST maxstacksize=20;
VAR stacksize: [0..maxstacksize];
    stack: ARAY[1..maxstacksize] OF INTEGER;

PROCEDURE Push(elem: INTEGER; VAR done: BOOLEAN);
BEGIN
  IF stacksize<maxstacksize
    THEN (*stack*)
      stacksize:=stacksize+1:
      stack[stacksize]:=elem;
      done:=TRUE;
    ELSE (*stack overflow*)
      done:=FALSE
  END;
END Push;

PROCEDURE Pop(FAR elem: INTEGER;VAR done: BOOLEAN);
BEGIN
  IF stacksize>0
    THEN (*unstack the top element of the stack*)
      elem:=stack[stacksize];
      stacksize:=stacksize-1;
      done:=TRUE;
    ELSE (*stack empty*)
      done:=FALSE
  END;
END Pop;
```

```
PROCEDURE IsEmpty: BOOLEAN;
 BEGIN
   RETURN stacksize=0;
 END IsEmpty;

BEGIN (*Initialization of the stack*)
 stacksize:=0;
END StackMod.
```

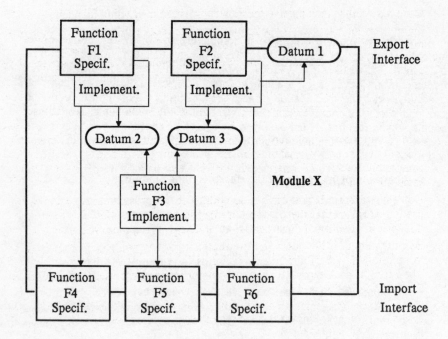

Illustration 6.1 Module Structure

This example shows that the module concept of Modula-2 corresponds exactly to the data and program control structures which have shown themselves to be the most suitable control structures for modular programming according to the analysis in section 5.3.6.

The modular decomposition chosen in the design may also be realized in the implementation. In this way every program system can be implemented as a hierarchy of modules. To show this a graphic representation of the module hierarchy of the file update program designed in section 5.3.6.2 is given in illustration 6.2.

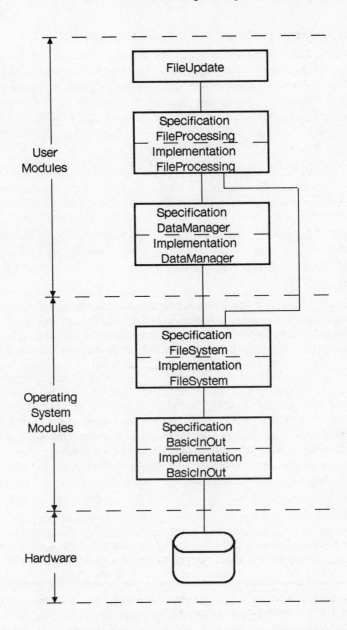

Illustration 6.2 Module Hierarchy of the File Update Program

6.4 Team Software Development and Separate Compilation

The production of complex program systems demands team software production, which means that a number of people are involved in the system development. It should therefore be required of a programming language in which large program systems are to be implemented that the individual components of the system be individually compilable. The technique of separate compilation as it is applied in older programming languages (for example Fortran or PL/1) has the disadvantage that each compilation unit is compiled independently of all the others. Consequently, it is not possible during compilation to check whether the interfaces of the system components are compatible. Independent compilation makes the test for the interactions of the modules more difficult and the programmer must check the compatibility of the interfaces himself.

Modula-2 permits a form of separate compilation of modules, in which the interfaces are checked for compatibility. For this, however, it is necessary to observe a certain compilation sequence.

As has already been emphasized, the definition and implementation sections of the modules in Modula-2 are separated. Both sections are compiled separately. The definition section contains all the names which are exported by a module and their declarations. The implementation section references the declarations in the definition section. Therefore the definition section of the module must always be compiled before the implementation section. The result of the compilation of a definition module is a "symbol table", which contains all constant, variable, type and procedure declarations of the definition module. This symbol table is stored in a symbol file, which is available to all modules. For the compilation of the implementation section it can therefore be checked whether the specification of the interface agrees with its implementation. In the compilation of a module which uses (imported) objects of other modules, the symbol tables of these modules must already be available so that the compatibility of the interfaces can be checked.

A change in the interface definition of a module thus requires a new compilation of all modules which use the module with the altered interface since the compatibility of the interfaces is no longer assured. In fact a test is made at execution time to determine whether the compilation sequence of the program system has been observed. Each change made in a definition module without recompilation of all modules which use the altered definition module therefore makes execution of the program system impossible. In this way the errors caused by incompatible interfaces, which are extremely difficult to localize, are avoided from the start. A change in the implementation section of a module, on the other hand, only requires its own recompilation because no change in the interface has occurred. These points are demonstrated in the example given in illustration 6.3.

Possible compilation sequences of the definition modules shown in illustration 6.3 are:

D-E-C-B   D-C-E-B
E-D-C-B   D-C-B-E

The compilation of an implementation module assumes the successful compilation of a definition module and the definition sections of those modules from which it imports objects. But otherwise, the compilation sequence of the implementation modules (module A inclusive) is arbitrary. For the example in illustration 6.3 this means in particular that:

* the compilation of the implementation modules D and E assumes only the successful compilation of their own definition sections,
* for the compilation of the implementation module B all definition modules must already by compiled,
* for the compilation of the program module A the definition modules B and C (and thus also D) must already be compiled. This means that A can be compiled before the definition module E,
* each implementation module can be changed and recompiled without the other modules (definition or implementation) being affected,
* if, for example, the definition module D is changed and recompiled, the definition and implementation modules B and C as well as the program module A must be recompiled.

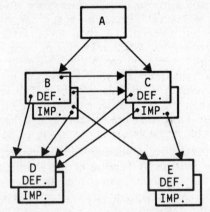

Illustration 6.3 Import Graph of a Program System

6.5 The Implementation of Data Capsules

It has already been shown in section 5.3 that the principle of *data encapsulation* (information hiding) takes on a great measure of importance in the implementation of reliable software systems. The problem of specially marking the *access procedures* of a data capsule is solved in Modula-2 by dividing the capsule into two parts: a *visible part* for the user of the data capsule (the specification or interface section), which contains the declarations of all access procedures and possibly exported data types, and a *part which is not visible* (the implementation section), which contains the declarations of the encapsulated data and all algorithms (procedures) of the capsule.

In general a data capsule is realized in Modula-2 as follows:

```
DEFINITION MODULE Capsulename;
   EXPORT QUALIFIED Exportlist;
   Declaration of the exported data types         interface
   Declaration of the interfaces of exported      section
   procedures (access procedures)
END Capsulename.

IMPLEMENTATION MODULE Capsulename;
   Declaration of the encapsulated data           implement-
   (concrete data structures)                     ation
   Declaration of all procedures
   (access procedures and internal procedures)
BEGIN
   statements for initialization
END Capsulename.
```

All objects (constants, data types) which are necessary for the declaration of the interfaces of the access procedures along with the interfaces themselves are declared in the *specificaton section*. But only those names which are contained in the export list are known to the outside. Everything else is contained in the *implementation section*, whose text is not visible to the user of the data capsule.

Export is not limited to procedures: type names, constants and variables can also be exported. If a variable is exported--for example to make the access to a single data element more efficient--the value of this variable can be *altered* by the importing module. In this way though, the principle of data encapsulation is compromised. The programmer must realize that he is now working with *global* data and that the effiency gained in this way is offset by the disadvantages of data exchange by means of *global* objects.

Modula-2 permits the implementation of data capsules but realizes the concept of data capsules only imperfectly because of the possibility of exporting data objects *together with their structure*. Examples of data capsules in Modula-2 are given in section 5.3.6. The example of the stack module from section 6.2 also shows the realization of a data capsule.

6.6 The Implementation of Abstract Data Types

Abstract data types are of just as great a practical importance as *data capsules* for software engineering. The concept and use of abstract data types are discussed in section 5.6.3. Abstract data types are a generalized form of data capsules and can be realized in Modula-2, like data capsules, by use of the facility of defining *opaque data types*. This concept is best explained by an example.

The example used is a data capsule which implements the abstract data type of a *stack*. The data capsule should offer the access procedures *Push*, *Pop* and *IsEmpty* and an access procedure for the generation of new stack instances (*NewStack*). This can be specified as follows:

```
DEFINITION MODULE StackMod;
  (*Data capsule for the abstract data type Stack*)
  EXPORT QUALIFIED Stack, NewStack, Push, Pop, IsEmpty;
  Type Stack;  (*opaque type*)

  PROCEDURE NewStack(VAR s: Stack);
    (*generates a new instance of a stack*)

  PROCEDURE Push(s: Stack; elem: INTEGER; VAR done: BOOLEAN);
    (*Places elem on the stack s, done=FALSE if stack s full,
      otherwise done=TRUE*)

  PROCEDURE Pop(s: Stack; VAR elem :INTEGER; VAR done: BOOLEAN);
    (*Yields the last element elem pushed onto s and done =TRUE.
      If the stack is empty: done=FALSE*)

  PROCEDURE IsEmpty(s: Stack): BOOLEAN;
    (*Yields the function value TRUE if the stack s is empty,
      otherwise the value FALSE*)

END StackMod.
```

The abstract data type is called "Stack" and is defined as an *opaque data type*, which means that its representation remains hidden to the user of the definition module and is first fixed in the implementation module. This does have the disadvantage, however, that at the time of compilation of the definition module the storage requirements for the objects of the abstract data type are unknown. Therefore Modula-2 requires that abstract data types be implemented as pointer types. It is thus not possible to implement fields or records as abstract data types directly. However, the objects of the concrete data type can be generated dynamically by using the *pointer* to them as their abstract data type. This makes the implementation a little less efficient, however.

The implementation of the data capsule could read:

```
IMPLEMENTATION MODULE StackMod;
  (*Implementation of the abstract data type Stack*)
  FROM Storage IMPORT ALLOCATE;
  CONST maxstacksize=20;
  TYPE Stack = POINTER TO stackinstance;
       stackinstance = RECORD
                          size: CARDINAL;
                          elem: ARRAY[1..maxstacksize] OF
                                      INTEGER;

  PROCEDURE NewStack(VAR s: stack);
  BEGIN
    NEW(s);  (*generate new stack instance)
    s↑.size:=0;  (*initialize stack length*)
  END NewStack;
```

```
PROCEDURE Push(s: Stack; elem: INTEGER; VAR done: BOOLEAN);
(*push elem onto stack s*)
BEGIN
  IF s↑.size<maxstacksize
    THEN (*push*)
      s↑.size:=s↑.size+1:
      s↑.elem[s↑.size]:=elem;
      done:=TRUE;
    ELSE (*stack overflow*)
      done:=FALSE
  END;
END Push;

PROCEDURE Pop(s: Stack; VAR elem: INTEGER; VAR done: BOOLEAN);
  (*return the top element from stack s*)
BEGIN
  IF s↑.size>0
    THEN (*pop the top element*)
      elem:=s↑.elem[s↑.size];
      s↑.size:=s↑.size-1;
      done:=TRUE;
    ELSE (*stack empty*)
      done:=FALSE
  END;
END Pop;

PROCEDURE IsEmpty(s: Stack): BOOLEAN;
  (*test if stack s is empty*)
BEGIN
  RETURN s↑.size=0;
END IsEmpty;

END StackMod.
```

The *abstract data type* has been realized here as a *pointer* to a record. With the procedure *NewStack* new instances of stacks are generated (dynamically) and their present length is initialized with zero. The pointer to the stack is returned as an output parameter. The remaining access procedures correspond to those of the data capsule for a stack given in section 6.3, with the difference that they have an additional parameter *s* which indicates which stack instance is to be accessed.

If three instances of a stack are needed in a module, for example, we write:

```
IMPLEMENTATION MODULE X;
  FROM StackMod IMPORT Stack, NewStack, Push, Pop, IsEmpty;
  ...
  VAR s1,s2,s3:Stack;
  ...
BEGIN
  NewStack(s1); NewStack(s2); NewStack(s3);
  ...
END X.
```

To push the element *y* in stack *s1* we write: Push(s1, y, done).

6.7 The Value of Strong Type Checking

In contrast to many other programming languages (for example PL/I, Fortran and Cobol) Modula-2 (like Pascal) is a programming language with *strong type checking*.

When an operator connects two operands, the operands must be *expression compatible* and the operation expressed by the operator must be admissible for the data types of the two operands. The same thing is true for the assignment statement. A value w represented by an expression can only be assigned to an object x if w and x are *assignment compatible*. (The concepts of *expression* and *assignment compatibility* are discussed in section 4.5.)

The programmer is thus compelled to use more discipline as he must always account for the data types of his objects. The observance of the rules of compatibility is checked by the compiler, the combination of objects whose data types do not correspond--a frequent source of error in programming--is thus already known at the time of compilation. The test effort is thereby reduced. This concept also increases the readability of the programs, because when studying expressions, statements and interfaces, no hidden rules of conversion need to be observed.

If it seems appropriate to the programmer to combine two objects of incompatible data type, he must arrange for the appropriate conversions himself by explicitly providing a conversion function (see section 4.10). The conversion is thus evident from the program text. In addition, the language definition is kept short because it is not burdened with complex rules of conversion (as is the case, for example, in PL/I).

Strong type checking helps to recognize sources of error early and therefore increases the degrees of correctness, testability and maintainability.

A comparison with the principles of software engineering given in chapter 5 shows that all these concepts can be realized in Modula-2 in a simple and elegant way, providing a strong correspondence between the design and the implementation of a software product. Modula-2 supports the implementation of modular program designs as well as the testing and maintenance of program systems; it enables quality gains and at the same time efficient software production.

7. Software Engineering Tools

In the previous chapters the author has shown how order can be brought into the running of software projects and how the production and operation of software products can be broken down into phases. For each phase of the software life cycle The author has described the associated activities and goals, and discussed methods and techniques for the achievement of these goals. It is also required of the science of software engineering that it provide *tools* which aid in the rationalization of software production (to reduce production, operation and maintenance costs) and *tools* which support project management and the individual phases of the software life cycle and contribute to quality assurance. An important task of research in the field of software engineering is thus the development of tools which support software production and the provision of techniques for implementing such tools.

When data processing was still a new discipline the only tools which were available for programming were assemblers, linkage editors and loaders. Parallel to the introduction of time sharing systems and desk top computers a wealth of software tools have been developed: simple tools and more sophisticated ones, tools which are tailored to a particular task only and tools which support an entire phase of the software life cycle. Today tools are even offered whith the claim that they are applicable to all phases of a software project.

There is no unity in the appearance of such universal tools--which are often referred to as *programming environments*. The systems offered are anything but mature and tested products; they are usually difficult to manage, only designed for special applications and seldom portable. They represent an unconvincing, makeshift solution, and give the impression that the fundamental problem has not been understood at all, in spite of the fact that a solution has been attempted.

There is therefore no mention of any *"new" universal programming environments* in this chapter. It simply provides a catalog of isolated tools for the *rationalization* and *quality assurance* of software production. To this end the ways in which they support the various activities carried out during the process of software development are described.

7.1 Simple Tools

There are a few *elementary tools* which are easy to produce and are still not available in many installations. These alone ease software production immensely. Two in particular fall into this category:

* tools for file administration
* tools for simple analysis and documentation tasks

7.1.1 Tools for File Administration

The individual program modules of a software product, and also the corresponding documents and data stocks are stored in *files* or *data bases* on external storage media (for example floppy disks, hard disks or tapes). For reasons of clarity and order it is useful to compile *file catalogs* and to organize them according to various aspects. Tools for file administration must permit *file catalogs* to be set up on one or more external storage units and to be made available in various ways:

* ordered by file type or file name
* with or without indication of storage space required
* with or without indication of access rights and owner

For the *administration* of files and for *error seeking* it is important to retain a number of generations of files and to determine if and in which way the various generations differ. Therefore tools for automatic *file saving* and for *file comparison* are of great value. Each file alteration should automatically trigger a "save" of the old file contents (creation of backups). Tools for file comparison should permit file contents to be made available with indications of changes, insertions and deletions.

To save space, the possibility of compressing the contents of files and, when needed, of expanding them again should be given. For this *file compression* and *expansion programs* are required.

These tools are taken for granted in modern operating systems such as *UNIX* (*Doltha* and *Mashey*, 1976, 1977), but oddly enough are absent from the operating systems of many large computers.

7.1.2 Simple Analysis Tools and Documentation Tools

For the simple *analysis* of programs in *seeking errors*, for the supervision of the observance of project conventions (for example number of comments, prescribed complexity bounds) and for quality control, it is necessary to provide information concerning structure anomalies and the frequency of certain program constructs.

This information is provided by tools for the analysis of the *static program profile*. In particular these tools should yield the following information:

(1) *Structure anomalies*
* complexity measures (for example according to *McCabe*, 1976 or *Halstead*, 1972)
* nesting levels of loops
* indications of modules, procedures and variables which are declared but not used
* all non-initialized objects
* all statements which cannot be reached from the start of the program (dead code)
* all statements from which the end of the program is not reachable

(2) *Number of program constructs*
* the length and number of modules and procedures
* the number of loops

* the number of GOTO's
* the length and number of comments

To facilitate the inspection of program listings, a *uniformly structured* output of program lists is of great value. If the required uniformity is not assured by the discipline of the programmers, and not compelled by other tools (for example structure oriented editors, see section 7.2.3), it is appropriate to bring all program lists into a standard form by the use of *Formatters* or *Pretty-Printers*.

For the analysis of any larger program modules a program listing, numbered according to lines or statements, and a cross reference list in which all objects, their type and declaration and their application are tabulated, are necessary. If this list is not automatically generated by the compiler, it is useful to employ a *cross reference list generator*. The same is true for the analysis of program descriptions and other documents. Documents are reference works. Study of them is greatly facilitated if an index is available. Therefore it is necessary to support the preparation and administration of indexes by tools (*index generators*).

7.2 Tools Related to Specific Project Phases

The software tools related to specific phases of a project should support methods which are applied in the individual phases of the software life cycle. They should help to recognize and correct errors at an early date and support the documentation and quality asurance of the products which arise in the individual phases.

7.2.1 Tools for Requirements Analysis and Specification

The classic techniques of requirements analysis (questionnaire, interviews, observations, etc.) are described in section 5.1. On the one hand tools which support and unify the documentation of the results of the analysis are required, and on the other hand tools which support the analysis itself are required.

For the *documentation of the analysis results* comfortable *text processors*--the requirements of these are discussed in section 7.2.5--and also *tools for the graphic representation of data and information flow* are required.

In the last few years data oriented thinking has come more and more to the foreground. Particularly in commercial and production applications, analysis begins with an examination of the data flow in addition to that of the functions. Thus tools for the preparation and management of *data flow diagrams*, where possible in graphic notation, are needed. These tools should permit screen oriented editing of data flowcharts and support their output on a printer.

For surmounting the communications difficulties between the system analysts and the users, and between the system analysts and the program designer, *data dictionaries* are increasingly being used. Tools which provide functions for *entering*, *deleting*, *searching* and *changing* data descriptions are required for the administration of these data dictionaries.

As special methods for the analysis phase, SADT (*Schoman* and *Ross*, 1977), SA (*Halsteadt*, 1972), HIPO (*IBM*, 1975) and PSL/PSA (*Teichrow* and *Hersley*, 1977) were mentioned in section 5.1. Usually these methods can only be used effectively, if software tools for their support are available. A good programming environment should offer tools for as many of these methods as possible because none of the methods has, as yet, become universally accepted. Such tools for example are discussed by *Alford* (1972), *Balzert* (1981), *Hruschka* and *Teichrow* and *Hersley*, (1977).

Because an unambiguous, complete and consistent requirements definition is of special importance for a software project, repeated attempts have been made to define special *specification languages* and to provide *prototyping tools*. *Jones* (1979) discusses important facts for the development of a specification language and some ideas for the field of prototyping can be found in *Budde* (1984). To date, however, no satisfactory solution to this problem exists, and none of these specification languages or prototyping methods has become generally accepted. The application of tools in the requirements definition phase is therefore mostly limited to that of text processing.

7.2.2 Design Tools

For efficient project development, and above all for the maintenance and expansion of software systems, a careful and complete documentation of the system structure and of all design decisions which lead up to it is of great importance. The following requirements are placed on a tool for the support of the design phase:

* support of the principle of stepwise refinement,
* wide freedoms in the formulation of the system design,
* automatic documentation of all levels of abstraction of the system design,
* comfortable facilities for changing and altering previously prepared designs,
* support in the choice of control structures,
* checking of the syntactic correctness of control structures as early as the design process,
* dialog orientation,
* support for the checking of interface consistency.

It should be possibile for the software engineer to formulate his system and module design in a simple *design language* at a high level without having to depart from his accustomed design style. The design tools should support interactive program development according to the principle of stepwise refinement so that the design can be formulated roughly or in detail, completely or incompletely, and in the process an immediate, that is input oriented, check of the control structures should take place. It must be possible to change, correct or refine the design simply and at any time.

The structure of program systems and algorithms can best be illustrated through graphic notation (a picture says a thousand words). Tools for *graphic representation of design documents* are of great value for the software engineer. Therefore generators for *flowcharts* and *Nassi Shneiderman diagrams* or--even better--design tools which permit diagrammatic designing are required. With the use of such tools, the design of program systems can be accomplished entirely on the computer, without pencil or paper. Tools of this type are described by *Frei* et al. (1978), *Pomberger* (1982), *Truöl* (1981) and *Willes* (1981), among others.

7.2.3 Tools for the Implementation Phase

For the *implementation phase,* tools which support the editing, compilation, loading and execution of programs are required.

For ease of coding, efficient (text) editors or, even better, *structure oriented editors* are needed. These enforce the formatted input of the program text and permit an automatic generation of the basic forms of statements, procedures and modules. The programmer need no longer bother himself with syntactic ballast, type in any keywords, nor can he forget to terminate statements correctly. Structure oriented editors should, in addition, permit structure oriented selection and--to provide an overview--the blending out of structure blocks. The disadvantage of these tools is that they only support the editing of programs in a single programming language. Unfortunately, the implementations of structure oriented editors known to date give grounds for much criticism. Examples of this type of tool can be found in *Teitelbaum* and *Reps* (1981) and *Donzeau-Gonge* et al. (1980).

Program template generators are also useful tools for the programmer. They support the automatic generation of program templates in which uniform program heads, interface descriptions and place holders for prescribed comments are contained (see section 5.4.2). This makes the observance of project standards simpler for the programmer.

The most important tool for the programmer is a *compiler* for compiling the source code into machine code. The quality of the compiler influences the production costs of a software product to a large extent. Good compilers must execute rapidly, generate efficient machine code and provide the programmer with as much information as possible concerning errors, error sources and the program structure. In particular the quality of a compiler is determined by the following criteria:

* its reliability,
* the compilation time, which should ideally be short,
* its ability to put out a program list with numbered source text lines and an indication of the level of nesting for each statement,
* its ability to mark each syntactically incorrect symbol and provide extensive commentary on the detected error; the error messages must be of such a nature that they are generally understandable,
* its ability to provide a separation between the source text and the information it produces,
* its ability generate a cross reference list which states for each name used in the program in which line of source text it is declared, what its type is and in which lines of source text it is used,
* the ability to give a minimal number of derivative error messages,

* the provision of the most complete syntax analysis of the program text possible, even in the event of an error,
* the provision of the separate compilation of program units with complete interface checking of the separately compiled units,
* the provision of options, for example the suppression of the output of certain program sections, for marking keywords and for the output of program lists with page numbers and uniform headers.

In the spirit of team development of modularly constructed program systems, separate compilation of program modules with complete *interface checking* is of great value. It is therefore necessary to have programming languages and compilers which support this concept (for example Ada or Modula-2). For older programming languages it is helpful to implement tools which handle interface checking through context checking of the separately compiled program units.

Further tools for the programmer are *linkage editors* and *loaders*. These tools serve to join the separately compiled modules of a program system into an executable program, and to load it. Linkers and loaders are prerequisites for work with module libraries.

7.2.4 Test Tools

All larger program systems contain errors, regardless of how carefully they are planned and designed by professional software engineers. It is well known that the costs devoured by testing are a very high percentage of the total costs. It is also known that correct testing is an art; how difficult it often is, to eliminate the source of an error without producing new errors in the process!

Tools which help in the tracking down and elimination of sources of errors are:

* static analyzers,
* debuggers,
* file comparison tools.

Static analyzers help the tester to obtain information about the composition and structure of the program system to be tested. They are therefore also of great importance for the documentation and maintenance of program systems. Simple static analyzers are discussed in section 7.1.2. These tools should be able to produce the following documents:

* a *module list,* which tabulates all module names for a programming system and the corresponding import/export interfaces,
* a *procedure list,* which tabulates the names of all procedures, to which module they belong and their interfaces,
* an *intermodular cross reference list,* which tabulates which object is exported by which module and by which modules it is imported,

* *hierarchy diagrams,* which are a graphic representation of the module hierarchy and the static nesting of the local modules and procedures of a compilation unit (an example is shown in illustration 7.1),

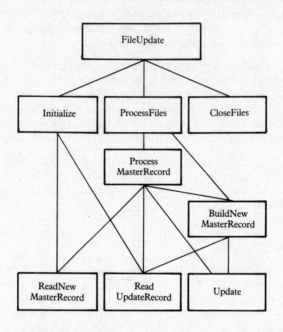

Illustration 7.1 Hierarchy Diagram for the File Update Program

* *control flowcharts,* which graphically illustrate the control structure, that is the branches of procedures (see illustration 7.2); the branches should be markable by another test tool (for example the debugger) during the execution of the test when they are traversed, and after the test, each branch should contain information concerning how often it was executed,

ProcessMasterRecord

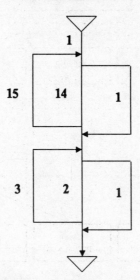

Illustration 7.2 Control Flowchart for the Procedure "ProcessMasterRecord"

* *call graphs,* which show the graphic representation of the dynamic nesting of the procedures of a module (see illustration 7.3),

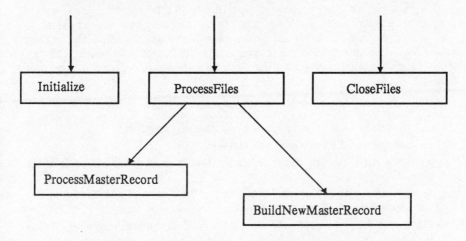

Illustration 7.3 Call Graph for the Module "File Processing"

* *import graphs,* which show the graphic representation of the static dependence between modules, that is the relation "*imports*" (see illustration 7.4). An import graph shows how many compilation units a program has and how they are connected.

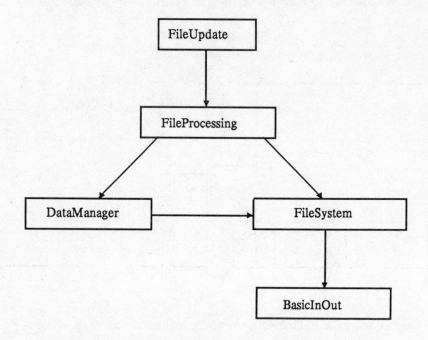

Illustration 7.4 Import Graph for the File Update Program

The *most important tool* for the *test specialist* is an efficient *debugger*. It should support the successive testing of programs by the analysis of the program status at any given point in time and at any given point in a program system. The analysis tables should be presented to the programmer in that notation in which he thinks. The debugger should also enable the alteration of storage contents for dynamic testing.

In particular, a debugger should be able to provide:

* an indication of the source of an error in case of a program halt,
* an indication of the error in the source text,
* an indication of the procedure call chain (that is the dynamic call chain at the time of the halt),
* an indication of the values and data types of the objects of all loaded modules and procedures at the time of the halt,
* the possibility of inspecting the contents of dynamically generated data structures,
* an indication of the storage contents in any desired representation,

* an indication of all loaded modules and processes,
* the possibility of altering the contents of storage and continuing the execution of the program.

There is an example of a good debugger in *Jacobi* (1982).

Test execution requires the comparison of the results of one test run with the results of earlier test runs. For large volumes of output this is difficult to manage manually. If the results are written onto files, they can be analyzed using *file comparison tools* (see section 7.1.1).

7.2.5 Tools for Documentation and Maintenance

Tools for documentation are used in many (usually in all) of the phases of the software life cycle. They are used by many users with differing needs, and therefore their design must be especially well thought out, and their operation must be conceptually simple and compatible with that of other tools.

A comfortable text processing tool should meet the following requirements:

* functions for inserting, deleting, searching for, copying and moving text,
* the provision of various type fonts and an editor for generating new characters and character sets,
* the possibility of showing and manipulating different parts of a document simultaneously,
* the possibility of showing and manipulating different documents simultaneously,
* flexible document positioning,
* provision of text processing functions such as adjusted margins, centering and the changing of fonts,
* the possibility of simultaneously processing text and pictures,
* the possibility of producing camera ready copy.

Descriptions of text editors which very nearly approach these requirements can be found in *Winiger* (1982) and *Gutknecht* and *Winiger* (1984).

In large software projects the documents as well as the module libraries are used and altered by a number of people. The objects in these libraries are thus usually present in different versions. Keeping such libraries up to date is a delicate task. Thus tools for *version control* must provide:

* indication of a new version,
* association of version numbers with documents and vice versa,
* comparison of two versions of a document,
* automatic documentation of the difference between two versions.

Examples of this can be found in *Feldman* (1979), *McGuffin* et al. (1979) and *Rochkind* (1975), among others.

The test tools described in section 7.4.2 are primarily important for the maintenance phase.

7.3 Project Management Tools

Project management tools should provide functions for the management of all products produced during the course of the project--that is project standards, documents, tables, plans, programs, etc.--and be able to manage network plans for progress control.

The prerequisite for these tools is a *common data base* which guarantees that all members of the project manipulate only those products for which they have the corresponding access rights and that all members work with the currently valid version of a product.

The *basic functions* of these tools are:

* the sketching and defining of a document,
* the assignation of project standards, that is the determination of the style of thedocuments, document templates, etc. for each product,
* the announcment, modifying, analyzing and merging of documents,
* assigning attributes such as version number, access rights, document style, release status, etc.

These tools are certainly the most costly and difficult to implement. A specification of a programming environment which contains this type of tools can be found in the *Stoneman Report* (Fisher, 1980).

A hierarchy diagram of the software engineering tools discussed above is shown in illustration 7.5.

7.4 Questions about the Implementation of Software Tools

Virtually all of the tools listed above, must be implemented as dialog programs if they are to be effective. The correct design of the user interface is of paramount importance for the acceptability of these tools. In the process it is important to decide *what* should be communicated to *whom* in *which way*. For the question "in which way", the tool maker must always keep an eye on the properties of the medium of communication employed. For software tools the primary means of communication is the screen. On a screen with graphic elements, a large amount of information can be expressed faster, more compactly and more understandably than through lengthy texts (compare *Nievergelt* and *Ventura*, 1983). In the development of tools, therefore, techniques of graphic data processing should be employed. This is usually overseen today, because of unsuitable hardware. Consequently, present man-machine dialogs do not come close to exhausting the possibilities of (graphic) screens.

Software tools must be modelled in such a way that they are "*accepted*" by software engineers. This once again presupposes that they are *simple* and do not infringe on his accustomed work methods by requiring too large an adaptation on his part. This in turn implies that the tools must be reliable, that they operate quickly, without hindering the work of the software engineer, and produce the results--whether on a screen or a printer--in an orderly and well measured fashion: not too little and not too much, in a pleasant, clear and aesthetically satisfying form.

In this connection it is also necessary to make a few remarks about the minimal requirements on the hardware components for an efficient man-machine communication. The minimal requirements are:

* a screen with graphic capability and a laser printer as output devices,
* a locator (mouse or joy stick) as an input device in addition to the usual keyboard,
* an efficient processor and, above all, also an efficient display controller with a high data transfer rate between main storage and the screen.

Waiving of these minimal requirements means attempting to implement tools of the present with the technology of the past.

In implementing tools one should start not with the most difficult tools, but rather with the simple tools. When these have proved to be reliable, more complicated tools can be added. Only then should the tools for project management be implemented. In other words, evolution rather than revolution should be the order of the day.

Software Engineering Tools

- **Simple Tools**
  - Tools for File Administration
    - Tools for Managing File Catalogs
    - Tools for File Saving
    - Tools for File Comparison
    - Tools for File Compression and Expansion
  - Analysis Tools
    - Tools for Determining the Static Program Profile
    - Cross Reference List Generators
  - Documentation Tools
    - Program Listing Formatters
    - Index Generators

- **Tools Related to Specific Project Phases**
  - Requirements Analysis and Definition
    - Text and Image Processing Tools
    - Tools for Managing Data Dictionaries
    - Tools for the Support of Special Methods
  - Design
    - Tools for the Support of Design Methods
      (e.g. SADT, HIPO, the Principle of Stepwise
      Refinement)
    - Diagram Editors
  - Implementation
    - Structure Oriented Editors
    - Program Template Generators
    - Compilers, Linkage Editors, Loaders
  - Test
    - Static Analyzers
    - Debuggers
    - File Comparison Tools

- **Non Phase Specific Tools**
  - Project Management Tools
    - Tools for the Administration of Project Libraries
    - Tools for the Enforcement of Project Standards
    - Tools for Version Administration
  - Documentation Tools
    - Text and Image Processing Tools

Illustration 7.5 Hierarchy Diagram of Software Engineering Tools

Further Reading

Miller, E.: Tutorial: Automated Tools for Software Engineering, IEEE Computer Society Press 1979.

Wasserman, A. (ed): Programming Environments, Computer Vol. 14(4); 1981.

Kernighan, B. W., Plauger, P. J.: Software Tools in Pascal; Adison-Wesley 1981.

8. Project Management

As a rule many people with different tasks and professional qualifications are involved in the production of complex software products. In order to achieve the goal of the *economic production* of software products, which is prescribed by our definition of the concept of *software engineering*, the organizational measures for producing a software product economically and on time must be just as well thought out as the technical measures for product development.

It is no rare occurrence that software projects are completed late and with much higher costs than were assumed at the start of the project, or that they fail completely. The cause of this is often to be found in lack of organization. The most important reasons for this are:

* *Poor Management*
  The project management is usually organized into a strict hierarchy, and the administration is incumbent upon either a qualified software engineer with little organizational and managerial experience or a qualified manager with little or no experience in the field of software engineering.

* *The Lack of Project Planning and Project Standards*
  Programmers are individualists. They refer to themselves often as artists and do not like to lay their cards on the table. This fact can be a great problem for team software development. The absence of project standards and milestones for project progress control often has devastating effects, because lack of quality of the individual system components and scheduling delays first become apparent at the time of the integration test.

* *The Lack of Up to Date Documentation*
  The neglect of accompanying documentation for a project is quite common. This hinders communication between the members of the project and prevents project progress control.

* *Lack of Project Progress and Quality Control*
  Complex software systems consist of subsystems which in turn consist of individual components (modules). As a rule these components are implemented by different people. Quality deficiencies in the individual components which are recognized too late usually require expensive retouching, and this causes increased cost and missed deadlines. The neglect of project progress and quality controls can lead to the interruption of the further progress of a project due to the late completion of individual system components, and an entire schedule may have to be thrown out.

* *The Lack of Economic Controls*
  If running expense checks are missing from a project, it is impossible to catch errors in cost planning and weak points in the course of the project in time, and thus to take the appropriate measures.

It is therefore just as important, especially in those cases where many people are involved in the production of a software product, to consider, in addition to the technical side, the organizational questions. In the following sections the objectives and tasks of the software project management are described and their realization is discussed.

8.1 The Aim of Project Management

The goal of *project management* is to guarantee that a software product which satisfies the quality requirements set down in the requirements definition is produced with the allotted resources (for example personnel, working material, tools), on time and at an economically justifiable cost. The *main tasks* of management are: *planning, organization* and the *professional* and *economic control* of the project.

8.1.1 Planning

Exact planning, appropriate for the project size, is of decisive importance for the success of a software project (compare also *Metzger* 1973, *Baker* and *Mills*, 1979). The effort and scope of planning (compare also *Gewald*, et al. 1977) are dependent on:

* the task (for example a short and precise requirements definition for a compiler project as opposed to a voluminous and informal requirements definition for commercial projects),
* the project size (the number of people presumably involved in the project),
* the experience and qualification of the project team (do those involved in the project already have the necessary expertise and have they already worked on similar projects),
* the constraints on the project (for example the availability of material and tools, fixed deadlines),
* the development methodology to be employed.

The *objective of planning* is to determine deadlines, costs, personnel deployment and measures for quality assurance. For this it is necessary to subdivide software projects so that the individual tasks are largely independent and so that they can be accomplished with economically justifiable expenditures of time and technical resources by the smallest teams possible. The basis for the subdivision of the project is the model of the software life cycle given in chapter 5.

Accordingly, the results of planning consist of:

* an organization and personnel deployment plan,
* a time line for the individual phases of the software development process,
* a cost plan,
* a documentation plan,
* a test plan and a plan of quality control measures of all intermediate products and of the final product.

Measures for test and documentation planning are described in chapter 5. Measures for cost estimation (for deadline and cost planning) and for organization planning are described later in this chapter.

8.1.2 Organization

Software products are distinguished from other technical products in that they are products of the mind, and their design cannot be as clearly separated from their manufacture as is the case for other technical products. For this reason, traditional forms of organization cannot be applied without hesitation to the development of software products. Thus there are no unified organizational models for software development. Despite this, a few basic organizational tasks can be delineated.

The most important organizational tasks of project management consist of:

* the distribution of the phases (or parts of phases) of the software development process over teams or individuals,
* the formation of teams (members, type of organization and leadership),
* the exact determination of the tasks, rights and duties of all people involved in the project,
* the determination of project standards, the methods to be employed (for example the principle of stepwise refinement, data encapsulation, etc.) and the measures for providing software tools,
* the regulation of communication (arranging conferences, guidelines for documentation, etc.),
* the provision of material (computers, office material, money and work space).

Besides the classical hierarchical organizational model, known from other technical projects--which as we mentioned earlier is only conditionally suitable for software development--there are, today, a few successful approaches to organizational models which positively influence the productivity and security of software development. The most well known is presented by *Baker* and *Mills* (1979). These models are discussed more thoroughly in section 8.4.

8.1.3 Technical Supervision

The most careful and intense planning is virtually worthless if the observance of the objectives prescribed in the project schedule are not continually supervised. The task of *technical supervision* is to check the technical properties of the intermediate products which arise in the individual phases *quantitatively* and *qualitatively*.

Quantitative supervision relates to the checking of the time dependent observance of the development goals laid down in the schedule. *Qualitative supervision* checks whether an intermediate product satisfies the functions and quality requirements given in the specification.

Technical supervision not only includes the verification of plan goals, but also the triggering of corrective measures if a plan goal is not achieved.

8.1.4 Economic Supervision

Economic supervision also has a *quantitative* and a *qualitative* aspect. *Quantitative supervision* must test whether the cost and time limits have been exceeded. *Qualitative supervision* should determine whether the intermediate products meet the conditions of the contract.

Cost control is only possible if the associated cost accounting is carried out. The project management must therefore take care that the incurred costs are continually recorded and documented.

Schnupp and *Floyd* (1976) note that "experience shows that the economic supervision of a software project is obviously the more difficult of the two tasks. Whereas, as a rule it is possible to complete a planned program sometime with satisfactory quality and to deploy it, the original time and cost estimates are only seldom even approximately realized."

This statement expresses the fact that *deadline* and *cost estimates* for software products are extremely *difficult* tasks. It is therefore appropriate to make a few statements concerning the fundamental difficulties of software management and the problems and prospects of cost estimation before turning to the organizational models.

8.2 Difficulties in Managing Software Projects

The fundamental difficulties in the management of software projects are:

* *The Uniqueness of Software Systems*
  Software systems are, as a rule, only developed once. The number of empirical values from previous projects is therefore too limited to make reliable cost estimates. The cost estimates are usually based on estimations, made by an experienced software engineer, of the scope (that is the number of instructions) of the software system to be developed. It is clear that this is a very unreliable foundation for computation.

* *The High Number of Possible Solutions*
  It has already been indicated in chapter 5 that there is an almost unlimited number of ways of solving a particular task. The development of software products is not subject to those limits which are given for other technical products (for example norms and material standards). The limits are primarily given by complexity and are difficult to establish in advance.

* *The Individuality of the Programmer*
  Even with the present level of software engineering it is still true that software development is more of an art than a science. Software engineers are individualists with large differences in productivity. Therefore it is especially difficult to estimate the effective personnel requirements. To make matters worse, individualists do not usually like to be forced into an organizational corset.

* *Rapid Technological Developments*
The rapid technological development of hardware, and recently that of software tools, impedes not only the planning but also the organization of software projects. It is not a rare occurence that, during the development of large software systems, new and more efficient hardware components (for example graphic screens or locators) enter the market making the system under development seem already out dated during the design. This can instigate design changes causing the schedule to be scrapped in the process. Quite often new software tools are deployed whose usefulnes is just as difficult to estimate.

* *The Immaterial Aspect of Software Products*
The intangibility of software products impedes supervision. It is possible to determine how much of a software product is actually finished only with difficulty, and the programmer has many opportunities to conceal the actual level of development. The task of supervising software projects is immeasurably more difficult than for other technical projects.

8.3 Cost Estimates

The necessity for cost estimations results from the requirements of deadline and cost planning. Cost estimations in the realm of software development are almost always based on a comparison of the project with earlier projects because of a lack of exact methods. The problem here is that, due to the uniqueness of software systems, the number of comparable projects is usually small, and, in addition, that quantitatively reliable empirical values are seldom available. But even if exact cost estimations are available for comparable projects, they are based on the technical and organizational conditions under which the comparison standard was developed. The technical and organizational conditions are parameters which may vary only within bounds, and this once again results in the empirical values of comparison standards being extremely unreliable foundations for estimation.

Because no universal standards are available, the factors involved in estimation must be carefully considered. The most important factors for cost and time estimations (compare also *Gewald* et al., 1977) are:

* the experience and qualification of the estimator,
* the type of software (for example algorithm oriented or input/output oriented, real time software with high efficiency requirements, control and surveillance software with high quality requirements),
* the expected complexity (for example the number of modules, the number of module interactions, the number of functions per module, the complexity of the functions),
* the expected programming volume (number of instructions),
* the experience and qualifications of the personnel (for example project experience, programming experience, knowledge of methods, experience in the use of tools, understanding of the problem),
* the methods and tools to be utilized (for example planning, design, documentation and test methods and tools, programming language),

* the size of the team.

The description of these factors indicates how difficult it is to quantify them. The person doing the estimation usually first estimates the volume, that is the number of program statements, of the software system to be implemented. For the cost estimation, the result of the volume estimation is then multiplied by the empirical value for the cost of one program statement, and for the time estimation the estimated volume is divided by an empirical value for the programming efficiency of a programmer in some unit of time (e.g. month, year).

These estimations are unreliable for a number of reasons:

* The estimation of the number of program statements is extremely difficult, requires much experience on the part of the estimator and in most cases is very wide of the mark.
* The strong variation in the productivity of the programmers has the result that the value for the average productivity can be only very imprecise. A study by *Sackmann* et al. (1968), which may also be found in *Schnupp* and *Floyd* (1976), revealed the following relations between the best and worst programmer production rate (for the same task):

```
program volume                        5 : 1
coding time                          25 : 1
required test time                   26 : 1
development CPU time                 11 : 1
run time of the completed program    13 : 1
```

One very important, and often little noticed, factor in cost estimation is the number of programmers deployed. *Brooks* (1975) mentions that the time required for each task accomplished in a team consists of two factors (see also *Schnupp* and *Floyd,* 1976):

(1) productive work and
(2) the communication between team members and their mutual co-ordination.

If no communication were necessary between the team members, the time required t for a project with n programmers would decline as: $t \sim 1/n$. But if one assumes that each member must exchange information with each other member and that the average time expended for the communicaton is k, then the result for the development time is a law of the form:

$$t \sim 1/n + k(n!/2!(n-2)!) \sim 1/n + n^2/2$$

The consequence of *Brooks Law* is, as Brooks puts it himself: "adding manpower to a late software project makes it later."

The majority of empirical values for cost estimations are kept secret by companies and are not published. Only a few results on empirical values are to be found in the literature, and they often vary considerably. Some of these values together with some of the author's own are given below.

Kopetz (1979) describes the distribution of the costs over the individual phases of a software project as shown in illustration 8.1.

Activity	Contractor			Average %
	Informatics %	Raytheon %	TRW [*] %	
Analysis	20	20	20	20
Design	16	20	20	18.7
Coding	16	25	24	21.7
Testing	32	25	28	28.3
Documentation	16	10	8	11.3
Composition:				
Mathematical	(60)	(0)	(100)	(53.3)
Commercial	(40)	(100)	(0)	(46.7)

[*] Strong Variation from Project to Project

Illustration 8.1 Distribution of the Costs Over the Individual Phases Software Development (Source *Kopetz*, 1979)

Gewald et al. (1977) detail the empirical values given in illustration 8.2 for cost distributions.

Software Type	Design * %	Coding * %	Test * %
System Software	30	20	50
System Software	33	17	50
"Command and Control Systems	46	20	30
Scientific Data Processing	44	26	30
Commercial Data Processing	55	10	35
SAGE Project	39	14	47
NTDS Project	30	20	50
Gemni Project	36	17	47
Saturn V Project	32	24	44
Average **	38.9	19.6	41.5

* The costs for documenting and administrating the functions is included proportionally.

** The so called "40-20-40 Rule" for cost destribution often used in the past.

Sources: *Aron* (1977), *Boehm* (1973), *Brooks* (1975), *Wolverton* (1974) and *Gewald* et al. (1977).

Illustration 8.2 Cost Distributions for Design, Coding and Testing (Source *Gewald* et al., 1977)

Brooks (1975) gives another cost distribution:

```
Planning and Design              35%
Coding                           15%
Component and first System Test  25%
System Test with all Components  25%
```

The author found the following distribution of time expenditures for the individual phases of software development (the documentation effort is included proportionately):

```
Requirements Analysis and
Requirements Definition   25%
Design                    25%
Implementation            15%
Test                      35%
```

Illustration 8.3 shows the results of *Schnupp* and *Floyd* (1976) concerning productivity figures for program development dependent on the type of software.

PROJECT		Total Costs in LOC [*]	Development Time in Months	Total Costs in MM [**]	Productivity in LOC/MM
Applications	Average of 174 Applications Program Designs	17,882 (various prog. lang.)	10	75	2,600
	New York Times Information Retrieval System	83,000 (PL/I)	22	132	6,900
	350 Applications Programs for a Real Time System	150,000 (Assembler)	unknown	738	2,240
Systems Programming	Control Program of a Real Time System	77,000 (Assembler)	unknown	595	1,140
	File Catalog System	7,000 (Assembler)	6	25	3,100
	SPOOL System	24,000 (Assembler)	9	70	3,800
	Data Base Compiler	7,000 (Assembler)	4	9	8,600
	Operating System	26,000 (Assembler)	24	115	2,530

[*] "Lines of Code"
[**] Man Months

Sources: *Martin* (unpublished), *Schnupp* and *Floyd* (1976) and *Weinwurm* (1970).

Illustration 8.3 Productivity Figures for Program Development

Empirical values for the time costs per instruction, dependent on the level of difficulty of a software project are given in *Metzelaar* (1971) and *Kopetz* (1979) (see illustration 8.4), and values for the cost per instruction dependent on the type of program are given in *Wolverton* (1974) (see illustration 8.5).

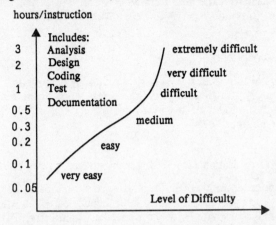

Illustration 8.4 Time Costs per Object Instruction as a Function of the Level of Difficulty (Sources *Metzelaar*, 1971 and *Kopetz*, 1979)

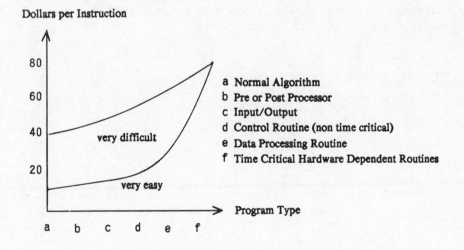

Illustration 8.5 Cost per Dollar per Instruction (Source *Wolverton*, 1974)

Clearly the empirical values given above can only be used as rough guidelines. They change continually as a result of technological changes--new programming languages, new methods and tools facilitate the production of software and alter the empirical values for cost estimation--but it is to be hoped that empirical data will become increasingly exact and reliable. An overview of the procedures used in the past for cost estimation can be found in *Schmith* (1975).

8.4 Project Organization

In the first part of this section the classical hierarchical model of organization is described and then its drawbacks for software development are discussed. In the second part another model of organization, the so called "chief programmer team" is examined in more detail.

8.4.1 Hierarchical Organization Model

There are a number of ways of organizing the members of a project. The organization of software projects has long been geared to the hierarchical organization that is common in other branches of industry. To this end, the division of software development into individual phases is granted special importance. A supervisor who is responsible for each phase is employed. He is supervised by the project manager, and in turn supervises either individuals or group leaders, depending on the size of the project. The project manager is generally provided with a project staff with advisory and administrative capacities. The larger the project, the larger the number of hierarchy levels in the organizational scheme. Illustration 8.6 provides an example of this (compare also *Metzger*, 1973, *Kimm* et al., 1979 and *Gewald* et al., 1977).

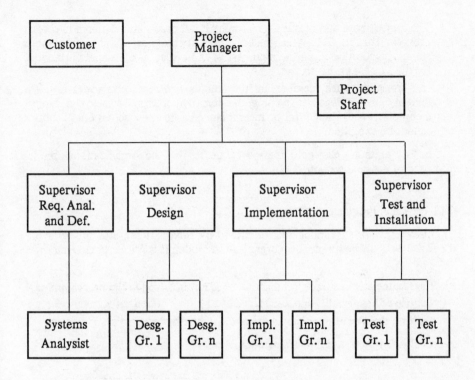

Illustration 8.6 Organigram for a Software Project

The *project manager* represents the project team externally and maintains the contact with the customer. His task is to select, deploy and supervise the personnel. In general he has complete powers of supervision over all members of the team and is responsible for the division of tasks in the project, the project progress control and for undertaking appropriate measures if costs are overrun or deadlines are not met.

The *project staff* includes members who advise the project manager in technical matters, who support him in the administrative tasks of project progress control, who undertake the preparation of project standards, who are responsible for the availability of operating material and who, if necessary, arrange schooling for the project members.

The *supervisors at the "middle level of management"* are responsible for the planning, execution and control of the phase related activities of the software life cycle (see chapter 5).

This form of organization exhibits some grave weaknesses:

* The project manager is too far removed from the actual programming and therefore can only perccive his planning and control tasks in a limited fashion.

* The many tiered organizational hierarchy hinders communication and project progress control. But it is precisely in software projects that frictionless communication between the members of the project is of crucial importance for the success of the project.

* In a hierarchy each member has the tendency to rise to his lowest level of inability, which leads to passing the buck on a grand scale. The project members rise to their level of incompetence, and their actual qualifications cannot be exploited.

One attempts to eliminate these weaknesses by the organizational model discussed in the next section.

8.4.2 The Chief Programmer Team

This organizational model, first described by *Baker* (1972), attempts to avoid the drawbacks of the hierarchical organization model. It is primarily characterized by:

* the renunciation of a project leader who is not involved in the programming,
* the use of high quality specialists,
* limiting the size of the team (maximum 10 members).

The chief programmer team is composed of

* the chief programmer,
* the project assistant,
* the project secretary,
* the specialists (language specialists, programmers, test specialists).

The *chief programmer* plans and designs the software system completely and implements the most important parts himself. He supervises the project progress, decides on all important questions and is responsible for everything. The professional requirements on the chief programmer are extremely high and there are surely only a few software engineers who actually satisfy these requirements.

The *project assistant* is the closest technical co-worker of the chief programmer. His task is to assist the chief programmer in all important activities, to support him on the one hand, and to replace him in his absence on the other. His professional qualifications should therefore be just as high as those of the chief programmer.

The *project secretary* has the task of relieving the chief programmer and also all other programmers of administrative tasks. He manages all programs and documents and is also drawn into the project progress control. He stands between the computer and the programmers. His main task is the administration of the project library.

The number of *specialists* is determined by the chief programmer as needed. They are called upon for the choice of implementation language, for the implementation of the individual system components (in as much as they are not implemented by the chief programmer himself), for the selection and deployment of software tools and for the conducting of the tests.

The chief programmer team and the role of the project secretary are shown in illustrations 8.7 and 8.8 (source *Schnupp* and *Floyd*, 1976).

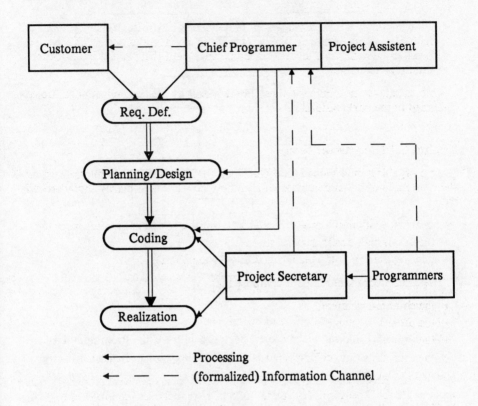

Ilustration 8.7 Chief Programmer Project Organization
(Source *Baker* and *Mills*, 1979)

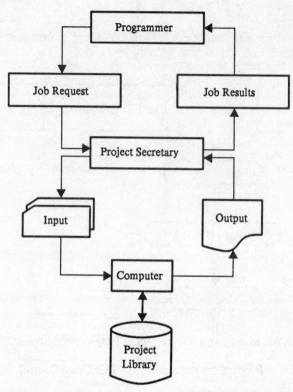

Illustration 8.8 The Role of the Project Secretary in the Chief Programmer Team

The advantages of this form of organization are:

* The chief programmer is directly involved in the programming and can therefore better perceive his control function .
* The communication difficulties which occur in the hierarchical organization are avoided.
* The communication channels concerning the project progress are much simpler.
* Smaller teams are as a rule more productive than large teams.

The disadvantages of this form of organization are:

* It is limited to small teams. Not every project can be realized with less than 10 members.
* The personnel requirements are practically impossible to satisfy. There are few software engineers who have the qualifications for a chief programmer or a project assistant.
* The project secretary has an extremely difficult and responsible task, but his job mostly consists of routine work: he therefore has a subordinate position. This has serious psychological drawbacks.

* Because of his central position the project secretary can easily become a bottleneck.
* The organizational model sees no replacement for the project secretary. However, if the project secretary is absent for some reason, the further course of the project can be seriously jeopardized.

Regardless of the disadvantages of the chief programmer organization model, experience shows that small teams consisting of experienced software engineers are much more productive, reliable and on time than large "software factories" (compare also *Gewald* et al., 1977).

Further Reading

Brooks, F.P.: The Mythical Man-Month. Essays on Software Engineering; Addison Wesley 1975.

Baker, F.T., Mills, H.D.: Chief Programmer Teams; In: Classics in Software Engineering; Yourdon Press 1979.

Metzger, P.W.: Managing a Programming Project; Prentice-Hall 1981.

Putman, L.: Software Cost Estimation and Life Cycle Control. IEEE Computer Society, 1980.

Reifer, D.T.: Tutorial: Software Management. IEEE Computer Society, 1979.

Riggs, J.: Production Systems Planning, Analysis and Control. Wiley, 1981.

Appendix 1

Report on The Programming Language Modula-2*

*Reprinted with permission from Springer Verlag from:
Wirth, N.: Programming in Modula-2, 2nd corrected Edition 1983, Text and
Monographs in Computer Science.
©Springer Verlag Berlin, Heidelberg, New York, Tokyo

1. Introduction

Modula-2 grew out of a practical need for a general, efficiently implementable system programming language for minicomputers. Its ancestors are *Pascal* and *Modula*. From the latter it has inherited the name, the important module concept, and a systematic, modern syntax, from Pascal most of the rest. This includes in particular the data structures, i.e. arrays, records, variant records, sets, and pointers. Structured statements include the familiar if, case, repeat, while, for, and with statements. Their syntax is such that every structure ends with an explicit termination symbol.

The language is essentially machine-independent, with the exception of limitations due to wordsize. This appears to be in contradiction to the notion of a system-programming language, in which it must be possible to express all operations inherent in the underlying computer. The dilemma is resolved with the aid of the *module* concept. Machine-dependent items can be introduced in specific modules, and their use can thereby effectively be confined and isolated. In particular, the language provides the possiblity to relax rules about data type compatibility in these cases. In a capable system-programming language it is possible to express input/output conversion procedures, file handling routines, storage allocators, process schedulers etc. Such facilities must therefore not be included as elements of the language itself, but appear as (so-called low-level) modules which are components of most programs written. Such a collection of standard modules is therefore an essential part of a Modula-2 implementation.

The concept of processes and their synchronization with signals as included in Modula is replaced by the lower-level notion of *coroutines* in Modula-2. It is, however, possible to formulate a (standard) module that implements such processes and signals. The advantage of not including them in the language itself is that the programmer may select a process scheduling algorithm tailored to his particular needs by programming that module on his own. Such a schedulaer can even be entirely omitted in simple (but frequent) cases, e.g. when concurrent processes occur as device drivers only.

A modern system programming language should in particular also facilitate the construction of large programs, possibly designed by several people. The modules written by individuals should have well-specified interfaces that can be declared independently of their actual implementations. Modula-2 supports this idea by providing separete *definition* and *implementation modules*. The former define all objects exported from the corresponding implementation module; in some cases, such as procedures and types, the definition module specifies only those parts that are relevant to the interface, i.e. to the user or client of the module.

This report is not intended as a programmer's tutorial. It is intentionally kept concise, and (we hope) clear. Its function is to serve as a reference for programmers, implementors, and manual writers, and as an arbiter, should they find disagreement.

2. Syntax

A language is an infinite set of sentences, namely the sentences well formed according to its syntax. In Modula-2, these sentences are called *compilation units*. Each unit is a finite sequence of symbols from a finite *vocabulary*. The vocabulary of Modula-2 consists of identifiers, numbers, strings, operators, and delimiters. They are called *lexical symbols* and are composed of sequences of characters. (Note the distinction between symbols and characters.)

To describe the syntax, an extended Backus-Naur Formalism called EBNF is used. Angular brackets [] denote optionality of the enclosed sentential form, and curly brackets {} denote its repetition (possibly 0 times). Syntactic entities (non-terminal symbols) are denoted by English words expressing their intuitive meaning. Symbols of the language vocabulary (terminal symbols) are strings enclosed in quote marks or words written in capital letters, so-called *reserverd words*. Syntactic rules (productions) are designated by a ß sign at the left margin of the line.

3. Vocabulary and representation

The representation of symbols in terms of characters depends on the underlying character set. The ASCII set is used in this paper, and the following lexical rules must be observed. Blanks must not occur within symbols (except in strings). Blanks and line breaks are ignored unless they are essential to separate two consecutive symbols.

1. *Identifiers* are sequences of letters and digits. The first character must be a letter.

   $ ident = letter {letter | digit}.

   Examples:

   x   scan   Modula   ETH   GetSymbol   firstLetter

2. *Numbers* are (unsigned) integers or real numbers. Integers are sequences of digits. If the number is followed by the letter B, it is taken as an octal number; if it is followed by the letter H, it is taken as a hexadecimal number; if it is followed by the letter C, it denotes the character with the given (octal) ordinal number (and is of type CHAR, see 6.1).

   An integer i in the range $0 <= i <= MaxInt$ can be considered as either of type INTEGER or CARDINAL; if it is in the range $MaxInt < i <= MaxCard$, it is of type CARDINAL. For 16-bit computers: MaxInt = 32767, MaxCard = 65535.

   A real number always contains a decimal point. Optionally it may also contain a decimal scale factor. The letter E is pronounced as "ten to the power of". A real number is of type REAL.

   $ number = integer | real.
   $ integer = digit {digit} | octalDigit {octalDigit}
   $ ("B" | "C") | digit {hexDigit} "H".
   $ real = digit {digit} "." {digit} [ScaleFactor].

```
$  ScaleFactor = "E" ["+" | "-"] digit {digit}.
$  hexDigit = digit | "A" | "B" | "C" | "D" | "E" | "F".
$  digit = octalDigit | "8" | "9".
$  octalDigit = "0" | "1" | "2" | "3" | "4" | "5"
$        | "6" | "7".
```

Examples:

```
1980    3768B    7BCH    33C    12.3    45.67E-8
```

3. *Strings* are sequences of characters enclosed in quote marks. Both double quotes and single quotes (apostrophes) may be used as quote marks. However, the opening and closing marks must be the same character, and this character cannot occur within the string. A string must not extend over the end of a line.

```
$  string = "'" {character} "'" | '"' {character} '"'.
```

A single-character string is of type CHAR, a string consisting of n>1 characters is of type (see 6.4)

```
ARRAY[0..n-1] OF CHAR
```

Examples:

```
"MODULA"    "Don't worry!"    'codeword "Barbarossa"'
```

4. *Operators* and *delimiters* are special characters, character pairs, or reserved words listed below. These reserved words consist exclusively of capital letters and MUST NOT be used in the role of identifiers. The symbols # and <> are synonyms, and so are & and AND.

+	=	AND	FOR	QUALIFIED
–	#	ARRAY	FROM	RECORD
*	<	BEGIN	IF	REPEAT
/	>	BY	IMPLEMENTATION	RETURN
:=	<>	CASE	IMPORT	SET
&	<=	CONST	IN	THEN
.	>=	DEFINITION	LOOP	TO
,	..	DIV	MOD	TYPE
;	:	DO	MODULE	UNTIL
(	)	ELSE	NOT	VAR
[	]	ELSIF	OF	WHILE
{	}	END	OR	WITH
↑			EXIT	POINTER	
		EXPORT	PROCEDURE	

5. *Comments* may be inserted between any two symbols in a program. They are arbitrary character sequences opened by the brackes (* and closed by *). Comments may be nested, and they do not affect the meaning of a program.

4. Declarations and scope rules

Every identifier occurring in a program must be introduced by a declaration, unless it is a standard identifier. The latter are considered to be predeclared, and they are valid in all parts of a program. For this reason they are called *pervasive*. Declarations also serve to specify certain permanent properties of an object, such as whether it is a constant, a type, a variable, a procedure, or a module.

The identifier is then used to refer to the associated object. This is possible in those parts of a program only which are within the so-called *scope* of the declaration. In general, the scope extends over the entire block (prodecure or module declaration) to which the object is local. The scope rule is augmented by the following cases:

1. If an identifier x defined by a declaration D1 is used in another declaration (not statement) D2, then D1 must textually precede D2.

2. A type T1 can be used in a declaration of a pointer type T (see 6.7) which textually precedes the declaration of T1, if both T and T1 are declared in the same block. This is a relaxation of rule 1.

3. If an identifier defined in a module M1 is exported, the scope expands over the block which contains M1. If M1 is a compilation unit (see Ch.14), it extends to all those units which import M1.

4. Field identifiers of a record declaration (see 6.5) are valid only in field designators and in with statements referring to a variable of that record type.

An identifier may be *qualified*. In this case it is prefixed by another identifier which designates the module (see Ch.11) in which the qualified identifier is defined. The prefix and the identifier are separated by a period.

```
$  qualident = ident {"." ident}.
```

The following are standard identifiers:

ABS	(10.2)	HIGH	(10.2)
BITSET	(6.6)	INC	(10.2)
BOOLEAN	(6.1)	INCL	(10.2)
CAP	(10.2)	INTEGER	(6.1)
CARDINAL	(6.1)	NEW	(10.2)
CHAR	(6.1)	NIL	(6.7)
CHR	(10.2)	ODD	(10.2)
DEC	(10.2)	ORD	(10.2)
DISPOSE	(10.2)	PROC	(6.8)
EXCL	(10.2)	REAL	(6.1)
FALSE	(6.1)	TRUE	(6.1)
FLOAT	(10.2)	TRUNC	(10.2)
HALT	(10.2)	VAL	(10.2)

5. Constant declarations

A constant declaration associates an identifier with a constant value.

```
$   ConstantDeclaration = ident "=" ConstExpression.
$   ConstExpression = SimpleConstExpr
$        [relation SimpleConstExpr].
$   relation = "=" | "#" | "<>" | "<" | "<=" | ">"
$        | ">=" | IN.
$   SimpleConstExpr = ["+" | "-"] ConstTerm
$        {AddOperator ConstTerm}.
$   AddOperator = "+" | "-" | OR.
$   ConstTerm = ConstFactor {MulOperator ConstFactor}.
$   MulOperator = "*" | "/" | DIV | MOD | AND | "&".
$   ConstFactor = qualident | number | string | set
$        | "(" ConstExpression ")" | NOT ConstFactor.
$   set = [qualident ] "{" [element {"," element}] "}".
$   element = ConstExpression [".." ConstExpression].
```

The meaning of operators is explained in Chapter 8. The identifier preceding the left brace of a set specifies the type of the set. If it is omitted, the standard type BITSET is assumed (see 6.6).

Examples of constant declarations are

```
N=100
limit=2*N-1
all={0..WordSize-1}
```

6. Type declarations

A data type determines a set of values which variables of that type may assume, and it associates an identifier with the type. In the case of structured types, it also defines the structure of variables of this type. There are three different structures, namely arrays, records, and sets.

```
$   TypeDeclaration = ident "=" type.
$   type = SimpleType | ArrayType | RecordType | SetType |
$        PointerType | ProcedureType.
$   SimpleType = qualident | enumeration | SubrangeType.
```

Examples:

```
Color = (red,green,blue)
Index = [1..80]
Card = ARRAY Index OF CHAR
Node = RECORD key: CARDINAL;
            left,right: TreePtr
       END
```

```
Tint = SET OF Color
TreePtr = POINTER TO Node
Function = PROCEDURE(CARDINAL):CARDINAL
```

6.1. Basic types

The following basic types are predeclared and denoted by standard identifiers:

1. A variable of type INTEGER assumes as values the integers between *MinInt* and *MaxInt*.

2. A variable of type CARDINAL assumes as values the integers between *0* and *MaxCard.*

3. A variable of type BOOLEAN assumes the truth values TRUE or FALSE. These are the only values of this type.

4. A variable of type CHAR assumes as elements values of the character set provided by the used computer system.

5. A variable of type REAL assumes as values real numbers.

For implementations on 16-bit computers, MinInt = -32768, MaxInt = 32767, and MaxCard = 65535.

6.2. Enumerations

An enumeration is a list of identifiers that denote the values which constitute a data type. These identifiers are used as constants in the program. They, and no other values, belong to this type. The values are ordered, and the ordering relation is defined by their sequence in the enumeration. The ordinal number of the first value is 0.

```
$   enumeration = "(" IdentList ")".
$   IdentList = ident {"," ident}.
```

Examples of enumerations:

```
(red,green,blue)
(club,diamond,heart,spade)
(Monday,Tuesday,Wednesday,Thursday,Friday,Saturday,Sunday)
```

6.3. Subrange types

A type T may be defined as a subrange of another, basic or enumeration type T1 (except REAL) by specification of the least and the highest value in the subrange.

```
$   SubrangeType = "["ConstExpression ".." ConstExpression"]".
```

The first constant specifies the lower bound, and must not be greater than the upper bound. The type T1 of the bounds is called the *base type* of T, and all operators applicable to operands of type T1 are also applicable to operands of type T. However, a value to be assigned to a variable of a subrange type must lie within the specified interval. If the lower bound is a non-negative integer, the base type of the subrange is taken to be CARDINAL; if it is a negative integer, it is INTEGER.

A type T1 is said to be *compatible* with a type T0, if it is declared either as T1 = T0 or as a subrange of T0, or if T0 is a subrange of T1, or if T0 and T1 are both subranges of the same (base) type.

Examples of subrange types:

```
[0..N-1]
["A".."Z"]
[Monday..Friday]
```

6.4. Array types

An array is a structure consisting of a fixed number of components which are all of the same type, called the *component type*. The elements of the array are designated by indices, values belonging to the *index type*. The array type declaration specifies the component type as well as the index type. The latter must be an enumeration, a subrange type, or one of the basic types BOOLEAN or CHAR.

$ ArrayType = ARRAY SimpleType {"," SimpleType} OF type.

A declaration of the form

```
ARRAY T1,T2,...,Tn OF T
```

with n index types T1..Tn must be understood as an abbreviation for the declaration

```
ARRAY T1 OF
    ARRAY T2 OF
        ...
        ARRAY Tn OF T
```

Examples of array types:

```
ARRAY[0..N-1] OF CARDINAL
ARRAY[1..10],[1..20] OF [0..99]
ARRAY[-10..+10] OF BOOLEAN
ARRAY WeekDay OF Color
ARRAY Color OF WeekDay
```

6.5. Record types

A record type is a structure consisting of a fixed number of components of possibly different types. The record type declaration specifies for each component, called field, its type and an identifier which denotes the *field*. The scope of these field identifiers is the record definition itself, and they are also accessible within field designators (see 8.1) refering to components of record variables, and within with statements.

A record type may have several variant sections, in which case the first field of the section is called the *tag field*. Its value indicates which variant is assumed by the section. Individual variant structures are identified by *case labels*. These labels are constants of the type indicated by the tag field.

```
$   RecordType = RECORD FieldListSequence END.
$   FieldListSequence = FieldList {";" FieldList}.
$   FieldList = [IdentList ":" type
$       | CASE [ident ":"] qualident OF variant
$       {"|" variant} [ELSE FieldListSequence] END].
$   variant = CaseLabelList ":" FieldListSequence.
$   CaseLabelList = CaseLabels {"," CaseLabels}.
$   CaseLabels = ConstExpression [".." ConstExpression].
```

Examples of record types:

```
RECORD
      day: [1..31];
      month: [1..12];
      year: [0..2000]
END

RECORD
      name,firstname: ARRAY[0..9] OF CHAR;
      age: [0..99];
      salary: REAL
END

RECORD
      x,y: T0;
      CASE tag0: Color OF
          red: a: Tr1; b: Tr2 |
          green: c: Tg1; d: Tg2 |
          blue: e: Tb1; f: Tb2
      END;
      z: T0;
      CASE tag1: BOOLEAN OF
          TRUE: u,v: INTEGER |
          FALSE: r,s: CARDINAL
      END
END
```

The example above contains two variant sections. The variant of the first section is indicated by the value of the tag field tag0, the one of the second section by the tag field tag1.

6.6. Set types

A set type defined as SET OF T comprises all sets of values of its base type T. This must be a subrange of the integers between 0 and N-1, or a (subrange of an) enumeration type with at most N values, where N is a small constant determined by the implementation, usually the computer's wordsize or a small multiple thereof.

```
$  SetType = SET OF SimpleType.
```

The standard type BITSET is defined as follows, where W is a constant defined by the implementation, usually the wordsize of the computer.

```
BITSET = SET OF [0..W-1]
```

6.7. Pointer types

Variables of a pointer type P assume as values pointers to variables of another type T. The pointer type P is said to be *bound* to T. A pointer value is generated by a call to the standard procedure NEW (see 10.2).

```
$  PointerType = POINTER TO type.
```

Besides such pointer values, a pointer variable may assume the value NIL, which can be thought as pointing to no variable at all.

6.8. Procedure types

Variables of a procedure type T may assume as their value a procedure P. The (types of the) formal parameters of P must be the same as those indicated in the formal type list of T. The same holds for the result type in the case of a function procedure.

Restriction: P must not be declared local to another procedure, and neither can it be a standard procedure.

```
$  ProcedureType = PROCEDURE [FormalTypeList].
$  FormalTypeList = "(" [[VAR] FormalType
$       {"," [VAR] FormalType}] ")" [":" qualident].
```

The standard type PROC denotes a parameterless procedure:

```
PROC = PROCEDURE
```

7. Variable declarations

Variable declarations serve to introduce variables and associate them with a unique identifier and a fixed data type and structure. Variables whose identifiers appear in the same list all obtain the same type.

```
$   VariableDeclaration = IdentList ":" type.
```

The data type determines the set of values that a variable may assume and the operators that are applicable; it also defines the structure of the variable.

Examples of variable declarations (refer to examples in Ch.6):

```
i.j: CARDINAL
k:   INTEGER
p,q: BOOLEAN
s:   BITSET
F:   Function
a:   ARRAY Index OF CARDINAL
w:   ARRAY[0..7] OF
         RECORD   ch: CHAR;
                  count: CARDINAL
         END
t:   TreePtr
```

8. Expressions

Expressions are constructs denoting rules of computation for obtaining values of variables and generating new values by the application of operators. Expressions consist of operands and operators. Parantheses may be used to express specific associations of operators and operands.

8.1. Operands

With the exception of literal constants, i.e. numbers, character strings, and sets (see Ch.5), operands are denoted by *designators*. A designator consists of an identifier referring to the constant, variable, or procedure to be designated. This identifier may possibly be qualified by module identifiers (see Ch.4 and 11), and it may be followed by selectors, if the designated object is an element of a structure. If the structure is an array A, then the designator A[E] denotes that component of A whose index is the current value of the expression E. The index type of A must be *assignment compatible* with the type of E (see 9.1). A designator of the form

```
A[E1,E2,...,En]    stands for    A[E1][E2]...[En].
```

If the structure is a record R, then the designator R.f denotes the record field f of R. The designator P↑ denotes the variable which is referenced by the pointer P.

```
$   designator = qualident {"." ident | "[" ExpList "]" |
$      "↑"}.
$   ExpList = expression {"," expression}.
```

If the designated object is a variable, then the designator refers to the variable's current value. If the object is a function procedure, a designator without parameter list refers to that procedure. If it is followed by a (possibly empty) parameter list, the designator implies an activation of the procedure and stands for the value resulting from its execution, i.e. for the "returned" value. The (types of these) actual parameters must correspond to the formal parameters as specified in the procedure's declarations (see Ch.10).

Examples of designators (see examples in Ch.7):

```
k              (INTEGER)
a[i]           (CARDINAL)
w[3].ch        (CHAR)
t↑.key         (CARDINAL)
t↑.left↑.right(TreePtr)
```

8.2. Operators

The syntax of expressions specifies operator precedences according to four classes of operators. The operator NOT has the highest precedence, followed by the so-called multiplying operators, then the so-called adding operators, and finally, with the lowest preecedence, the relational operators. Sequences of operators of the same procedence are executed from left to right.

```
$   expression = SimpleExpression [relation SimpleExpression].
$   SimpleExpression = ["+" | "-"] term {AddOperator term}.
$   term = factor {MulOperator factor}.
$   factor = number | string | set | designator
$       [ActualParameters] | "(" expression ")" | NOT factor.
$   ActualParameters = "(" [ExpList] ")".
```

The available operators are listed in the following tables. In some instances, several different operations are designated by the same operator symbol. In these cases, the actual operation is identified by the types of the operands.

8.2.1. Arithmetic operators

```
symbol          operation
-----------------------------------
  +             addition
  -             subtraction
  *             multiplication
  /             real division
  DIV           integer division
  MOD           modulus
```

These operators (except /) apply to operands of type INTEGER, CARDINAL, or subranges thereof. Both operands must be either of type CARDINAL or a subrange with base type CARDINAL, in which case the result is of type CARDINAL, or they must both be of type INTEGER or a subrange with base type INTEGER, in which case the result is of type INTEGER.

The operators +, -, and * also apply to operands of type REAL. In this case, both operands must be of type REAL, and the result is then also of type REAL. The divison operator / applies to REAL operands only. When used as operators with a single operand only, - denotes sign inversion and + denotes the identity operation. Sign inversion applies to operands of type INTEGER or REAL. The operations DIV and MOD are defined by the following rules:

x DIV y is equal to the truncated quotient of x/y
x MOD y is equal to the remainder of the division x DIV y (for y>0)
x = (x DIV y)*y + (x MOD y)

8.2.2. Logical operators

```
symbol          operation
---------------------------------
OR        logical conjunction
AND       logical disjunction
NOT       negation
```

These operators apply to BOOLEAN operands and yield a BOOLEAN result.

p OR q   means "if p then TRUE, otherwise q"
p AND q   means "if p then q, otherwise FALSE"

8.2.3. Set operators

```
symbol          operation
-------------------------------------
+        set union
-        set difference
*        set intersection
/        symmetric set difference
```

These operations apply to operands of any set type and yield a result of the same type.

```
x IN (s1 + s2)    iff    (x IN s1) OR (x IN s2)
x IN (s1 - s2)    iff    (x IN s1) AND NOT (x IN s2)
x IN (s1 * S2)    iff    (x IN s1) AND (x IN s2)
x IN (s1 / s2)    iff    (x IN s1) # (x IN s2)
```

8.2.4. Relations

Relations yield a BOOLEAN result. The ordering relations apply to the basic types INTEGER, CARDINAL, BOOLEAN, CHAR, REAL, to enumerations, and to subrange types.

```
symbol          relation
---------------------------------------------
  =             equal
  #             unequal
  <             less
  <=            less or equal (set inclusion)
  >             greater
  >=            greater or equal (set inclusion)
  IN            ontained in (set membership)
```

The relations = and # also apply to sets and pointers. If applied to sets, <= and >= denote (improper) inclusion. The relation IN denotes set membership. In an expression of the form x IN s, the expression s must be of type SET OF T, where T is (compatible with) the type of x.

Examples of expressions (refer to examples in Ch.7):

```
1980            (CARDINAL)
k DIV 3         (INTEGER)
NOT p OR q      (BOOLEAN)
(i+j) * (i-j)   (CARDINAL)
s - {8,9,13}    (BITSET)
a[i] + a[j]     (CARDINAL)
a[i+j] * a[i-j] (CARDINAL)
(0<=k) & (k<100)(BOOLEAN)
t↑.key = 0      (BOOLEAN)
{13..15}<=s     (BOOLEAN)
i IN {0,5..8,15}(BOOLEAN)
```

9. Statements

Statements denote actions. There are elementary and structured statements. Elementary statements are not composed of any parts that are themselves statements. They are the assignment, the procedure call, and the return and exit statements. Structured statements are composed of parts that are themselves statements. These are used to express sequencing, and conditional, selective, and repetitive execution.

```
$    statement = [assignment | ProcedureCall | IfStatement
$             | CaseStatement | WhileStatement | RepeatStatement
$             | LoopStatement | ForStatement | WithStatement
$             | EXIT | RETURN [expression]].
```

A statement may also be empty, in which case it denotes no action. The empty statement is included in order to relax punctuation rules in statement sequences.

9.1. Assignments

The assignment serves to replace the current value of a variable by a new value indicated by an expression. The assignment operator is written as ":=" and pronounced as "becomes".

    $ assignment = designator ":=" expression.

The designator to the left of the assignment operator denotes a variable. After an assignment is executed, the variable has the value obtained by evaluating the expression. The old value is lost (overwritten). The type of the variable must be *assignment compatible* with the type of the expression. Operand types are said to be assignment compatible, if either they are compatible or both are INTEGER or CARDINAL or subranges with base types INTEGER or CARDINAL.

A string of length n1 can be assigned to a string variable of length n2>n1. In this case, the string value is extended with a null character (0C).

Examples of assignments:

    i:=k
    p:=i=j
    j:=log2(i+j)
    F:=log2
    s:={2,3,5,7,11,13}
    a[i]:=(i+j)*(i-j)
    t↑.key:=i
    w[i+1].ch:="A"

9.2. Procedure calls

A procedure call serves to activate a procedure. The procedure call may contain a list of actual parameters which are substituted in place of their corresponding formal parameters defined in the procedure declaration (see Ch.10). The correspondence is established by the positions of the parameters in the lists of actual and formal parameters respectively. There exist two kinds of parameters: *variables* and *value parameters*.

In the case of variable parameters, the actual paramter must be a designator denoting a variable. If it designates a component of a structured variable, the selector is evaluated when the formal/actual parameter substitution takes place, i.e. before the execution of the procedure. If the parameter is a value parameter, the corresponding actual parameter must be an expression. This expression is evaluated prior to the procedure activation, and the resulting value is assigned to the formal parameter which now constitutes a local variable. The types of corresponding actual and formal parameters must be compatible in the case of variable parameters and assignment compatible in the case of value parameters.

    $ ProcedureCall = designator [ActualParameters].

Examples of procedure calls:

```
Read(i)      (see Ch.10)
Write(j*2+1,6)
INC(a[i])
```

9.3. Statement sequences

Statement sequences denote the sequence of actions specified by the component statements which are separated by semicolons.

```
$  StatementSequence = statement {";" statement}.
```

9.4. If statements

```
$  IfStatement = IF expression THEN StatementSequence
$       {ELSIF expression THEN StatementSequence}?
$       [ELSE StatementSequence] END.
```

The expressions following the symbols IF and ELSIF are of type BOOLEAN. They are evaluated in the sequence of their occurrence, until one yields the value TRUE. Then its associated statement sequence is executed. If an ELSE clause is present, its associated statement sequence is executed if and only if all Boolean expressions yielded the value FALSE.

Example:

```
IF (ch>="A") & (ch<="Z") THEN ReadIdentifier
ELSIF (ch>="0") & (ch<="9") THEN ReadNumber
ELSIF ch='"' THEN ReadString('"')
ELSIF ch="'" THEN ReadString("'")
ELSE SpecialCharacter
END
```

9.5. Case statements

Case statements specify the selection and execution of a statement sequence according to the value of an expression. First the case expression is evaluated, then the statement sequence is executed whose case label list contains the obtained value. The type of the case expression must be a basic type (except REAL), an enumeration type, or a subrange type, and all labels must be compataible with that type. Case labels are constants, and no value must occur more than once. If the value of the expression does not occur as a label of any case, the statement sequence following the symbol ELSE is selected.

```
$  CaseStatement = CASE expression OF case {"|" case}
$       [ELSE StatementSEquence] END.
$  case = CaseLabelList ":" StatementSequence.
```

Example:

```
CASE i OF
  0: p:=p OR q; x:=x+y |
  1: p:=p OR q; x:=x-y |
  2: p:=p AND q; x:=x*y
END
```

9.6. While statements

While statements specify the repeated execution of a statement sequence depending on the value of a Boolean expression. The expression is evaluated before each subsequent execution of the statement sequence. The repetition stops as soon as this evaluation yields the value FALSE.

```
$  WhileStatement = WHILE expression DO StatementSequence
END.
```

Examples:

```
WHILE j>0 DO
  j:=j DIV 2; i:=i+1
END

WHILE i#j DO
  IF i>j THEN i:=i-j
  ELSE j:=j-i
  END
END

WHILE (t # NIL) & (t↑.key # i) DO
  t:=t↑.left
END
```

9.7. Repeat statements

Repeat statements specify the repeated execution of a statement sequence depending on the value of a Boolean expression. The expression is evaluated after each execution of the statement sequence, and the repetition stops as soon as it yields the value TRUE. Hence, the statement sequence is executed at least once.

```
$  RepeatStatement = REPEAT StatementSequence
$        UNTIL expression.
```

Example:

```
REPEAT k:=i MOD j; i:=j; j:=k
UNTIL j=0
```

9.8. For statements

The for statement indicates that a statement sequence is to be repeatedly executed while a progression of values is assigned to a variable. This variable is called the *control variable* of the for statement. It cannot be a component of a structured variable, it cannot be imported, nor can it be a parameter. Its value should not be changed by the statement sequence.

```
$  ForStatement = FOR ident ":=" expression TO expression
$      [BY ConstExpression] DO StatementSequence END.
```

The for statement

```
FOR v:=A TO B BY C DO SS END
```

expresses repeated execution of the statement sequence SS with v successively assuming the values A, A+C, A+2C,...,A+nC, where A+nC is the last term not exceeding B. v is called the control variable, A the starting value, B the limit, and C the increment. A and B must be assignment compatible with v; C must be a constant of type INTEGER or CARDINAL. If no increment is specified, it is assumed to be 1.

Examples:

```
FOR i:=1 TO 80 DO j:=j+a[i] END
FOR i:=80 TO 2 BY -1 DO a[i]:=a[i-1] END
```

9.9. Loop statements

A loop statement specifies the repeated execution of a statement sequence. It is terminated by the execution of any exit statement within that sequence.

```
$  LoopStatement = LOOP StatementSequence END.
```

Example:

```
LOOP
  IF t1↑.key>x THEN t2:=t1↑.left; p:=TRUE
  ELSE t2:=t1↑.right; p:=FALSE
  END;
  IF t2=NIL THEN
    EXIT
  END;
    t1:=t2
END
```

While, repeat, and for statements can be expressed by loop statements containing a single exit statement. Their use is recommended as they characterize the most frequently occurring situations where termination depends either on a single condition at either the beginning or end of the repeated statement sequence, or on reaching the limit of an arithmetic progression. The loop statement is, however, necessary to express the continuous repetition of cyclic processes, where no termination is specified. It is also useful to express situations exemplified above. Exit statements are contextually, although not syntactically bound to the loop statement which contains them.

9.10. With statements

The with statement specifies a record variable and a statement sequence. In these statements the qualification of field identifiers may be omitted, if they are to refer to the variable specified in the with clause. If the designator denotes a component of a structured variable, the selector is evaluated once (before the statement sequence). The with statement opens a new scope.

    $ WithStatement = WITH designator DO StatementSequence END.

Example:

```
WITH t↑ DO
   key:=0; left:=NIL; right:=NIL
END
```

9.11. Return and exit statements

A return statement consists of the symbol RETURN, possibly followed by an expression. It indicates the termination of a procedure (or a module body), and the expression specifies the value returned as result of a function procedure. Its type must be assignmant compatible with the result type specified in the procedure heading (see Ch.10).

Function procedures require the presence of a return statement indicating the result value. There may be several, although only one will be executed. In proper procedures, a return statement is implied by the end of the procedure body. An explicit return statement therefore appears as an additional, probably exceptional termination point.

An exit statement consists of the symbol EXIT, and it specifies termination of the enclosing loop statement and continuation with the statement following that loop statement (see 9.9).

10. Procedure declarations

Procedure declarations consist of a *procedure heading* and a block which is said to be the *procedure body*. The heading specifies the procedure identifier and the *formal parameters*. The block contains declarations and statements. The procedure identifier is repeated at the end of the procedure declaration.

There are two kinds of procedures, namely *proper procedures* and *function procedures*. The latter are activated by a function designator as a constituent of an expression, and yield a result that is an operand in the expression. Proper procedures are activated by a procedure call. The function procedure is distinguished in the declaration by indication of the type of its result following the parameter list. Its body must contain a RETURN statement which defines the result of the function procedure.

All constants, variables, types, modules and procedures declared within the block that constitutes the procedure body are *local* to the procedure. The values of local variables, including those defined within a local module, are undefined upon entry to the procedure. Since procedures may be declared as local objects too, procedure declarations may be nested. Every object is said to be declared at a certain level of nesting. If it is declared local to a procedure at level k, it has itself level k + 1. Objects declared in the module that constitutes a compilation unit (see Ch.14) are defined to be at level 0.

In addition to its formal parameters and local objects, also the objects declared in the environment of the procedure are known and accessible in the procedure (with the exception of those objects that have the same name as objects declared locally).

The use of the procedure identifier in a call within its declaration implies recursive activation of the procedure.

```
$   ProcedureDeclaration = ProcedureHeading ";" block ident.
$   ProcedureHeading = PROCEDURE ident [FormalParameters].
$   block = {declaration} [BEGIN StatementSequence] END.
$   declaration = CONST {ConstantDeclaration ";"}
$       | TYPE {TypeDeclaration ";"}
$       | VAR {VariableDeclaration ";"}
$       | ProcedureDeclaration ";" | ModuleDeclaration ";".
```

10.1. Formal parameters

Formal parameters are identifiers which denote actual parameters specified in the procedure call. The correspondence between formal and actual parameters is established when the procedure is called. There are two kinds of parameters, namely *value* and *variable parameters*. The kind is indicated in the formal parameter list. Value parameters stand for local variables to which the result of the evaluation of the corresponding actual parameter is assigned as initial value. Variable parameters correspond to actual parameters that are variables, and they stand for these variables. Variable parameters are indicated by the symbol VAR, value parameters by the absence of the symbol VAR.

Formal parameters are local to the procedure, i.e. their scope is the program text which constitutes the procedure declaration.

```
$   FormalParameters = "(" [FPSection {";" FPSection}] ")"
$       [":" qualident].
$   FPSection = [VAR] IdentList ":" FormalType.
$   FormalType = [ARRAY OF] qualident.
```

The type of each formal parameter is specified in the parameter list. In the case of variable parameters it must be compatible with its corresponding actual parameter (see 9.2), in the case of value parameters the formal type must be assignment compatible with the actual type (see 9.1). If the parameter is an array, the form,

```
ARRAY OF T
```

may be used, where the specification of the actual index bounds is omitted. The parameter is then said to be an *open array parameter*. T must be the same as the element type of the actual array, and the index range is mapped onto the integers 0 to N-1, where N is the number of elements. The formal array can be accessed elementwise only, or it may occur as actual parameter whose formal parameter is without specified index bounds. A function procedure without parameters has an empty parameter list. It must be called by a function designator whose actual parameter list is empty too.

Restriction: If a formal parameter specifies a procedure type, then the corresponding actual parameter must be either a procedure declared at level 0 or a variable (or parameter) of that procedure type. It cannot be a standard procedure.

Examples of procedure declarations:

```
PROCEDURE Read(VAR x:CARDINAL);
  VAR i:CARDINAL; ch:CHAR;
BEGIN i:=0;
  REPEAT ReadChar(ch)
  UNTIL (ch>="0") & (ch<="9");
  REPEAT i:=10*i + (ORD(ch)-ORD("0"));
    ReadChar(ch)
  UNTIL (ch<"0") OR (ch>"9");
  x:=i
END Read

PROCEDURE Write(x,n:CARDINAL);
  VAR i:CARDINAL;
    buf: ARRAY[1..10] OF CARDINAL;
BEGIN i:=0;
  REPEAT INC(i); buf[i]:=x MOD 10; x:=x DIV 10
  UNTIL x=0;
  WHILE n>i DO
    WriteChar(" "); DEC(n)
  END;
  REPEAT WriteChar(CHR(buf[i] + ORD("0")));
    DEC(i)
  UNTIL i=0;
END Write
```

```
PROCEDURE log2(x:CARDINAL):CARDINAL;
  VAR y:CARDINAL; (*assume x>0*)
BEGIN x:=x-1; y:=0;
  WHILE x>0 DO
    x:=x DIV 2; y:=y+1
  END;
  RETURN y
END log2
```

10.2. Standard procedures

Standard procedures are predefined. Some are *generic* procedures that cannot be explicitly declared, i.e. they apply to classes of operand types or have several possible parameter list forms. Standard procedures are

ABS(x)

> absolute value; result type = argument type.

CAP(ch)

> if ch is a lower case letter, the corresponding capital letter; if ch is a capital letter, the same letter.

CHR(x)

> the character with ordinal number x. CHR(x) = VAL(CHAR,x).

FLOAT(x)

> x of type CARDINAL represented as a value of type REAL.

HIGH(a)

> high index bound of array a.

ODD(x)

> x MOD2 # 0.

ORD(x)

> ordinal number (of type CARDINAL) of x in the set of values defined by type T of x. T is any enumeration type, CHAR, INTEGER, or CARDINAL.

TRUNC(x)

> real number x truncated to its integral part (of type CARDINAL).

VAL(T,x)

> the value with ordinal number x and with type T. T is any enumeration type, CHAR, INTEGER, or CARDINAL.
> VAL(T,ORD(x))=x, if x of type T.

DEC(x)

> x:=x-1

```
DEC(x,n)
```
```
    x:=x-n
```
```
EXCL(s,i)
```
```
    s:=s-{i}
```
```
HALT
```
terminate program execution

```
INC(x)
```
```
    x:=x+1
```
```
INC(x,n)
```
```
    x:=x+n
```
```
INCL(s,i)
```
```
    x:=s+{i}
```

The procedures INC and DEC also apply to operands x of enumeration types and of type CHAR. In these cases they replace x by its (n-th) successor or predecessor.

NEW and DISPOSE are translated into calls to ALLOCATE and DEALLOCATE, procedures that are either explicitly programmed or imported from another module.

```
NEW(p)                  = ALLOCATE(p,TSIZE(T))
DISPOSE(p)              = DEALLOCATE(p,TSIZE(T))
NEW(p,t1,t2,...)        = ALLOCATE(p,TSIZE(T,t1,t2,...))
DISPOSE(p,t1,t2,...)    = DEALLOCATE(p,TSIZE(T,t1,t2,...))
```

TSIZE is defined in Chapter 12, and p is declared as "VAR vp: POINTER TO T". These procedures must be compatible with the type

```
PROCEDURE(VAR ADDRESS,CARDINAL)
```

11. Modules

A module constitutes a collection of declarations and a sequence of statements. They are enclosed in the brackets MODULE and END. The module heading contains the module identifier, and possibly a number of *import lists* and an export list. The former specify all identifiers of objects that are declared outside but used within the module and therefore have to be imported. The export-list specifies all identifiers of objects declared within the module and used outside. Hence, a module constitutes a wall around its local objects whose transparency is strictly under control of the programmer.

Objects local to a module are said to be at the same scope level as the module. They can be considered as being local to the procedure enclosing the module but residing within a more restricted scope.

```
$   ModuleDeclaration = MODULE ident [priority] ";" {import}
$       [export] block ident.
$   priority = "[" ConstExpression "]".
$   export = EXPORT [QUALIFIED] IdentList ";".
$   import = [FROM ident] IMPORT IdentList ";".
```

The module identifier is repeated at the end of the declaration.

The statement sequence that constitutes the *module body* is executed when the procedure to which the module is local is called. If several modules are declared, then these bodies are executed in the sequence in which the modules occur. These bodies serve to initialize local variables and must be considered as prefixes to the enclosing procedure's statement part.

If an identifier occurs in the import (export) list, then the denoted object may be used inside (outside) the module as if the module brackets did not exist. If, however, the symbol EXPORT is followed by the symbol QUALIFIED, then the listed identifiers must be prefixed with the module's identifier when used outside the module. This case is called qualified export, and is used when modules are designed which are to be used in coexistence with other modules not known a priori. Qualified export serves to avoid clashes of identical identifiers exported from different modules (and presumably denoting different objects).

A module may feature several import lists which may be prefixed with the symbol FROM and a module identifier. The FROM clause has the effect of unqualifying the imported identifiers. Hence they may be used within the module as if they had been exported in normal, i.e. non-qualified mode.

If a record type is exported, all its field identifiers are exported too. The same holds for the constant identifiers in the case of an enumeration type. If a module identifier is exported, then all identifiers occurring in that module's export list are also exported.

Standard identifiers are always imported automatically. As a consequence, standard identifiers can be redeclared in procedures only, but not in modules, including the compilation unit (see Ch.14).

Examples of module declarations:

The following module serves to scan a text and to copy it into an output character sequence. Input is obtained characterwise by a procedure inchr and delivered by a procedure outchr. The characters are fiven in the ASCII code; control characters are ignored, with the exception of LF (line feed) and FS (file separator). They are both translated into a blank and cause the Boolean variables eoln (end of line) and eof (end of file) to be set respectively. FS is assumed to be preceded by LF.

```
MODULE LineInput;
  IMPORT inchr,outchr;
  EXPORT read,NewLine,NewFile,eoln,eof,lno;
  CONST LF=12C; CR=15C; FS=34C;
```

```
VAR lno: CARDINAL;  (*line number*)
  ch: CHAR;  (*last character read*)
  eof,eoln: BOOLEAN;
PROCEDURE NewFile;
BEGIN
  IF NOT eof THEN
    REPEAT inchr(ch) UNTIL ch=FS;
  END;
  eof:=FALSE; eoln:=FALSE; lno:=0
END NewFile;

PROCEDURE NewLine;
BEGIN
  IF NOT eoln THEN
    REPEAT inchr(ch) UNTIL ch=LF;
      outchr(CR); outchr(LF)
  END;
  eoln:=FALSE; INC(lno)
END NewLine;

PROCEDURE read(VAR x:CHAR);
BEGIN  (*assume NOT eoln AND NOT eof*)
  LOOP inchr(ch); outchr(ch);
    IF ch>=" " THEN
      x:=ch; EXIT
    ELSIF ch=LF THEN
      x:=" "; eoln:=TRUE; EXIT
    ELSIF ch=FS THEN
      x:=" "; eoln:=TRUE; eof:=TRUE; EXIT
    END
  END
END read;

  BEGIN eof:=TRUE; eoln:=TRUE
  END LineInput
```

The next example is a module which operates a disk track reservation table, and protects it from unauthorized access. A function procedure NewTrack yields the number of a free track which is becoming reserved. Tracks can be released by calling procedure ReturnTrack.

```
MODULE TrackReservation;
  EXPORT NewTrack,ReturnTrack;
  CONST ntr=1024;  (*no. of tracks*)
    w=16;  (*word size*)
    m=ntr DIV w;

  VAR i:CARDINAL;
    free: ARRAY[0..m-1] OF BITSET;

  PROCEDURE NewTrack():INTEGER;
```

```
           (*reserves a new track and yields its index as result, if
            a free track is found, and -1 otherwise*)
           VAR i,j:CARDINAL; found:BOOLEAN;
        BEGIN found:=FALSE; i:=m;
          REPEAT DEC(i); j:=w;
            REPEAT DEC(j);
              IF j IN free[i] THEN found:=TRUE END
            UNTIL found OR (j=0)
          UNTIL found OR (i=0);
          IF found THEN EXCL(free[i],j); RETURN i*w+j
          ELSE RETURN -1
          END
        END NewTrack;

        PROCEDURE ReturnTrack(k:CARDINAL);
        BEGIN  (*assume 0<=k<ntr*)
          INCL(free[k DIV w], k MOD w)
        END ReturnTrack;

     BEGIN  (*mark all tracks free*)
        FOR i:=0 TO m-1 DO free[i]:={0..w-1} END
     END TrackReservation
```

12. System-dependent facilities

Modula-2 offers certain facilities that are necessary to program *low-level* operations referring directly to objects particular of a given computer and/or implementation. These include for example facilities for accessing devices that are controlled by the computer, and facilities to break the data type compatibility rules otherwise imposed by the language definition. Such facilities are to be used with utmost care, and it is strongly recommended to restrict their use to specific modules (called low-level modules). Most of them appear in the form of data types and procedures imported from the standard module SYSTEM. A low-level module is therefore explicitly characterized by the identifier SYSTEM appearing in its import list.

Note: Because the objects imported from SYSTEM obey special rules, this module must be known to the compiler. It is therefore called a pseudo-module and need not be supplied as a separate definition module (see Ch.14).

The module SYSTEM exports the types WORD, ADDRESS, PROCESS, and the procedures ADR, SIZE, TSIZE, NEWPROCESS, TRANSFER, and possibly other identifiers depending on the implementation being used (see Ch.13).

The type WORD represents an individually accessible storage unit. No operation except assignment is defined on this type. However, if a formal parameter of a procedure is of type WORD, the corresponding actual parameter may be of any type that uses one storage word in the given implementation. This includes the types CARDINAL, INTEGER, BITSET and all pointers. If a formal parameter has the type ARRAY OF WORD, its corresponding actual parameter may be of any type; in particular it may be a record type to be interpreted as an array of words.

The type ADDRESS is defined as

```
ADDRESS = POINTER TO WORD
```

It is compatible with all pointer types, and also with the type CARDINAL. Therefore, all operators for integer arithmetic apply to operands of this type. Hence, the type ADDRESS can be used to perform address computations and to export the results as pointers. The following example of a primitive storage allocator demonstrates a typical usage of the type ADDRESS.

```
MODULE Storage;
  FROM SYSTEM IMPORT ADDRESS;
  EXPORT Allocate;

  VAR lastused: ADDRESS;

  PROCEDURE Allocate(VAR a:ADDRESS; n:CARDINAL);
  BEGIN a:=lastused; INC(lastused,n)
  END Allocate;

  BEGIN lastused:=0
END Storage
```

The function ADR(x) denotes the storage address of the variable x and is of type ADDRESS. SIZE(x) denotes the number of storage units assigned to the varaible x. TSIZE(T) is the number of storage units assigned to any variable of type T. SIZE and TSIZE are of type CARDINAL.

Examples:

```
ADR(lastused)    SIZE(a)    TSIZE(Node)
```

Besides those exported from the pseudo-module SYSTEM, there are two other facilities whose characteristics are system-dependent. The first is the possiblity to use a type identifier T as a name denoting the *type transfer function* from the type of the operand to the type T. Evidently, such functions are data representation dependent, and they involve no explicit conversion instructions.

The second facility is used in variable declarations. It allows to specify the absolute address of a variable and to override the allocation scheme of a compiler. This facility is intended for access to storage locations with specific purpose and fixed address, such as e.g. device registers on coumputers with "memory-mapped I/O". This address is specified as a constant integer expression enclosed in brackets immediately following the identifier in the variable declaratioan. The choice of an appropriate data type is left to the programmer. For examples, refer to 13.2.

13. Processes

Modula-2 is designed primarily for implementation on a conventional single-processor computer. For multiprogramming it offers only some basic facilities which allow the specification of quasi-concurrent processes and of genuine concurrency for peripheral devices. The word *process* is here used with the meaning of *coroutine*. Coroutines are processes that are executed by a (single) processor one at a time.

13.1. Creating a process and transfer of control

A new process is created by a call to

```
PROCEDURE NEWPROCESS(P:PROC; A:ADDRESS; n:CARDINAL;
                     VAR p1:PROCESS)
```

P   denotes the procedure which constitutes the process,
A   is the base address of the process' workspace,
n   is the size of this workspace,
p1 is the result parameter.

A new process with P as program and A as workspace of size n is assigned to p1. This process is allocated, but not activated. P must be a parameterless procedure declared at level 0.

A transfer of control between two processes is specified by a call to

```
PROCEDURE TRANSFER(VAR p1,p2:PROCESS)
```

This call suspends the current process, assigns it to p1 , and resumes the process designated by p2. Evidently, p2 must have been assigned a process by an earlier call to either NEWPROCESS or TRANSFER. Both procedures, as well as the type PROCESS, must be imported from the module SYSTEM. A program terminates, when control reaches the end of a procedure which is the body of a process.

Note: assignment to p1 occurs after identification of the new process p2; hence, the actual parameters may be identical.

13.2. Device processes and interrupts

If a process contains an operation of a peripheral device, then the processor may be transferred to another process after the operation of the device has been initiated, thereby leading to a concurrent execution of that other process with the *device process*. Usually, termination of the device's operation is signalled by an interrupt of the main processor. In terms of Modula-2, an interrupt is a transfer operation. This interrupt transfer is (in Modula-2 implemented on the PDP-11) programmed by and combined with the transfer after device initiation. This combination is expressed by a call to

```
PROCEDURE IOTRANSFER(VAR p1,p2:PROCESS; va:CARDINAL);
```

In analogy to TRANSFER, this call suspends the calling device process, assigns it to p1, resumes (transfers to) the suspended process p2, and in addition causes the interrupt transfer occurring upon device completion to assign the interrupted process to p2 and to resume the device process p1. va is the interrupt vector address assigned to the device. The procedure IOTRANSFER must be imported from the module SYSTEM, and should be considered as PDP-11 implementation-specific.

It is necessary that interrupts can be postponed (disabled) at certain times, e.g. when variables common to the cooperating processes are accessed, or when other, possibly time-critical operations have priority. Therefore, every module is given a certain priority level, and every device capable of interrupting is given a priority level. Execution of a program can be interrupted, if and only if the interrupting device has a priority that is greater than the priority level of the module containing the statement currently being executed. Whereas the device priority is defined by the hardware, the priority level of each module is specified by its heading. If an explicit specification is absent, the level in any procedure is that of the calling program. IOTRANSFER must be used within modules with a specified priority only.

The following example (programmed for the PDP-11) shows a module with a process that acts as a driver for a typewriter. The module contains a buffer B for N characters.

```
MODULE Typewriter[4];   (*typewriter interrupt priority=4*)
  FROM SYSTEM IMPORT

PROCESS,NEWPROCESS,TRANSFER,IOTRANSFER,LISTEN,WORD,ADR,SIZE;
  EXPORT typeout;

  CONST N=32;

  VAR n:INTEGER;  (*no. of chars in buffer*)
    in,out: [1..N];
    B: ARRAY[1..N] OF CHAR;
    PRO: PROCESS;  (*producer*)
    CON: PROCESS;  (*consumer = typewriter driver*)
    wsp: ARRAY[1..50] OF WORD;
    TWS[177564B]: BITSET;  (*status register*)
    TWB[177566B]: CHAR;  (*buffer register*)

  PROCEDURE typeout(ch:CHAR);
  BEGIN INC(n);
    WHILE n>N DO LISTEN END;
    B[in]:=ch; in:=in MOD N+1;
    IF n=0 THEN TRANSFER(PRO,CON) END
  END typeout;
```

```
    PROCEDURE driver;
    BEGIN
      LOOP DEC(n);
        IF n<0 THEN TRANSFER(CON,PRO) END;
        TWB:=B[out]; out:=out MOD N+1;
        TWS:={6}; IOTRANSFER(CON,PRO,64B); TWS:={}
      END
    END driver;


  BEGIN n:=0; in:=1; out:=1;
    NEWPROCESS(driver,ADR(wsp),SIZE(wsp),CON);
      TRANSFER(PRO,CON)
    END Typewriter
```

LISTEN must be a procedure that lowers the processor's priority level so that pending interrupts may be accepted.

14. Compilation units

A text which is accepted by the compiler as a unit is called a *compilation unit*. There are three kinds of compilation units: main modules, definition modules, and implementation modules. A main module constitutes a main program and consists of a so-called *program module*. In particular, it has no export list. Imported objects are defined in other (separately compiled) program parts which themselves are subdivided into two units, called definition module and implementation module.

The *definition module* specifies the names and properties of objects that are relevant to clients, i.e. other modules which import from it. The *implementation module* contains local objects and statements that need not be known to a client. In particular the definition module contains the export list, constant, type, and variable declarations, and specifications of procedure headings. The corresponding implementation module contains the complete procedure declarations, and possibly further declarations of objects not exported. Definition and implementation modules exist in pairs. Both may contain import lists, and all objects declared in the definition module are available in the corresponding implementation module without explicit import.

```
$   DefinitionModule = DEFINITION MODULE ident ";" {import}
$         [export] {definition} END ident ".".
$   definition = CONST {ConstantDeclaration ";"}
$         | TYPE {ident ["=" type] ";"}
$         | VAR {VariableDeclaration ";"}
$         | ProcedureHeading ";".
$   ProgramModule = MODULE ident [priority] ";"
$         {import} block ident ".".
$   CompilationUnit = DefinitionModule
$         | [IMPLEMENTATION] ProgramModule.
```

The definition module evidently represents the interface between the definiton/implementation module pair on one side and its clients on the other side.

Definition modules require the use of qualified export. Type definitions may consist of the full specification of the type (in this case its export is said to be transparent), or they may consist of the type identifier only. In this case the full specification must appear in the corresponding implementation module, and its export is said to be *opaque*. The type is known in the importing client modules by its name only, and all its properties are hidden. Therefore, procedures operating on operands of this type, and in particular operating on its components, must be defined in the same implementation module which hides the type's properties. Opaque export is restricted to pointers and to subranges of standard types.

Appendix 2

Revisions and Amendments to Modula-2 *

N.Wirth, ETH Zürich.

On November 21, 1983, a meeting was held with participants from several firms who had implemented Modula-2. Numerous features and facilities were proposed for addition or correction. The following subset was agreed upon. These rules should be regarded as revisions of Modula-2. Future implementors are encouraged to comply with these revisions, and existing compilers should be adapted. Although any change in a language is subject to resentment, the number of changes adopted here is very small and, I believe, each one is a genuine improvement.

1. Restrictions and Clarifications

1.1. The types of a formal VAR-parameter and that of its corresponding actual parameter must be *identical* (i.e. not merely compatible). This rule is relaxed in the case of a formal parameter of type ADDRESS, which is also compatible with all pointer types, and in the case of the type WORD, where the compatible types are specified for each implementation.

1.2. The types of the expressions specifying the starting and limiting values of the control variable in a for statement must be *compatible* (i.e. not merely assignment compatible) with the type of the control variable.

1.3. A process initiated in a module at priority level n must not call a procedure declared in a module at priority level m<n. Calls of procedures declared without priority are allowed.

1.4. Pointer types can be exported from definition modules as opaque types. Opaque export of other types may be subject to implementation restrictions. Assignment and test for (in)equality are applicable to opaque types.

1.5. All imported modules are initialized *before* the importing module is initialized. If there exist circular references, the order of initialization is not defined.

*Reprinted with permission from Springer Verlag from:
Wirth, N.: Programming in Modula-2, 2nd corrected Edition 1983, Text and Monographs in Computer Science.
©Springer Verlag Berlin, Heidelberg, New York, Tokyo

2. Changes

2.1. *All* objects declared in a definition module are exported. The explicit export list is discarded. The definition module may be regarded as the implementation module's separated and extended export list.

```
DefinitionModule = DEFINITION MODULE ident ";" {import}
    {definition} END ident ".".
```

2.2. The syntax of a variant record type declaration with missing tag field is changed from

```
FieldList = | CASE [ident ":"] qualident OF ...
```

to

```
FieldList = | CASE [ident] ":" qualident OF ...
```

The fact that the colon is always present makes it evident which part was omitted, if any.

3. Extensions

3.1. The syntax of the case statement and the variant record declaration is changed from

```
case = CaseLabelList ":" StatementSequence.
variant = CaseLabelList ":" FieldListSequence.
```

to

```
case = [CaseLabelList ":" StatementSequence].
variant = [CaseLabelList ":" FieldListSequence].
```

The inclusion of the empty case and the empty variant allows the insertion of superfluous bars similar to the empty statement allowing the insertion of superfluous semicolons.

3.2. A string consisting of n characters is said to have length n. A string of length 1 is assignment compatible with the type CHAR.

3.3. The syntax of the subrange type is changed from

```
SubrangeType = "[" ConstExpression ".." ConstExpression
    "]".
```

to

```
SubrangeType = [ident] "[" ConstExpression ".."
    ConstExpression "]".
```

The optional identifier allows to specify the base type of the subrange. Example: INTEGER[0..99].

3.4. Elements of sets habe been restricted to be constants. This restriction is now relaxed. The syntax of sets and factors changes to

```
ConstFactor = ... | ConstSet | ... .
ConstSet = [qualident] "{" [ConstElement {","
     ConstElement}] "}".
ConstElement = ConstExpression [".." ConstExpression].
factor = ... | set | ... .
set = [qualident] "{" [element {"," element}] "}".
element = expression [".." expression].
```

3.5. The character "~" is a synonym for the symbol NOT.

3.6. The identifiers LONGCARD, LONGINT, and LONGREAL denote standard types (which may not be available on some implementations).

3.7. The type ADDRESS is compatible with all pointer types and with either CARDINAL or LONGCARD. The interpretation of addresses as numbers depends on the implementation.

3.8. The standard functions MIN and MAX take as argument any scalar type (including REAL). Their value is the type's minimal resp. maximal value.

Appendix 3

The Syntax of Modula-2

```
ident = letter {letter I digit}.
number = integer I real.
integer = digit {digit} I octalDigit {octalDigit} ("B" I "C") I
    digit {hexDigit} "H".
real = digit {digit} "." {digit} [ScaleFactor].
ScaleFactor = "E" ["+" I "-"] digit {digit}.
hexDigit = digit I "A" I "B" I "C" I "D" I "E" I "F".
digit = octalDigit I "8" I "9".
octalDigit = "0" I "1" I "2" I "3" I "4" I    "5" I "6" I "7".
string = "'" {character} "'" I '"' {character} '"'.
qualident = ident {"." ident}.

ConstantDeclaration = ident "=" ConstExpression.
ConstExpression = SimpleConstExpr [relation SimpleConstExpr].
relation = "=" I "#" I "<" I "<=" I ">" I ">=" I IN.
SimpleConstExpr = ["+" I "-"] ConstTerm {AddOperator ConstTerm}.
AddOperator = "+" I "-" I OR.
ConstTerm = ConstFactor {MulOperator ConstFactor}.
MulOperator = "*" I "/" I DIV I MOD I AND I "&".
ConstFactor = qualident I number I string I ConstSet I
    "(" ConstExpression ")" I NOT ConstFactor.
ConstSet = [qualident] "{" [ConstElement {"," ConstElement}] "}".
ConstElement = ConstExpression [".." ConstExpression].

TypeDeclaration = ident "=" type.
type = SimpleType I ArrayType I RecordType I SetType I
    PointerType I ProcedureType.
SimpleType = qualident I enumeration I SubrangeType.
enumeration = "(" IdentList ")".
IdentList = ident {"," ident}.
SubrangeType = [ident] "[" ConstExpression ".."
    ConstExpression "]".
ArrayType = ARRAY SimpleType {"," SimpleType} OF type.
RecordType = RECORD FieldListSequence END.
FieldListSequence = FieldList {";" FieldList}.
FieldList = [IdentList ":" type I
    CASE [ident] ":" qualident OF variant {"I" variant}
    [ELSE FieldListSequence] END].
variant = [CaseLabelList ":" FieldListSequence].
```

```
CaseLabelList = CaseLabels {"," CaseLabels}.
CaseLabels = ConstExpression [".." ConstExpression].
SetType = SET OF SimpleType.
PointerType = POINTER TO type.
ProcedureType = PROCEDURE [FormalTypeList].
FormaltypeList = "(" [[VAR] FormalType {"," [VAR] FormalType}] ")"
     [":" qualident].

VariableDeclaration = IdentList ":" type.
designator = qualident {"." ident | "[" ExpList "]" | "↑"}.
ExpList = expression {"," expression }.
expression = SimpleExpression [relation SimpleExpression].
SimpleExpression = ["+" | "-"] term {AddOperator term}.
term = factor {MulOperator factor}.
factor = number | string | set | designator [ActualParameters] |
     "(" expression ")" | NOT factor.
set = [qualident] "{" [element {"," element}] "}".
element = expression [".." expression].
ActualParameters = "(" [ExpList] ")".

statement = [assignment | ProcedureCall | IfStatement |
          CaseStatement | WhileStatement | RepeatStatement |
          LoopStatement | ForStatement | WithStatement | EXIT |
          RETURN [expression] ].
assignment = designator ":=" expression.
ProcedureCall = designator [ActualParameters].
StatementSequence = statement {";" statement}.
IfStatement = IF expression THEN StatementSequence
     {ELSIF expression THEN StatementSequence}
     [ELSE StatementSequence] END.
CaseStatement = CASE expression OF case {"|" case}
     [ELSE StatementSequence] END.
case = [CaseLabelList ":" StatementSequence].
WhileStatement = WHILE expression DO StatementSequence END.
RepeatStatement = REPEAT StatementSequence UNTIL expression END.
ForStatement = FOR ident ":=" expression TO expression
     [BY ConstExpression] DO StatementSequence END.
LoopStatement = LOOP StatementSequence END.
WithStatement = WITH designator DO StatementSequence END.

ProcedureDeclaration = ProcedureHeading ";" block ident.
ProcedureHeading = PROCEDURE ident [FormalParameters].
block = {declaration} [BEGIN StatementSequence] END.
declaration = CONST {ConstantDeclaration ";"} |
     TYPE {TypeDeclaration ";"} | VAR {VariableDeclaration ";"} |
```

```
    ProcedureDeclaration ";" | ModuleDeclaration ";".
FormalParameters = "(" [FPSection {";" FPSection}] ")"
    [":" qualident].
FPSection = [VAR] IdentList ":" FormalType.
FormalType = [ARRAY OF] qualident.
ModuleDeclaration = MODULE [priority] ";" {import} [export]
    block ident.
priority = "[" ConstExpression "]".
import = [FROM ident] IMPORT [IdentList] ";".
export = EXPORT [QUALIFIED] IdentList ";".

DefinitionModule = DEFINITION MODULE ident ";" {import}
    {definition} END ident ".".
definition = CONST {ConstantDeclaration ";"} |
    TYPE {ident ["=" type] ";"} |
    VAR {VariableDeclaration ";"} |
    ProcedureHeading ";".
ProgramModule  = MODULE ident [priority] ";"{import}
    block ident ".".
CompilationUnit = DefinitionModule |
    [IMPLEMENTATION] ProgramModule.
```

Bibliography

Ada: The Programming Language Ada; Reference Manual; Lecture Notes in Computer Science Nr.106; Springer 1981.

Aho, A.V., Ullman, J.D.: The Theory of Parsing, Translation and Compiling; Prentice-Hall 1972.

Alford, M.W.: A Requirements Engineering Methodology for Real Time Processing Requirements; IEEE Transactions on Software Engineering, SE-3(1); 1972.

Aron, J.D.: Estimating ressources for large programming systems; Software Engineering Techniques; Nato Scientific Affairs Division, Brüssel; 1972.

Baase, S.: Computer Algorithms, Introduction to Design and Analysis; Addison-Wesley 1978.

Baker, F.T.: Chief Programmer Team Management of Production Programming; IBM Systems Journal 11/1; 1972.

Baker, F.T.: Organizing for Structured Programming; In: Lecture Notes in Computer Science, Programming Methodology; Springer 1974.

Baker, F.T., Mills, H.D.: Chief Programmer Teams; In: Classics in Software Engineering; Yourdon Press 1979.

Balzert, H.: Das Software-Entwicklungssystem PLASMA; Angewandte Informatik 5/1981.

Bauer F.L.: Software Engineering; In: Software Engineering As An Advanced Course; Springer 1975.

Bell, T.E., et al.: An Extendable Approach to Computer Aided Software Requirement Engineering; IEEE Transactions on Software Engineering, SE-3; 1977.

Boehm, B.W.: Software and its Impact. A Quantitative Assessment; Datamation 19; 1973.

Boehm, B.W.: Experience with Automated Aids to the Design of Large Scale Reliable Software; Proc. of the Internat. Conf. on Reliable Software; Los Angeles 1975a.

Boehm, B.W.: The High Cost of Software; Practical Strategies for Developing Large Software Systems; Addison-Wesley 1975b.

Boehm, B.W., et al.: Quantitative Evaluation of Software Quality; Proc. of 2nd Internat. Conf. on Software Engineering; IEEE Comp.Soc.; 1976.

Boehm B.W., et al.: Characteristics of Software Quality; North Holland 1978.

Boehm B.W.: Software Engineering; In: Classics in Software Engineering; Yourdon Press 1979.

Boehm, B.W.: Software Engineering As It Is; In: Software Engineering; Academic Press 1980.

Böhm, D., Jacopini, G.: Flow diagrams, turing machines and languages with only two formation rules; Comm. of the ACM, Vol.9; 1966.

Bons, H., van Megen, R.: Zur Festlegung von Qualitätszielen als Grundlage der Qualitätsplanung und -Kontrolle; German Chapter of the ACM, Bericht 9; 1982.

Bowen, J.B.: Are Current Approaches Sufficient for Measuring Software Quality; Proc. Software Quality Assurance Workshop, San Diego; 1978.

Brooks, F.P.: The Mythical Man-Month. Essays on Software Engineering; Addison Wesley 1975.

Brown, P.J.: Software Portability; Cambridge University Press 1977.

Brown, R.R.: The Techniques and Practice of Structured Design a la Constantine; Structured Design, Infotech State of the Art Conference; London 1972.

Budde, R., et. al.: Approaches to Prototyping, Springer Verlag 1984.

Buxton, J.N., Randell B. (Eds.): Software Engineering Techniques, Report on a Conference, Rome; Brüssel: NATO Scientific Affairs Division; 1969.

Cavano, J.P.: Framework for the Measurement of Software Quality; ACM Software Quality Assurance Workshop Proceedings; 1978.

Congar, J.R.: Evolution of Business Systems Analysis Techniques; Computing Surveys Vol.5; 1973.

Dahl, O.J., et al.: Structured Programming; Academic Press 1972.

Dennis, J.B.: Modularity; Lecture Notes in Economics and Mathematical Systems Nr.81; Springer 1973.

Dennis, J.B.: The Design and Construction of Software Systems; In: Software Engineering As An Advanced Course; Springer 1975.

Dijkstra, E.W.: A constructive approach to the problem of program correctness. BIT 8; 1968a.

Dijkstra, E.W.: Goto Statements considered Harmful. Comm. of the ACM Vol.11; 1968b.

Dijkstra, E.W.: Structured Programming; Software Engineering Technique; Report on a Conference; Rome 1969.

Dijkstra, E.W.: The Humble Programmer; Comm. of the ACM, Vol.15, No.10; New York 1972a.

Dijkstra, E.W.: Notes on Structured Programming; Academic Press 1972b.

Dijkstra, E.W.: A Discipline of Programming; Prentice-Hall 1976.

Dolotha, T.A., Mashey, J.R.: An Introduction to the Programmer's Work Bench; 2nd Internat. Conf. on Software Engineering, San Francisco; IEEE Oct. 1976.

Dolotha, T.A., Haigth, R.C.: PBW/UNIX - Overview and Synopsis of Facilities; Bell Laboratories, Napervill; Illinois 1977.

Donzeau-Gouge, V., et al.: Programming Environments based on structured Editors: the mentor exprience; INRIA Research Report 26, Rocquencourt, France; 1980.

Dwyer, B.: One More Time - How to Update a Master File; Comm. of the ACM Vol.24, No.1; 1981.

Elben, W.: Entscheidungstabellentechnik; Walter de Gruyter 1973.

Elspas B., et al.: An assessment of techniques for proving program correctness; Computing Surveys 4; 1972.

Erbesdobler, R., et al.: Entscheidungstabellen-Technik; Springer 1976.

Fagan, M.E.: Design and code inspections to reduce errors in program development; IBM Systems Journal, Vol.15(3); 1976.

Feldman, S.I.: MAKE - A Program for Maintaining Computer Programs; Software Practice and Experience, Vol.9; 1979.

Fisher, D.A.: Requirements for Ada Programming Support Environments "Stoneman"; US Department of Defense; 1980.

Floyd, R.W.: Assigning meanings to programs; Mathematical Aspects of Computer Science Vol.19; 1967.

Frei, H.P., et al.: Graphics-Based Programming Support Systems. Computer Graphics, ACM Siggraph, Vol.12/3; 1978.

Gerhart, S., et al.: Observations of Fallibility in Applications of Modern Programming Methodologies; IEEE Transactions on Software Engineering, Vol.SE-2,3; 1976.

Gewald, K., et al.: Software Engineering; Grundlagen und Technik rationeller Programmentwicklung; Oldenbourg 1977.

Gibson, C.G., et al.: Verification Guidelines; TRW Software Series Report; Redondo Beach 1971.

Goos, G.: Hierarchies. In: Software Engineering As An Advanced Course. Springer 1973a.

Goos, G.: Systemprogrammiersprachen und strukturiertes Programmieren. Lecture Notes in Computer Science Nr.23; Springer 1973b.

Goos, G.: Language Characteristics - Programming Languages as a Tool in Writing System Software; Software Engineering; Springer 1977.

Goos, G.: ADA - Zweck, Entwicklung und Zukunft einer Programmiersprache; Angewandte Informatik 2/82; Vieweg 1982.

Gries, D.: Compiler Construction for Digital Computers; Wiley 1971.

Gutknecht, J., Winiger, W.: Andra: The Document Preparation System of the Personal Workstation Lilith; Software Practice and Experience, Vol.14; 1984.

Guttag, J.V.: The Specification an Application to Programming of Abstract Data Types; Ph.D.Thesis, Univ. of Toronto; Rep. CSRG-59, 1975.

Guttag, J.V.; Horning, J.J.: The Algebraic Specification of Abstract Data Types; Acta Informatica 12,3; 1977.

Halsteadt, M.H.: Natural Laws Controlling Algorithm Structure; Sigplan Notices Vol.7,2; 1972.

Haney, F.M.: Module connection analysis - A tool for scheduling software debugging activities; Fall Joint Computer Conference 1972.

Henderson, P., Snowdon, R.: An experiment in structured programming; BIT 1972.

Heninger, K.L.: Specifying Software Requirements for Complex Systems; New Techniques and Their Application; IEEE Transactions on Software Engineering, SE-6; 1980.

Herschel, R.: Einführung in die Theorie der Automaten, Sprachen und Algorithmen; Oldenbourg 1974.

Hesse, W.: Methoden und Werkzeuge zur Software-Entwicklung - Ein Marsch durch die Technologie-Landschaft; Informatik Spektrum, Vol.4; 1981.

Hoare, C.A.R.: An Axiomatic basis for computer programming; Comm. of the ACM Vol.12; 1969.

Hopcroft, J.E., Ullman, J.D.: Introduction to Automata Theory, Languages and Computation; Addison Wesley 1969.

Horning, J.J.: Some Desirable Properties of Data Abstraction Facilities; Sigplan Notices, Special Issue 1976.

Hruschka, P.: Fallstudie: Die Softwareproduktionsumgebung PROMOD; GEI Aachen.

Hughes, J.K., Michtom J.I.: A Structured Approach to Programming; Prentice-Hall 1976.

IBM: HIPO - A Design Aid and Documentation Technique; GC 20-1851-11, White Plains; N.Y. 1975.

Ichbiah, J.D., et al.: Rational for the Design of the ADA Programming Languages; Sigplan Notices 14; 1979.

Jackson, M.A.: Principles of Program-Design; Academic Press 1975.

Jacobi, C.: The Debugger. In: Lilith Handbook - A Guide for Lilith Users and Programmers; Institut für Informatik, ETH Zürich; 1982.

Jeffords, R.D.: Updating a Master File - Yet Another Time; Comm. of the ACM Vol.25, No.6; 1982.

Jones, C.: A Survey of Programming Design and Specification Techniques; Proceedings Specification of Reliable Software; IEEE New York 1979.

Kimm, R., et al.: Einführung in Softwareengineering; Walter de Gruyter 1979.

Knuth, D.E.: Semantics of Context-free Languages; Mathematical Systems Theory 2; 1968.

Knuth, D.E.: Examples of Formal Semantics; Symposium on Semantic of Algorithmic Languages; Springer 1971.

Knuth, D.E.: The Art of Computer Programming; Vol.1-3; Addison Wesley 1968, 1969, 1973.

Knuth, D.E.: Structured Programming with GOTO-Statements; Computing Surveys 6(4); 1974.

Kopetz, H.: Software Reliability; Macmillan Press 1979.

Lauesen, S.: A Large Semaphore Based Operating System; Comm. of the ACM, Vol.18; 1975.

Levy, M.R.: Modularity and the Sequential File Update Problem; Comm. of the ACM Vol.25, No.6; 1982.

Lewis, P.M., et al.: Compiler Design Theory; Addison-Wesley 1976.

Lientz, B.P., Swanson, E.B.: Software Maintenance Management; Addison Wesley 1980.

Liskov, B., Zilles, S.: Programming with Abstract Data Types. Sigplan Notices 94; 1974.

Liskov, B., Zilles, S.; Specification Techniques for Data Abstractions; IEEE Transactions on Software Engineering, SE-1; 1975.

Manna, Z.: The Correctness of Programs; Journal of Computer and System Science Vol.3; 1969.

Marcotty, M., et al.: A Sampler of Formal Definitions; Computing Surveys 8/2; 1976.

Martin, J.: Objectives and Design of a Real-Time Controll Program. Unpublished.

McCabe, T.J.: A Complexity Measurement; IEEE Transactions on Software Engineering, SE-2; 1976.

McCall, J.A., et al.: Factors in Software Quality, Vol.II; RADC-TR-77-369, Rome Air Development Center; New York 1977a.

McCall, J.A., et. al.: Factors in Software Quality, Vol.I; Concepts and Definitions of Software Quality; California 1977b.

McCarthy, J.: Towards a mathematical science of computation; Proc. IFIP Congress, Amsterdam; North-Holland Publications 1962.

McGuffin, R.W., et al.: CADES - Software Engineering in Practice; Proceedings 4th Internat. Conf. on Software Engineering; München 1979.

Meek, B., Heath P.: Guide to Good Programming Practice; Ellis Horwood Limited 1980.

Metzelaar, P.N.: Cost estimation graph; TRW Systems Group, Redondo Beach, Calif.; 1971.

Metzger, P.W.: Managing a Programming Project; Prentice-Hall 1973.

Miller, E.F.: Software Testing and Validation techniques; IEEE Computer Society; California 1978.

Mills, H.D.: Mathematical Foundations for Structured Programming; IBM FSC 72-6012; 1972.

Mitchell, J.G.: Mesa Language Manual; Xerox PARC, CSL-78-1; 1978.

Nassi, I., Shneiderman, B.: Flowchart Techniques for Structured Programming; Sigplan Notices 88; 1973.

Naur, P.: Proof of algorithms by general snapshots; BIT 6; 1966.

Naur, P., Randell, B. (Eds.): Software Engineering. Report on a Conference, Garmisch, 1968; Brüssel: NATO Scientific Affairs Division; 1969.

Nievergelt, J., Ventura, A.: Die Gestaltung interaktiver Programme; Teubner 1983.

Parnas, D.L.: On the Criteria to be Used in Decompositing Systems into Moduls. Comm. of the ACM Vol.15, No.12; 1972.

Parnas, D.L.: Software Engineering or Methods for the Multi-Person Construction of Multi-Version Programs; Lecture Notes in Computer Science, Programming Methodology; Springer 1974.

Pomberger, G.: Lexikalische Analyse und Syntaxanalyse; In: Prinzipien des Übersetzerbaus; Schriftenreihe der Österreichischen Computer Gesellschaft Nr.6; Wien 1979.

Pomberger, G., Blaschek, G.: STRUCT - Ein dialogorientiertes Programmsystem zur Unterstützung des Programmentwurfs und der -dokumentation; Techn.Bericht 3/81, Univ. Linz, Inst.f.Informatik; 1981.

Pomberger, G.: Ein Werkzeug zur interaktiven Programmentwicklung und -dokumentation; Elektronische Rechenanlagen; Oldenbourg 1982.

Pressman, R.S.: Software Engineering. A Practitioner's Approach; McGraw-Hill International Student Edition, 1982.

Räihä, K.J.: On Attributed Grammars and their Use in a Compiler Writing System; Report A-1977-4; Univ. Helsinki, Dept. of Computer Science; 1977.

Ramamoorthy, C.V., et al.: Reliability and Integrity of Large Computer Programs; Lecture Notes in Computer Science - Fachtagung Prozeßrechner 1974. Springer 1974.

Ramamoorthy, C.V., et al.: Techniques in Software Quality Assurance; Proc. of the German Chapter of the ACM, Vol.9; Teubner 1982.

Rechenberg, P.: Programmieren für Informatiker mit PL/I; Oldenbourg 1974.

Rechenberg, P.: Attributierte Grammatiken als Werkzeug der Softwaretechnik; Techn.Bericht 3/80, Univ. Linz, Inst.f.Informatik; September 1980.

Rechenberg, P.: Anleitung zur Beschreibung von Programmsystemen; Techn.Notiz 1/81, Univ. Linz, Inst.f.Informatik; 1981.

Rechenberg, P.: Context Conditions for Modula-2; Techn.Bericht 2/82, Univ. Linz, Inst.f.Informatik; 1982.

Rechenberg, P.: Ada und Modula-2 - Programmiersprachen der achtziger und neunziger Jahre? Zeitschrift der Johannes-Kepler-Universität Linz, 4.Jahrgang, Heft 4; Linz 1983a.

Rechenberg, P.: Daten- und Programm-Kontrollstrukturen; In: Software-Engineering; Schriftenreihe der Österreichischen Computer Gesellschaft Nr.19; Oldenbourg 1983b.

Rochkind, M.J.: The Source Code Control System; IEEE Transactions on Software Engineering SE-1(4); 1975.

Rohlfing, H.: Simula;. BI-Taschenbuch 747; Bibliographisches Institut, Mannheim 1973.

Sackmann, H., et al.: Exploratory Experimental Studies Comparing Online and Offline Programming Performance; Comm. of the ACM, Vol.11; 1968.

SADT: An Introduction to SADT Structured Analysis and Design Technique; Woltham Messachusetts. Softech Inc.; 1976.

Sammer, W., Schwärtzel, H.: Chill - eine moderne Programmiersprache für die Systemtechnik; Springer 1982.

Sommerville, I.: Software Engineering; Addison-Wesley 1982.

Schmith, R.L.: Estimating software project ressource requirements; Structured Programming Series, Vol.11; 1975.

Schmitz, P., et al.: Workshop "Ausgewählte Methoden und Verfahren für das Testen und für die Aufwandsschätzung"; Köln 1980; Projektgruppe Softwaretechnologie, Rechenzentrum der Universität zu Köln; 1980.

Schnupp, P., Floyd, Ch: Software; Walter de Gruyter 1976.

Schoman, K., Ross, D.T.: Structured Analysis for Requirements Definition; IEEE Transactions on Software Engineering, SE-3; 1977.

Schulz, A.: Methoden des Softwareentwurfs und strukturierte Programmierung; Walter de Gruyter 1982.

Stevens, W.P., Myers, G.J., Constantine, L.L.: Structured Design; IBM System Journal 13; 1974a.

Stevens, W. et al.: Structured Design. IBM Systems Journal 2/74; 1974b.

Strunz, H.: Entscheidungstabellen und ihre Anwendung bei Systemplanung, -implementierung und -dokumentation; Elektronische Rechenanlagen; Oldenbourg 1970.

Tanenbaum, A.S., et al.: Guidelines for Software Portability; Software Practice and Experience, Vol.8; 1978.

Schmitz, P., et al.: Software-Qualitätssicherung - Testen im Software-Lebenszyklus; Vieweg 1982.

Teichrow, D., et al.: An Introduction to PSL/PSA; IDOS Working Paper No.86; University of Michigan; 1974.

Teichrow, D., Hersley, E.A.: PSL/PSA: A Computer Aided Technique for Structured Documentation and Analysis of Information Processing Systems; IEEE Transactions on Software Engineering, SE-3; 1977.

Teitelbaum, T., Reps, T.: The Cornell program synthesizer: A syntax- directed programming environment; Comm. Ass. Comput. Mach., Vol.24; 1981.

Truöl, K.: DIPROTOR - ein Softwarewerkzeug zur Erstellung von Diagrammen und Programmrahmen für die Datenstruktur-orientierte Methode des Programmentwurfs; Informatik Fachberichte, Vol.43; Springer 1981.

Walt, D.A., Madson, O.L.: Extended Attributed Grammars; Report Nr.10; Univ. Glasgow, Dept. of Computer Science; 1977.

Warnier, J.D.: Logical Construction of Programs; Leiden 1974.

Wasserman, A.L.: A top-down view of Software engineering; Proceedings 1st Nat. Conf. on Software Engineering; Washington DC 1975.

Wedekind, H.: Systemanalyse; Carl Hanser 1973.

Weinwurm, G.F.: On the Economic Analysis of Computer Programs, and On the Management of Computer Programming; Auerbach 1970.

Willis, R.R.: AIDES: Computer Aided Design of Software Systems; Software Engineering Environments; North-Holland 1981.

Winiger, W.: The Editor. In: Lilith Handbook - A Guide for Lilith Users and Programmers; Institut für Informatik, ETH Zürich; 1982.

Wirth, N.: Programming and Programming Languages; Proc. Internat. Computer Symp.; Bonn 1970.

Wirth, N.: Program Development by Stepwise Refinement; Comm. of the ACM, Vol.14, No.4; 1971.

Wirth, N.: Systematic Programming; Prentice-Hall 1973.

Wirth, N.: Compilerbau; Teubner 1977.

Wirth, N.: Systematisches Programmieren; Teubner 1978.

Wirth, N.: Modula-2; Institut für Informatik, ETH Zürich, Bericht Nr.36; 1980.

Wirth, N.: The Personal Computer Lilith; Bericht Nr.40 der Eidgenössischen Technischen Hochschule Zürich, Institut für Informatik; 1981.

Wirth, N.: Programming in Modula-2; Springer 1982.

Wolverton, R.W., et al.: Assessment of Software Reliability; TRW Software Report (TRW-SS-72-4); California 1972.

Wolverton, R.W.: The Cost of Developing Large Scale Software;. IEEE Transactions on Computers, Vol.23; 1974.

Wulf, W., Shaw, M.: Global Variable Considered Harmful; Sigplan Notices 2; 1973.

Yin, B.H., Winchester, I.W.: The Establishment and Use of Measures to Evaluate the Quality of Software Designs; Proc. Software Quality Assurance Workshop, San Diego; 1978.

Yourdon, E., Constantine, L.: Structured Design; Prentice-Hall 1979.

Zelkowitz, M., et al.: Principles of Software Engineering and Design; Prentice-Hall 1979.

Index

The index contains also the names of the syntax rules written in a standard programming font (i.e. AddOperator).